Reservation: Policy, Practice and Its Impact on Society

Reservation: Policy, Practice and Its Impact on Society

Vol. I

Scheduled Castes and the Scheduled Tribes

Anirudh Prasad
and
Dr Chandra Sen Pratap Singh

Foreword: Professor Upendra Baxi

KALPAZ

ISBN: 978-93-5128-217-4

Price : ₹ 2550 (set of 2 Vols)
₹ 1050 (Vol–I)

First Published, 2016

Published by

Kalpaz Publications
C-30, Satyawati Nagar,
Delhi – 110052
E-mail: kalpaz@hotmail.com
Ph.: 9212142040

Printed at: G. Print Process, Delhi

Cataloging in Publication Data—DK
Courtesy: D.K. Agencies (P) Ltd. <docinfo@dkagencies.com>

Prasad, Anirudh, author.
Reservation policy, practice and its impact on society : a critical study of problems and prospects in relation to preferential treatment for other backward classes / Anirudh Prasad and Dr. Chandra Sen Pratap Singh.
volumes cm
Contents: volume - I. Scheduled castes and the schedule tribes — volume - II. Other backward classes.
ISBN 9789351282174 (v. 1)
ISBN 9789351282181 (v. 2)

1. Caste—India. 2. People with social disabilities—Government policy—India. 3. Reverse discrimination—India. I. Singh, Chandra Sen Pratap, 1976- author. II. Title.

DS422.C3R47 2016 DDC 305.51220954 23

Contents

Dedicated

In the honour of
The two living legends
With commitment to the
Emancipation of Marginalised Groups
In Ambedkaritc Vision-
-P.B. Sawant J.
-K. Ramaswamy J.
And
To the thorny memory of
-Immortal Shambuka,
-Invictus Eklabya,
-Mrityunjaya Karna,
-Un-blossomed fragrance of Vemula
-Many, many unwept, unsung
And unknown victims of the
Persecution by
Our Graded and Degraded
Hierarchical Social System

Acknowledgements

"Honour to those whose words or deeds.
Thus, help us in our daily needs.
And by their overflow,
Raise us from what is low!"

– **H.W. Longfellow**

Authors put on record a sense of gratitude and thankfulness to all those who have been helpful in this enterprise in one way or the other. The excellent academic works of Marc Galanter and articles of Professor Upendra Baxi, have been inspiring force to view spade and spade, we owe more than mere words of gratitude to these two great social engineer legal luminaries. The autobiography "Ceaseless and Relentless Journey" coming from the living legend justifying only the wearer knows where the shoe pinches, Justice K. Ramaswamy, has influenced our thinking on the issue of social reservation from realistic angel, the authors are immensely thankful to him.

Associate Professor Dr Anand Pawar and Assistant Professor, Rajiv Gandhi National University of Law Punjab, (Patiala), and Ms Gurmanpreet Kaur need special mention who have helped ungrudgingly by typing a part of the hand written manuscript in spite of their busy schedule of teaching and non-teaching works. Authors express their thankfulness to them. Authors are also thankful to Sri Rama Shankar Shukla, former P.A. to the V.C., D.D.U. Gorakhpur University, Gorakhpur who tirelessly typed the handwritten manuscript.

Thanks are also due to library staff of R.G.N.U.L. Punjab, (Patiala) Sri Yogendra Paul, Sri Arjun and Yashpal who promptly provided every help by making available the relevant books and reports on demand; library staff of Central Library of D.D.U. Gorakhpur University, library staff of Rajiv Gandhi P.G. Government College, Ambikapur (C.G.). Authors are also thankful to Sri Rakesh Gupta, Advocate, High Court of Judicature at Allahabad who provided relevant data for use in the book writing.

The senior author Anirudh Prasad expresses his sincere thanks to Professor Paramjit S. Jaswal, Vice-Chancellor, R.G.N.U.L. Punjab (Patiala) for his due encouragement both by words and deeds to do something significant and Professor G.I.S. Sandhu, Registrar of the same institution for his helping and encouraging smilingly respectful behaviour with all. Senior Professors like Professor Gurpal Singh and Mr M.R. Garg have also been appreciative, inspiring and encouraging, we owe respectful gratitude to them. We are also thankful to Professor B.S. Malhi, Controller of Examination, Dr V.K. Anand, Librarian and other colleagues for their good gesture in work culture and ever inspiring **Subhashitani** i.e. memoriable sayings, daily displayed on board on the entering point of the grand modern library.

The authors are extremely grateful to Professor Upendra Baxi for his most illuminating Foreword with critical search light on the book and thankful to Kalpaz Publications, New Delhi for publishing the book most promptly and expeditiously in presentable form. All efforts have been made to make the study crystal clear with sufficient authorities cited to prove the view point, even at the cost of repetition of some of glaring and blatantly incidents of ignoring merit in the name of merit appointment. If somebody feels over assertion or personal value preference dominance, comment with evidentiary proof is always welcome.

Let the noble Thoughts come to us from every side **(Ano Bhadrah Kratvo Yantu Vishwatah).**

CSP Singh **Anirudh Prasad**

Authors' Caveat

Vedic India was a casteless and classless society. Caste system came into being as special feature of Brahminical culture and priests were its strongest advocates and "after investing it with a sacred character in the eyes of the people, they expanded into an immense spider's web, which separated class from class, family from family, man from man and which, while it rendered all united action impossible, enabled the watchful priests to pounce upon all who dared to disturb the threads of their social tissue and to wither them to death."[1] Entrenched caste-ridden society could be termed as a non-contractual status 'society'.[2] The evil of caste system has been that "*hitherto for centuries, there have been cent- per cent reservations in practice in all fields, in favour of high castes and classes, to the total exclusion of others. It was a purely caste and class-based reservation.*"[3] Any attempt at ensuring reservational justice to the deprived backward classes is bound to pay attention to the above-hard reality and its presence in one form or the other like unwritten reservation at the present by polarised caste solidarity — working silently for upper caste people and putting severest resistance to any attempt to implement schemes beneficial to the disadvantaged section of society — backward classes.

The hard reality of the Indian society is that there has been collective contempt for merit and virtue in view of asserting unearned superiority. Recognition of virtue and help of the weaker sections had been left to the God, who is deemed to be bound from time to time, to come down to the earth and restore law and justice. To elaborate it: Draupadi was bound to get humiliated in front of the galaxy of eminent virtuous personalities like Bhishma, Dronacharya, Kripacharya, etc. and it was left to Lord Krishna to protect her honour. Similarly, it was left to Lord Krishna to recognise and appreciate virtues to Eklabya and Karna.[4] The worldly virtuous men like Dronacharya had to persecute them and humiliate them like anything.

The premise that only meritorious come through merit pool is demolished in actual practice. Sometimes, less meritorious are appointed on open/general/merit posts and most meritorious are adjusted in reserved category. Constitutionally social reservation is envisioned and posts are to be reserved for SCs/STs and OBCs. In practice, it is made threefold reservations — SCs/STs, OBCs and upper dominant castes. Where merit is said to prevail, but merit determination is peculiarly in-genuine.[5]

Recently in the most glorious institution like B.H.U. which is the outcome of efforts of the great humanist Pt. Mahamana Madan Mohan Malviya, selection for the Assistant Professors in Law was held for general category out of 79 candidates [Form No. 3706-0-3306-154] with eligibility twenty were shorted out for two posts (Post Code 3306 (Gen. 02)). Out of these twenty, there were many candidates with Ph.D. and NET along with many years teaching experience including in some Central University. The appointees were non-Ph.Ds. of the same elite caste of which all the members of the Selection Committee belonged. Obviously the reactions on faceblook flared up terming that well-known institution as "...Banaras Hindu University." This incident leaves million dollar question: where will the creamy layer of SEBCs with better credentials, achievements and experience go? Have creamy layer of SEBCs any future for justice after being stamped as creamy layer? So be the case of non-creamy layer of OBCs and SCs STs. with better career in view of invisible reservation for upper castes on merit/open posts.

Sometimes, the ways and means of the claimants of the reservational benefit by certain caste groups is not approvable either. The Patidars agitation headed by an immature not to brilliant student Hardik Patel Jat agitation of Haryana in February 2016 causing many thousand crore loss of national property and like can never be approved by any standard by any sensible citizen interested in national cause.

In such agitations the real and genuine cause looses public sympathy. It is true that Patidars have problems due to uneconomic agriculture and closing of many diamond factories. All Jats are not Chaudhari Charan Singh, Ajit Singh, Devilal, Om Prakash Chautala and so on. But the way they expressed grievance is not a way at all. But the role of vote catcher politicians, motivated bureaucracy and governments is more to blame. Inspite of the clear judicial directions, the governments announce reservations without following caring of Ashok Kumar Thakur's verdict[6] and the price paid by backwards when judiciary frustrates the ill-thought governmental move.[7]

The aftermath Jat movement governmental move will prove nothing but great deception. Not only politicians come to show their loyalty and support for Jat cause, the government assured the reservation for certain caste groups in Haryana without effecting the existing 27 per cent reservation for OBCs. Will not any law to this effect be a fraudulent exercise of power in view of Balaji[8] ruling approved by nine judge bench in Mandal case[9]?

To make it clear 15 per cent + 7.5 per cent = 22.5 per cent for SCs/STs + 27 for SEBCs = 49.5 per cent. Permissible 50 per cent - 49.5 per cent = 0.5 per cent. If the Haryana legislature passes law for Jats and others, it will exceed 50 per cent. Certainly it will be social reservation adjustable within 50 per cent. It will not be non-social reservation to be adjusted in quotas of SCs/STs/OBCs and General. Nor will it be legislative attempt like some of southern states. What will be the fate of Law? Declaration of unconstitutionality and nothing less and desirous claimants will have to rub their hands and nothing more than that. The message of Haryana proposed lesson is very damaging – *firstly*, it may encourage other caste groups to resort to the same technique and *second,* the reservation will be nicknamed for politicalisation without any benefit to the reserved category people.

The general mindset, elite preferences and overall unconscious forces operating in thinking process appear to dominate even the judicial mind. To start with the very first case dominating reservation issue decided by Madras High Court Full Bench and approved by the apex court was entertained in teeth of facts that the petitioner had graduation in 1934 and after a long period of 16 years had made up her mind to pursue medical study without applying for that. On her mere conjecture based on enquiry about admission and knowing the policy of the communal order and likelihood of her denial of admission, the petition was allowed.[10] Even the government did not raise preliminary issue as to the non-maintainability of the petition as well as after 16 years lapse of study the knowledge of subjects might have become zero. Inspite of the apex court decision by a nine judge bench in famous *Mandal Case*[11] that there should be no reservation on the post of professor and above if any, one judge of the High Court denied reservation on the post of an intermediate lecturer in chemistry.[12] A division bench[13] comprising of that judge along with another judge in the apex court allowed an appeal against reservation even though likely to be affected two appellants had not been party at the High Court level, one challenger was an unincorporated body rendering social service purporting to espouse the cause of merit in appointments in government service and public undertakings and fourth party was the Public Service Commission itself which constitutionally envisioned to make the constitutional scheme effective. There was specific provision that if an SC/ST/OBC candidate is so meritorious that even if he is not treated as SC/ST/OBC he would still qualify in the open merit then he would not be treated as an SC/ST/OBC candidate and he would be adjusted in 10 seats meant for open merit candidates. In other words, he will not take away the seats reserved for SC/ST/OBC candidates. It was clearly established by the constitution bench decision in *R.K. Sabharwal v. State of Haryana*.[14] But, the learned judge limited the application of this rule to unit of 20 candidates and not for total vacancies. Rule provided that out of 20 seats, 2 seats for SC/ST transferable to S.C. in case of non-availability of suitable S.T. candidate, 8 OBC and rest 10 was open for merit. Reservation starts where the merit border ends. Merit/General category is meant for all meritorious irrespective of their belonging to the reserved category or unreserved category. The single judge of the High Court applied this normal rule of reservation. The Division Bench of the High Court approved that. But, the two judge division bench of the Supreme Court of India set aside the High Court decision. Practically the decision of the Supreme Court converted reservation policy from three categories – SCs/STs and OBCs to three categories – SCs/STs, OBCs and upper castes. One judge of a High Court made observation in one case before him that, "If I am asked by any one to name two things which have destroyed this country or, rather have not allowed the country to progress in the right direction, then the same are, (i) Reservation and (ii) Corruption. It is very shameful of any citizen of this country to task for reservation after 65 years of independence."[15] Caste dominance underlies even in the merit slogan – to quote I.P. Desai, "the recourse to merit appears to be a progressive slogan, it is in fact a weapon for defending the moribund Hindu hierarchy and maintaining social and economic *status quo*."[16]

Any attempt to provide reservational justice to the depressed classes should have to identify clearly the value preferences i.e., whether it wishes to ameliorate the deplorable condition of individual backward people through reservational justice or it proposes to ensure class interest by enabling their partnership in administration and power sharing. The problem can be viewed differently in cases of SCs/STs and OBCs. In case of the former it is said that the benefit of reservation is captured by heady berth occupant among SCs/STs. If such people are denied the benefit of reservation will their quota of 15+7.5= 22.5 per cent be filled in? OBCs are subject to creamy layer rule. If individualist connotation is taken into account economic ceiling and creamy layerisation will have top priority. But, if power sharing is the value preference creamy layer formula will be totally unattractive unless the adequate share of OBCs i.e. 27 per cent of services is ensured to them. Though in principle there is much force in the argument that "elite sections among the OBCs are exploiting them for their own gains in a manner in no way different from those of communal organisations of the past."[17] Thus, the danger of emergence of neo-brahminical class among OBCs is to be minimised by skimming off the creamy layer of OBCs. But, the real problem is: Is the non-creamy layer of OBCs in a position to take the benefit of 27 per cent reservations in their favour? The real issue to be decided shall always remain: the reservational scheme after skimming off creamy layer should not result into taking away by one hand what has been given by the other.

The real problem of India, has been, is, and appears to continue till posterity, is how to adopt compromistic view so as to minimise the rigour of one or few dominant castes/classes' dominance everywhere and absence of bulk of population in administration. The object of social reservation is not only to give service to certain disprivilaged groups but to provide their share in governance of the country too, when he applied Mandal commission report. Dr Ambedkar had talked of the same situation when he was explaining the reservation in service for backward classes. One of the considerations was to ensure reservation in favor of certain communities which had not, so far, a proper look in into administration. He made clear that, for historical reasons- the administration had been controlled by one community or a few communities, and that situations should disappear and the others also must have an opportunity of getting in to the public services. Majority decision of B.P. Jeevan Ready J. In Mandal case also noted that the object behind clause (4) of article 16 was the sharing of state power. It was exposed that, the state power which was almost exclusively monopolised by the upper castes i.e. a few communities, who were till then kept, out of apparatus of power, were sought to be inducted there into. Jeevan Ready J. made clear that, the object behind article 16(4) is empowerment of the deprived backward communities- to give them a share in the administrative apparatus and in the governance of the country. Similar was the view of P.B. Sawant J. in Mandal Case. The learned judge observed, 'neither democracy nor unity will become real, unless all sections of the society have an equal and effective voice in the affairs and the governance of the country. Similar was the opinion of Pandian J. in that case. Thus, the objective of participation in governance of the country was shared by six hon'ble justices, e.g., B.P. Jeevan Ready, J. M.H Kania, C.J. and M.N. Venkatachalaiah, A.M. Ahmadi, Pandian and Sawant JJ. As a result by two-third majority of the nine judge bench, the objective of participation in the administration of the country through reservation was approved. But, in practice, it has lost sight of the vehement opponent of the social reservation.

One obvious result is that even after sixty-eight years of the independence and vesting of political power in the hands of the people, the same section, which dominated the nation's affairs earlier, continues to do so today.

The tryst with destiny appears to have not been fulfilled. The victims are the same; the perpetuators are also the same, which had been in the historical perspective. The mode has changed. Casteism has got more entrenched. Barring a few exceptions, the SCs/STs are still discriminated, persecuted and deprived of their genuine claims. To quote from Ramaswamy J., the former judge, the Supreme Court, the glorious history of our country was converted into hierarchical structure among Hindus due to moral decadence and social degeneration. The reality being, no one ever bargained to be born in particular religion, caste or sub-caste. Birth is the result of the biological act of parenthood. Man is born free but is chained in India everywhere. Men, perchance, born in different castes or religions speak different languages or profess different religions. The result is that the society has disintegrated, mutual distrust is ever deepening ascending scale of respect in social hierarchy and descending scale of disdain is being perpetuated. The status of Dalit from the cradle to the grave is linked and tied with Castes".

The real impact of reserved and general category has to be evaluated on factual studies like *Brandies Brief*[18] – fact-based justification of certain claims. It should not be based on pre-conceived notions – either as that the candidates coming in reserved category are less meritorious or those coming through general category are more meritorious. To quote Pandian J., the intelligence, merit, ability, competence, meritocracy, administrative efficiency and achievement cannot be measured by skin-pigmentation or by surname of an individual indicating his caste.[19] The cry of merit is made by those "who are in and want to keep out those who are out" from taking advantages. In India such bald conclusions may prove to be untenable and wrong. Data-based factual study becomes imperative. In some cases merit may not be consideration in open selections. Rather it may be casualty and a dominant casteless meritorious candidate with minimum statutory qualifications may be preferred to the best available non-dominant caste candidates. That is to say, unwritten reservations may have upper hand in filling in vacancies in the general category. Likewise the talk of equality etc. after initial appointment may prove to be a slogan mongering by allowing unwritten reservational preferences in favour of dominant castes in the services for purposes of promotions.

The authors were inspired by certain observations in the judgment of justice Sawant giving recognition to caste-based unwritten reservations in the past[20] and repeated warning of P.B. Jeevan Reddy J. in *Mandal case* delivering the leading judgment that while drawing the line between the creamy and non-creamy layer "it should be ensured that it does not result in taking away with one hand what is given by the other."[21] As a matter of fact Marc Galanter[22] concluded his study with note that: (i) a set of beneficiaries (or potential beneficiaries) failed to get much benefits as the law seemed to promise due to deficiencies in laws and harbouring of attitudes unfavourable to their claims; and (ii) absence of suitable legal services i.e., presence of lawyers or others capable of providing such clients with continuing strategic legal services. By it, Marc Galanter, means persistence and inventiveness in pursuing long range goals of client groups – that are organised and capable of using more aggressive, more continuous and more inventive lawyering.[23] There are certain studies which prove that presence of all communities in different walk of life would be necessary to ensure fair treatment. A survey of Kakatiya University students revealed that "while differences between the internal and external evaluations of BC and SC candidates were not found to be significant statistically, the differences in the internal and the external assessments of the performance of FC(forward caste) candidates was found to be significant statistically. It can be concluded that the Forward Caste (students) get relatively higher rate of boosting by the internal evaluators than the BCs and SCs."[24] This outcome was significant in view of the number of teachers belonging to different communities i.e., FC 126; BC 36 and SC 3. A similar trend is discernible from the assessment of merit of candidates coming from different sections of society at the level of jobs. "When a candidate is interviewed, the prejudice of the social class of the examiner is still active, and in many cases the examiners instead of more sympathetic questioning in cases of those who come from less well-endowed background, want to embarrass the candidates in manner that even performance one ordinarily shows he is not able to exhibit to the rest of the examiners."[25] Sawant J. himself noted that one of the major reasons why during all these years after Independence, the lot of the downtrodden has not even been marginally improved and why majority of the schemes for their welfare have remained on paper, is perceptibly traceable to the fact that "*the implementing machinery, dominated as it is by the high classes is indifferent to their problems.*"[26] (emphasis added)

The book deals with reservational issues with empirical outlook and new realist dimension reaching to the core of the problems inviting all who feel concern themselves to think, rethink and again think over the real social problems and their solutions. Recent trends in the country with scams and elitist flavour of services has put question mark on meritocracy and its importance in the nation-building. Mr N.C. Saxena, Director, Lal Bahadur Sastri National Academy of Administration, Mussorie has shown in his paper: "Whatever little virtue the I.A.S. possessed – integrity, political neutrality, courage and his morals – are showing sign of decay, unfortunately many I.A.S. officers are accepting a diminished role of themselves by becoming agents of exploitation in a state structure which is callous to the needs of the poor. The prime motivating factor for joining I.A.S. is ample opportunity of making money. Most of them are like parasites – they are taking too much from the system and contributing too little." Merit sans sincerity and patriotism is becoming danger signal to the country and therefore, too much, can no more be made out of meritocratic slogans. The issue has to be viewed in broader national perspective. In India, even the civilian awards like Padma Bhibhushan, Padma Bhushan and Padma Shree have been getting degenerated with the passage of time and it prompted Justice Kuldip Singh to query whether the purpose for which these awards were instituted has been achieved or, these are being conferred on the deserving persons, or being given to "well known, less known or even unknown".[27] Thus, not only in services, in every walk of life there is marked deterioration. In services too either merit is ignored or if merit is honoured the meritorious become threat to national cause in view of the race of money building leading to scams after scams. Does not C.B.I. consist of brains undiluted by reservation so far? The diluted F.I.R. against former J.M.M. M.Ps. Suraj Mandal, Shibu Soren, Shailendra Mahato and Simon Marandi for taking bribe for voting in favour of Narasimha Rao Government during no-confidence motion in 1993 was registered by whom? Compensatory discrimination is the constitutional necessity. Its justification is threefold[28] – compensatory, utilitarian and distributive justice. Compensatory Justice requires elimination of existing inequalities as well as compensating the unequals for injustices and discrimination they have suffered. It is remedial action to right wrong already committed to depressed classes. It is opposed on account of unsustainability of intergenerational justice and reverse discrimination, Utilitarian justice widens chances of disadvantages people in education, employment and promotion and would promote overall equality. It provides society the benefit of utilisation of wide range talents and human resources. The distributive Justice encourages proportional equality and representation of at all levels of income and achievements. It is accepted fact that no scheme may be foolproof. Compensatory discrimination may develop, rather has developed vested interest, capture of benefits by elite among depressed, claim by many groups through agitations etc. But, they cannot provide justification for doing away with it. They provide chances for ensuring genuine implementation of policy.

What is the pressing need of the Indian society is the change in elitist mindset, adoption of social justice - orientation, response to the human situation to combat social evils and large-heartedness guided by reason to maintain the bland of change and continuity of order. Positivistic view need to give way to social engineering. Seed of change in right perspective was sown in the decision of honourable justice Somasundram (though not pressed) in *Smt. Chanpkam Dorairajan v. State of Madras*[29], asserted by Subba Rao J. in his strong dissent in *T. Devadasan* v. *Union of India*[30] declaring the provision of Article 16(4) not an exception to clause (1) of that Article but as much emphatic way to enforce equality, reiterated by majority opinion in *State of Kerala* v. *N.M. Thomas*[31] and given full exposition in the decisions of K. Ramaswamy J.[32] Nothing is good or bad thinking makes it so and thinking depends on way to view the problem, of course with education, upbringing and social outlook. Differing view among honourable Supreme Court decisions and extra judicial writings of justices are obvious example. Take instance of the application of government reservation policy in unaided private educational institutions. In spite of the specific constitutional amendment on the point one hon'ble judge of the Supreme Court viewing complete immunity in view of Article 19(1) (g) on plea of declaring Article 19(1)(g) as a basic structure declared the Constitution amendment unconstitutional even though no unaided institution had asked for such drastic action.[33] He found at least four problems in government move to provide reservation in such educational institutions viz., suffering of academic standard; attracting and retaining good faculty becoming more difficult; severe diminution of incentive to establish a first rate unaided institution and ultimate compromising of the global reputation of our unaided institutions.[34] On the other hand, unaided private educational institutions (which have outnumbered government colleges) have been criticised by Justice V.R. Krishna Iyer as "degree distribution shops"[35] and by K. Ramaswamy J. as 'Commercialisation of Education'.[36]

Present is the time facing hostile attitude towards compensatory discrimination without ensuring fair deal with depressed people. Even the judiciary has gone to condemn governmental attempts under Articles 15(4) and 16(4) and suggested determination of backwardness on criterion like poverty and occupation, even politically undeserved sections based on disability or gender, that is transgender, in spite of the fact that such reservation will fall in vertical reservation and not in horizontal reservation, which is meant for social reservation that is SCs/STs and OBCs.[37]

Such move is appreciated even by some academician[38] without caring that such reservation does not fall under Articles 15(4) and 16(4) i.e. social reservations. They fall in the category of non-social reservation to be conceded horizontally and adjusted in General, OBC and SC/ST as the claimant belonged.

The content of the book relates to Social reservation. There is all round reaction against it. In hue and cry extreme form is prevalent. Objectivity, judiciousness and critical view has gone far off. The very informative, in-depth and spade a spade study was presented during early 1980s by Marc Galanter.[39] He himself had some change in his approach in his latter, article.[40] After Galanter no book like that is available. An in-depth and ground reality with grassroots, analysis has been a long due. Authors, though belong to SEBC category, are not benefitted by that. Though during formative stage (upto matriculation) they suffered all stresses and strains and handicaps of backward community-social and educational. But never could claim the benefit of social reservation. The co-author lost many opportunities in competitive examinations due to being so called creamy layer and missed the bus by few marks in general category. Still, the practical experience shows that everything is not right with merit claim – more particularly having the practical and conscience pricking experience with merit of general category scholars like one P.G. with 52.3 per cent and Ph.D. in other Faculty enjoying cream of Merit pool post-Professorship inspite of Supreme Court decisions on the point speaking otherwise[41] or search of merit through screening examination resulting in 98 per cent marks by wards of some M.L.As., belonging to a ruling party,[42] as has been discussed earlier. All efforts have been made to be as objective as possible and pinpoint the living law of the Indian society dealing with social reservation. In this backdrop, the authors were prompted to endeavour to write a book which does not deal only with technical arguments niceties but also presents social reality and ways to frustrate constitutional mission of establishing a strong nation with co-operation of all sections of the society, and ensure reflective participatory democracy in decision-making process.

There is all round confusion with respect to social reservation i.e. reservation for SCs/STs and OBCs. Will they be continued or be reviewed as voices have been being raised from time to time from different quarters of the society? Recently, the Prime Minister of India, has unequivocally asserted that nobody can take away the right of reservation from the Dalits.This itself shows that something is going on, in some quarters, against the social reservation and in opinion of our popular P.M, the likely to be affected section is allay in apprehensions. Sometimes, even the over enthusiastic sympathy of governments unconsciously perpetuate the discrimination, that is to say, financing of and construction of separate cremation-ground for Dalit in Gujarat and some other states.

The issue of SCs/STs was so deplorable that the framers of our Constitution accepted/provided special treatment to them. The fault lies with implementation and social mores, disallowing them to come forward in the job of national building. The Constitution is superb, the laws have very laudable objectives, but social mores have not changed. Nearly one hundred eighty years earlier, what Alexis de Tocqueville remarked of American society still holds good of our society. He remarked, "If I consider the US of our days, I see clearly that in a certain part of the country the legal barrier, that separates the two races is tending to fall, but not that of mores. Is slavery receding: the prejudices to which it gave birth is immovable."[43]

The problem of other backward classes is quite different from SCs STs. They suffer a different kind of discrimination. As the Supreme Court of India pointed out in *Chatter Singh* V. *State of Rajasthan*[44] 'though OBCs are not socially and educationally forward, they do not suffer the same social handicaps inflicted upon scheduled castes and scheduled tribes. Articles 15(2) and 17 furnish historical and social dissatisaction inflicted on them. The object of reservation for the scheduled castes and scheduled Tribes is to bring them into the mainstream of national life, while the objective in respect. Therefore, they are always treated dissimilar and they do not form an integrated class with Dalits and Tribes for the purpose Aarticles 16(4) 15 (4).

They are different in the sense that SCs suffer from acute social indignity whereas OBCs have social acceptability. SCs are persecuted, tortured and often deprived the right to live in house of their choice inspite of payment for that, so on, so forth. Sometimes, they are victims of the OBCs wrath too.There is some dissimilarity between the SCs and STs. STs do not suffer from that indignation as the SCs suffer due to lack of entrencherd hierarchical structure in their society. There have less cases coming to the courts in relations to STs in comparisons to SCs. Still their fate is likewise-economic deprivation, acute backwardness, faraway living from civilised society, lower status, economic exploitation, forced eviction for big projects, all bring them nearer to SCs. But, OBCs share similar discrimination like SCs/STs so far as unfair treatment at the hands of upper castes and power that be, are concerned. They sail on the same boat so far as their representation in services, teaching jobs, Vice Chancellorships, judiciary and other places are concerned. Even the most brilliant SCs/STs and OBCs candidates can not compete with most mediocre dominant caste candidate in merit pool they have to suffer the burnt of reserved posts being left un-filled inspite of eligibility and good academic records.

In spite of discrimination similarity of all the social reservation beneficiaries, the hard reality is that SCs and STs are quite different in social status, dealings and almost all walks of life. They are really and indisputably backwards attracting the attention of the framers of the Constitution, judiciary etc. I necessitates to deal with the problems of different social reservation groups in different books – volume one dealing with reservation policy, practice and its impact on society – SCs and STs and volume two dealing with reservation policy, practice and its impact on society –OBCs.Though two different volumes have been devoted separately for SCs/STs and OBCs but some discusssions in each volume may be relevant for both and will explain the common experience, that is to say, Authors Caveat Preface written by Professor Upendra Baxi, Chapters 2and 3 of volume 1 dealing with –Problems of Discrimination and Compensatory Discrimination/Preferential Treatment: What, Why and How Long? And Chapters 7 of volume 11 dealing with-Meritocracy Pro and Con and Ground Reality in India.

The expression socially and educationally backward classes and other backward classes have been used interchangeability both communicate the same idea - the former is constitutional expression used in Articles 5(4) and 340 and other used in common parlances and media. Reservation is part of preferential treatment and some writers have preferred to call it compensatory discrimination. Therefore, the terms compensatory discrimination and preferential treatment have been explained and used in the book interchangeably.

Referances

1. Max Muller, Chips from a German Workshop, Vol. II.
2. Henry Summer Maine.
3. Per Sawant J. in Indra Sawhney v. Union of India, 1992 S.C.C. (L. and S.) Supp. 1 at p. 211.
4. Lord Krishna was very much appreciative of the virtuous Karna but his words "Chaturvarnya Mayakritam, Guna Karam Vibhagshah" have been reduced to chaturvanya based on caste and Lord Krishna has been misinterpreted for entrenching the caste evil.
5. The search sometimes ignores even minimum eligibility and sometimes gives impression of tilting the balance of the scale of Justice in favour of power that

be. Recently in the month of January, 2016 one National Law University intended to appoint two general category Assistant Professors. Since the applicants' number reached beyond proportion, the university decided to hold screening examination test. No course was prescribed. If no course is prescribed normal prudence requires test on pattern of NET or question from Constitution and Jurisprudence which are most essential and prominent subjects of study at graduation level. But, most questions related to the subject expertise of the Vice-Chancellor - international law. Surprisingly one candidate scored 48 and the other 47 out of 49, (one question being cancelled due to incorrectness). The topper with 98 per cent belonged to the host university itself. The most outstanding scholar candidates scoring 98 per cent happened to be daughter of sitting M.L.A.

6. Ashok Kumar Thakur v. Union of India, (2008)6 SCC 1.
7. Ram Singh v. Union of India (2015) 4SCC687.
8. M.R. Balaji v. Union of India, AIR 1963 SC 649.
9. Indra Sahwaney v. Union of India, AIR 1993 SC 477.
10. Srimati Champkam Dorairajan v. State of Madras A.I.R. 1951/Mad. 120 (D/on 27.7.1950). The F.B. consisted of Rajamannar, C.J., Vishwanath Sastri and Samasundrama JJ. Somasundram J. agreed with order written by C.J. hesitantly but his observation to the effect that omission of language in Article 29(2) similar to Article 16(4) "does not preclude the state from giving effect to the principle contained in Art. 46, which are bound to do" is very much instructive.
11. A.I.R. 1993 S.C. 477.
12. Naresh Chand v. District Inspector of School, Ghaziabad 1992 Lab. IC 2613 (All.) For critical analysis of the judgment See, P S Soman, "Reservation in Scientific Fields: A Critique of Naresh Chand Case (1994) 36 (2) JILI Pages 231-236.
13. Nair Service Society v. Dr T. Beermasthan (2009) 5 SCC 545. The bench consisted of R.V. Raveendran and Markandey Katju JJ. The judgment was delivered by Katju J.
14. (1995) 2 SCC 745.
15. Justice J.B. Pardiwala of Gujarat High Court. Rajya Sabha members took notice of the observation Treating it as objectionable and moved impeachment motion. Ultimately, the learned judge himself removed para 62 of his judgment as not 'relevant and necessary' for disposal of the petition. *Impeachment move Against Judge*, The Hindu, 19.3.2015, p. 12.
16. I.P. Desai, 'Anti Reservation Agitation' (in), *Caste, Caste Conflict and Reservations*, Ajanta Publications, Delhi, 1985, p. 135.
17. Meenakshi Jain, "High Caste Fight Back in North", *The Times of India*, Sept. 5, 1985.
18. Brandies- Brief is popularly associated with historic briefest legal argument (brief) of two pages and factual reports of Commission/Committees, factories inspectors on the ill effect of Women's ten hours duty is factories which covered 107 pages in Muller v. Oregon US 412 (1908) and he won the case.
19. Per Pandian J. in Indra Sahwney v. Union of India, 1992 S.C.C. (L. and S.) Supp. 1 at p. 108 (para 159).
20. Sawant J. in *Mandal Case*, quoted earlier.

21. Jeevan Reddy J. in *Mandal Case*, p. 428 (para 792).
22. Marc Galanter, 'Law and Society in Modern India' (Oxford Univ. Press) 1989, p. 233.
23. *Ibid.*
24. Parmaji; *Caste: Reservation and Performance*, Mamata Publications, Warrangal, 1985, p. 60.
25. Gautam, Mathur, *The Rectification of Positive Discrimination*, Institute of Applied Manpower Research, New Delhi, 1982.
26. Per Sawant J., *Mandal Case*, p. 211 (para 406).
27. 'Question Mark on Padma awards' credibility, *The Times of India*, 18.12.95, p. 5.
28. For detail see, Swati Deva (ed.) Law And (In) Equalities – Contemporary Perspective E.B.C. 2010, pp. 8-9 (Permanand Singh, The Ideal of equality and Reservation Policy: A Critical Review, pp. 3-24 at pp. 8-9).
29. A.I.R. 1951 Mad. 120.
30. A.I.R. 1964 S.C. 149.
31. A.I.R. 1976 SC 490.
32. Discussed in detail in Annexure, namely "Justice K. Ramaswamy: The Great Sociological jurist Judge."
33. *Ashok Kumar Thakur* v. *Union of India* (2008) 6 SCC 1. at 710 (Bhandari J.).
34. *Ibid*, pp. 678-679 (para 534-538).
35. V.R. Krishna Iyer, "Unequal Access to Professional Forces" and "Ten Commandments of Higher Education" (In) Indian Law- Dynamic Dimensions of the Abstract, Universal Law Publishing Company, New Delhi 2012, pp. 418-433
36. Ceaseless and Relentless Journey, EBC, 2008, p. 211.
37. Ram Singh v. Union of India (2015) 4 SCC 697.
38. For appreciation of Ram Singh's case C, K L Bhatia, "Affirmative Action Serving The Deserving Under Privileged Groups of the Society Which Truly Deserve Palliative Action: A Neo-Identification of Backwardness (2015) 51 (4) CMLJ pp. 395-405.
39. Marc Galanter. Competing Equalities, Oxford Univ. Press (1984).
40. Marc Galanter, Missed Opportunities: The Use and Non-use of Law Favourable to untouchables and other especially vulnerable Groups (in) I.L.I. Publication "Law and Social Change – Indo American Reflections", N.M. Tripathi, Bombay, 1988 pp. 183-206.
41. See University Education, Administration and Law, Deep and Deep Publications, New Delhi, 2000.
42. K.L. Bhatia, "Affirmative Action Serving the Deserving underprivileged Groups of the Society which they truly Deserve Palliative Action: A New-Identification of Backwardness" 51(4) C.M.L.J. pp. 395-405.
43. Alexis de Tocqueville, Democracy in America, Vol. I Liberty fund, Indiana Polis (1835, 1942 ed.).
44. (1996) 1SCC 742=AIR 1977 SC 303.

List of Abbreviations

AIR	- All India Reporter
AAP	- Affirmative Action Programme
BC	- Backward Classes
BCC	- Backward Classes Commission
CAD	- Constituent Assembly Debates
EPW	- Economic and Politically Weekly
GO	- Government Order
JILI	- Journal of India Law Institute
OBC	- Other Backward Classes
PCR Act	- The Protection of Civil Rights Act, 1955
POA Act	- Scheduled Castes and Scheduled Tribes (Prevention of Atrocities) Act, 1989
RCSCST	- Report of the Commissioner for Scheduled Castes and Scheduled Tribes
SC	- Supreme Court
SCC	- Supreme Court Cases
SC	- Scheduled Castes
SEBC	- Socially and Educationally Backward Classes
ST	- Scheduled Tribes
UGC	- University Grants Commission
UPSC	- Union Public Service Commission
US	- United States (Supreme Court)

Foreword

I had the privilege to write a Preface to Professor (Dr) Anirudh Prasad's earlier brilliant book entitled *Reservation Policy and Practice in India: A Means to an End* (1991) where he seriously presents contradictions—material, institutional, normative, cultural, and hermeneutical— in the tasks of justification of affirmative action.

Dr Anirudh Prasad there identifies six dimensions of the dialectics of equality. The first is offered by the need to continuously weigh ameliorative, social justice interests with the necessity to prevent "disproportionate protective discrimination". Second, howsoever that expression may be construed, "merit and efficiency stand compromised in any (but especially the Indian variety) measure of protective discrimination". Third, the distinctive reality of caste system, and the increasing role it plays in the construction of "backwardness", poses the problem of the revitalisation of "caste consciousness". Fourth, inherent to protective discrimination policies is the prospect of perpetuation of caste based quotas; the problem arises of ways of their conversion into "self-abolition in course of time". Fifth, India witnesses the problem of "losing the identity of non-reservational equality" in the process of extending the specific principle of redress to ever increasing sections of society. The articulation of runaway reservations policies leads the author to lament (here to offer a poignant amendment of Coleridge) "reservation, reservation everywhere but not a single prop to stand?" And, sixth, remains the worrisome aspect of the stigmatisation of communities in the construction and reconstruction of backwardness by state policies; stigmatisation, as this process operates in India, threatens equality gains of reservation policies.

This work, a companion Volume by Anirudh Prasad and Chandra Sen Pratap Singh offering a sound exposition of law, is haunted by the production of continuing social indifference towards untouchables and sets the mood for a sad contemplation of realties of caste prejudice, discrimination, repression, and even violence against the lower castes, especially the untouchables. A steadfast but mournful awareness of poignant social realties provides the analytic context for studying what politics and justicing has really accomplished in the name of reservations.

Of course, in a class and caste divided society reservation will always evoke public debates, mostly acrimonious and often violent. But movements for redressing past wrongs are struggles for justice against all 'justifications' offered for social exclusion, very often wounding, cruel and lived. Whereas the Constitution of India guarantees a vision of good life to all its citizens, most beneficiaries live a life that political philosopher Thomas Hobbes in *Leviathan* long time ago described as 'solitary, poor, nasty, brutish, and short'. Social exclusion, and violent practices of racial discrimination (apartheid) constitute both a scar and wound. To paraphrase George Deleuze, the difference between a scar and a wound is not only anatomical or physiological, where it involves the differentiation of depth, scale, and healing); it is also cultural and historical. If a scar is trace of the hurtful past and is the memory of a collective wound, the untouchables live and embody the reiterated wound itself.

People have different views about almost everything associated with reservations. There are many axes along which the contention moves. The first concern the nomenclature and worries exist about how these should be called: affirmative action, quotas, preferential and compensatory discrimination, or even reparation for past historic wrongs. Second, there is debate over the constituencies for reservations or the beneficiaries: should it be for ancient past wrongs (such as scheduled cases and tribes) or for new groups compendiously called as "socially and educationally backward classes" and "other backward classes"? And, in turn, how they are to be identified? Third, deeply contested remain the justifications for change for various types of benefits to be offered: constitutional political elites and Justices continue to differ on how policies may be fashioned, how class and ethnicity may be constructed, and the scale and duration of reservations. Fourth, the problem of social costs: how long the benefits are to continue? And at whose/what costs? Fifth, and in particular, the debates over merit and efficiency and how exclusion is to be the other side of inclusion (the problem of ceilings and of constructions of 'creamy layer'—or as an 'inclusive exclusion' as an Italian Philosopher Gorgio Agamben would call this.) Sixth, the issues of the shrinking public sector; if the government share of educational and employment is no more than once it was, is the other sector (the beneficiary of de-nationalisation, disinvestment, and deregulation—the three Ds of contemporary globalisation) to be bound by a social contract of constitutional morality whereunder those who inherit the state wealth are bound to follow the core obligations of the State, at least for a prescribed period? Or should constitutional obligations give place merely to the so-called corporate social responsibility? Or simply, the riot of free market enterprises? Seventh, how far should adjudicatory hermeneutic leadership extend to this area, even granting the last word in constitutional interpretation to the Supreme Court of India?

Eighth, what are the justifications for reservation insurgency and the justice of various state responses? How is the potential for social violence to be assessed and what mechanisms exist as well to constrain state violence in a civil war situation? Are reservation movements to be considered as states of civil war (Agamben in a slender book on Hobbes recently draws our attention to a paradigm of the State as permanent civil war)? Or (to use political scientist Paul Brass's metaphor) an 'institutionalised riot system'? Or further as social justice movement, a constitutional insurgency for social inclusion and equality?

Authors face almost all these questions – in itself a huge academic achievement for it is not easy to describe such a vast terrain. Their recognition of other writers in the field is exemplary and the range of comparative constitutional materials, in the Anglo-American orbit, is vast. And they write with admirable critical grasp, not just erudition, about Indian constitutional hermeneutics in this forbiddingly difficult terrain. A resolute 'socio-ethical conviction' (to borrow a term form the jurisprudential veteran Julius Stone) shines through: reservations—the authors believe— are the only, if not always the best, means India has to combat past, especially millennial, wrongs.

There are several reasons animating this perspective. The learned authors are pained by the amount of injustices and atrocities against the scheduled castes and tribes, although they remain subjects of affirmative action and compensatory discrimination. It is, indeed, a cruel paradox of contemporary India that atrocities increase even as the social protection of vulnerable individuals and communities is sought to be achieved by reservations. Normative exuberance is witnessed at the same moment with indifferent enforcement, even non-implementation of the law as it stands. This contradiction comes alive in business-as-usual caste repression. Recently, some state legislatures (Haryana and Rajasthan, for example) have begun to legislatively exclude even the scheduled castes if they do not meet the required academic qualifications and other unconstitutional conditions on the right to contest, an integral aspect of democracy and rule of law constituting the basic structure of the Constitution. Even the Supreme Court of India has very recently sanctioned this unconstitutional tendency.

The learned authors believe that even today, "[C]aste dominance underlies even in the merit slogan" and quote a great Indian thinker Professor I.P. Desai who says that while "the recourse to merit appears to be a progressive slogan", it is "in fact a weapon for defending the moribund Hindu hierarchy and maintaining social and economic status quo". These are strong words, indeed; but is the constitutional commitment thereby rendered vulnerable? It is well known that the Indian constitutional secularism, and its democratic modes, disallow any form of what is known as 'IQ-ism' and widespread justifications for social inequality based on innate caste or class superiority.

Authors' analysis of 'merit' and 'efficiency' logics and languages as de-justifying reservations is indeed worth pondering even if you hold a different view. They do not say, at least I read this work, that there is no such thing as merit but they are against 'meritocracy' which proceeds endlessly to manufacture new political myths against redressing the accumulated past wrongs. In the company of gifted socialist thinkers, Authors urge us to think that what is called 'merit' and 'efficiency' are virtues socially caused and learnt and should not become masks for dominant caste or class power.

It is not just individual biography but also the social text that matters. Authors also urge us to rethink 'efficiency' as an integral aspect of justice. They admiringly quote Justice Chinnappa Reddy: "Why not ask ourselves why 35 (now 68) years after Independence, the position of the Scheduled Cases etc. has not greatly improved? Is it not a legitimate question to ask whether things might have been different, had the District Administrators and the State and Central Bureaucrats been drawn in larger numbers from these classes". Justice Sawant brilliantly supplemented, as the authors note, these questions in *Indira Sawhney v. Union of India.* These socio-jural interrogations still await responses from the votaries of merit and efficiency.

The study is in two Volumes. Chapter-6 of Volume-1 and chapter-4 of Volume-2 present a detailed narration of the "burning issues arising out of preferential treatment in India" and chapters-7 & 8 of Volume-1 and chapters-5 & 6 of Volume-2 of the book in your hands analyse 'resentment, circumvention and resistance'. Under these rubrics stand analysed a range of critical issues. Chapter-6 of Volume-1 is primarily concerned with reservations "confined to initial stage of appointment or covering promotional stage too." the "famous Rangachari Ruling, its reign upto Mandal decision", "constitutional attempts" and "judicial setback given to reserved category people". Chapter-4 of Volume-2 deals with "extent of reservation, carry forward rule, matter of reservation against a single post and superspecialities, nature of Articles 15(4) and 16(4), their exhaustiveness on the issue of preferential treatment and the real objective of preferential treatment".

Chapter-7 (Volume-1) presents violent reactions against "Dalit upliftment", the resistance against reservation policy through the "restrictive interpretation of roster rule, insistence on Department or faculty-wise reservation, dereservation of roster posts and threat to SCs/STs claim by false caste certificates". Likewise, Chapter-5 (Volume-2) deals with resentment: spontaneous, pre-emptive and violent against Mandal Commission Report's implementations in services and later on in educational institutions.

Chapters 6, 7 & 8 (Volume 1) and Chapters 5 & 6 (Volume 2) constitute, as it were, the bleeding heart of the work. A patient reading is required; even the dull details of law and interpretation need to be fully recoursed to experience , even vicariously, the heartbeats of reservation policies in action. The learned authors offer many a creative and sensible suggestion that urge not "abolition" as the way ahead but "honest, effective and purposeful implementation of reservation policy". Although the 2014 Scheduled Castes (SCs) and the Scheduled Tribes (STs) Prevention of Atrocities (PoA) Act, 1989, and the Rules 2016, deserve normative applause, the affected communities know better through the sad wisdom of experience that prosecution, punishments and the happenings of a general deterrence are few and far between. Yet, all suggestions in this regard deserve urgent attention and support: particularly worthy are the authors' suggestions for even further amendments to the atrocities Act that would make punishable social boycott and economic blackmail.

The learned authors do not shy away from making political and sociological judgements. The difference between the two respectively lies in judgements about the competitive practices of power and in following the protocols of sequence of description, analysis, and evaluation (most social theorists avoid the last stage of prediction associated with 'natural' sciences). If a value-neutral method of doing social theory stops short of making political judgements, Authors feel it constitutionally mandatory to do so. The reader may or may not share the political judgements but the authors command respect for doing a superb sociology of the Indian reservational theory, policy, and practice. And I say this being 'blest' with a ringside perspective of the Mandal maelstrom (movement/agitation) at the University of Delhi!

Even those of diametrically opposed viewpoints will learn from this painstaking and honest work which expresses the constitutional itineraries of reservations. They will know more about what the Supreme Court of India actually said against caricatures that misrepresent what their Lordships actually said. And if the readers of differing views will be as patient and indulgent to honest difference of opinion as the authors are, they will find some old and some new questions to ponder, if not to answer. This is one of the very few books on the subject of justice as care in modern India worth reading repeatedly and with anxious care for the future of constitutionalism and human rights.

Upendra Baxi
Emeritus Professor of Law
University of Warwick and Delhi

14 May 2016

Chapter - 1

Introduction

On mid night of August 14-15, 1947 India began tryst with its destiny with golden aspiration to wipe out every tear from every eye. The Constitution of India, framed by Indians dreamt to secure to all its citizen justice –social, economic and political and liberty, equality and fraternity was to be signature tune of our national life. Dr Ambedkar, the main architect of the Constitution and messiah of the Schedule Castes and the Scheduled Tribes spoke of Constitution in our socio-economic perspective. In the Constitution Assembly he made clear:

"We must make our political democracy a social democracy as well. Political democracy cannot last unless there lies at the base of it social democracy. What does social democracy mean? It means a way of life which recognises liberty, equality and fraternity as the principles of life. These form a union of trinity in the sense that to divorce one from the other is to defeat the very purpose of democracy. Liberty cannot be divorced from equality; equality cannot be divorced from liberty Nor can liberty and equality be divorced from fraternity. With fraternity liberty and equality could not become a natural course of things. It would require a constable to enforce them. We must begin by knowledge the fact that there is complete absence of two things in Indian society. One of these is equality. On the social plane, we have in India a society based on the principle of graded inequality which means elevation of some and degradation for other. On the economic plane, we have a society in which there are some who have immense wealth as against many who live in abject poverty. On the 26th January 1950 we are going to enter in to a life on contradictions. In politics we will have equality and in social and economic life, we will have inequality. In politics we will be recognising the principles of one man one vote and one vote on value. In our social and economic life, we shall, by reason of our social and economic structure, continue to deny the principle of the one man one value. How long shall we continue to live this life of contradiction? How much shall we continue to deny equality on our social and economic life? If we continue to deny for long, we will do so only by putting out political democracy in peril. We must remember this contradiction at the earliest possible moment for else those who suffer from inequality will blow up the structure of political democracy which this assembly has so laboriously built up."[1]

Untouched ability was treated as the root cause of the Indian social disintegration and vulnerability of the depressed classes. Untouchbility had added to not only social degradation but the economic deprivation too. As Dr Ambedker explained "untouchbility is not only a system of unmitigated economic exploitation but it is also a system of uncontrolled economic exploitation. That is, because there is no independent public opinion to condemn it and there is no important machinery of administration and restraint."[2]

With a view to ameliorate the condition of deprived, disprivileged, discriminated and persecuted untouchables many a programmers were adopted by the framers of the constitution. **First** step was to abolish untouchbility. The **second** step was to forbid its practice in any form. The **third** step was the declaration that enforcement of any disability arising out of untouchability shall be an offence punishable in accordance with law.[3] To make the commitment of the framers' of the Constitution effective, the parliamentary laws- Untouchability Offences Act (renamed in 1976 as Protection of Civil Rights Act) 1955 and the Scheduled Castes and Scheduled Tribes (Prevention of Atrocities) Act, 1989 and Rules there in have been enacted.[4] The **fourth** step was to prohibit any kind of discrimination or impose any disability as to access to public places,[5] service,[6] educational institutions[7] or eligibility in electoral roll.[8] The **fifth** step was to provide constitutional guarantee through special provisions[9] including reservations in Lok Sabha[10] and Vidhan Sabhas[11] of the various states. The **sixth** was to provide for reservation in services under the state with a view to ensure the adequate representation of SCs and STs and STs as they belong to definitely backward class. The **seventh** step was added in 1951 by the Constitution first Amendment Act inserting clause (4) to Article 15 providing for special provision for SCs and STs. The **eighth** step has been added by the Constitution 73rd and 74th Amendment Acts, 1992 providing for reservation of SCs and STs in the Panchayats[12] and the Municipalities.[13]

Over governmental commitment is enshrined in Article 46, one of the Directive Principles of State Policy, it states "The State shall promote with special care the educationally and economic interests of the weaker sections of the people and it particular, of the Scheduled Castes and Scheduled Tribes and shall protect them from all social injustice and all forms of exploitation." The Governments–Union and the States, have devised a number of ways and means to safeguard the interests of Scheduled Castes and Scheduled Tribes and push their development. They have adopted carry forward rule and allowed exchange of unfilled quotas between the Scheduled Castes and Scheduled Tribes. A number of concessions and relaxations have been provided to the Scheduled Castes and the Scheduled Tribes:[14] A number of institutional safeguards have been provided by appointment of Commissions, Committees, Corporations, and Liaision Officers.[15] The University Grants Commission provides for SC/ST Cells in the Universities/Remedial Coaching, relaxation up to 10 per cent cut off marks for grant of Junior Research Fellowship with all SC/ST candidates getting scholarship. There are pre-matric scholarship, post-matric scholarship and book bank schemes for the SC/ST students along with schemes for girls/ boys hostels for them. SC/STs well educated candidate also enjoy national oversees scholarship and passage grants and so on and so forth.

When one confronts with the issue of the efficacy of the constitutional guarantees in favour of the Scheduled Castes and Scheduled Tribes and different governmental schemes to ameliorate their conditions so as to become the equal partner in the nation building, the hope does not remain the same as it was in 1950.

Due to entrenched social mores and mindset social discrimination is rampant. Equality is only on paper. Even at this stage of modern sophistication and pronounced commitment of equal treatment to all we hear of the washing of the statute of Sampoornanand by Gangajal after the unveiling ceremony performed by Babu Jagjivan Ram. We also find the case of the requirement of purification of Harijans by 'Gangajal' and 'Tulsidal' prior to the entry in temple of 'Sree Nath Ji' near Udaipur which prompted Justice J.S. Verma of Rajasthan High Court to expose the problem of hypocratic social behaviour. "It is tragic that on the eve of Gandhi Jayanti we are debating a Harijan's right to enter a public temple for worship as an equal, and directions of the Court be needed for enforcement of this right to equality. All men are born equal and classification between them thereafter is man-made and artificial against the divine dictate. To present them as unequal before God is, therefore, injustice and insult to our Maker beside being contrary to the guarantee and mandate to equality in our

Constitution and a basic human right. To name them 'Harijans' and then discriminate them for entry into a public temple to worship 'Hari' is not merely violation of a constitutional guarantee or insult to them but sheer hypocrisy and insult to 'Hari' rendering their name a misnomer."[16] Above all gangrape of Bhanwari, a backward caste Saathin and judicial observation crossed all limits of decency and expressed status bias outbrust. On Nov. 5, 1995 District and Sessions Court Jaipur acquitted all the accused of gang-raping. The Court said, "since the offenders were upper caste men and included a Brahmin, the rape could not have taken place because Bhanwari was from a lower caste."[17]

The recent suicide committed by a brilliant S.C. research scholar – Sri Rohith Vemula on Jan. 17, 2016 on the campus of Hyderabad Central University has raised many unanswered questions for consideration of those who choose to talk on review of social reservation. Mr Vemula was admitted not on the basis of reservation but on the basis of his merit. Still, he fell victim of hostile discrimination for his being a scheduled caste scholar. His was not isolated case. His was sixth since 2008 in that university. Due to unbearable hostile discriminatory attitude of the university by not providing even a guide and a lab Senthil Kumar committed suicide in 2008; so did Balraj in the same year; Swaran Singh committed suicide in 2012 and Pulayala Raju and Madri Venkatesh in 2013 and ultimately Rohith Vemula in 2016. Our Prime Minister rightly expressed a human touch that mother India has lost a brilliant son. But question is still looming large how long shall it continue?

In the above backdrop it is obviously clear that the dreams of our framers of the Constitution to wipe out very tear from every eye and insure a civic society without discrimination along with establishment of social democracy has remained a long distant aspiration and the living law, practices and social mores are not aligned the fulfillment of the aspirations of the founding fathers to make India a great country with contribution of all the segments of society. With a view to expose the fault lines in our constitutional functioning and social democracy the present book has become the felt necessities of the time.

Thus, the present book deals with the constitutional provisions relating to the reservation for the Schedule Castes and the Schedule Tribes, the practice and outcome of such efforts. The book has been divided in to four parts. Part **one** deals with general considerations containing three chapters –one –problem of discrimination, two – compensatory discrimination/ preferential treatment: What, Why, How Long? and three- vision of the framers of the Indian Constitution. Part **two** deals with preferential treatment to SCs/STs and contains one chapter – Chapter IV under the same caption. Part **three** deals with issues relating to reservation for SCs and STs and contains one chapter – **five** which deals with the issues of reservation in promotions and allied issues. Part **four** deals with conclusion and suggestion.

In this enterprise some articles of Dr Upendra Baxi, at present Professor of Law at Warwick University, U.K. served as a guiding force. After Galanter, Dr Baxi is the legal luminary who dauntlessly has preferred to call spade a spade to move in direction envisioned by Dr Ambedkar. Dr Baxi's article, "Emancipation of Justice: Babasaheb Ambedkar's Legacy and Vision" presents the solution of the present day darkness prevailing in the Indian society including the highest places of learning like Universities. The concluding words read, "For those who (perhaps vainly in the eye of the history) believe in the possibilities of emancipator politics, there is no escape of discovery of India- and un-Nehruvian 'discovery', for a change for the real Atisudras of India[18] an equally real expression came from Dr Baxi's pen when the conversion of Supreme Court ordained Law Day was converted into an executive ordered Constitution Day last year. In his briefest exposition under caption, "Constitution Day After", Dr Baxi wished, "Parliament would better celebrate Ambedkar by declaring war on unconstitutional evils like untouchability.[19] This book is humble effort to deal with the living law on social reservation- reservations for SCs/STs.[20]

We proceed to work with a note of Justice V. R. Krishna Iyer.[21] The Great Jurist Judge with Human Sympathy and Above all a Great Man with compassion to all creatures-

"Those members handicapped by numbers or social disability have the right of special concern. It is their land and equalisation, through particular fillip, shall lift them to equality. This process is equalisation to attain equality.

> Full many a gem of purest ray serene,
> The dark unfathom'd caves of ocean bear,
> Full many a flower is born to blush unseen,
> And waste its sweetness on the desert air.
>
> —Thomas Gray

Notes

1. Dhananjay Keer, Dr Ambedkar: Life and Mission, 1954, p. 143.
2. Constituent Assembly Debate, Vol. X- XII, p. 979.
3. Article 17, the Constitution of India provides. "Untouchbility" is abolished and its practice in any form is forbidden. The enforcement of any disability

arising out of "untouchability" shall be an offence punishable in according us the law".

4. Laws have been enacted by Parliament under Article 17 read with Article 35(a) (ii).
5. Article 15(1) and (2).
6. Article 16(2).
7. Article 29(2).
8. Article 325.
9. Part XVI (Articles 330-342).
10. Article 330.
11. Article 332.
12. Part XI, the Constitution of India.
13. Part XI A, the Constitution of India 1950.
14. Concessions and Relaxations–
    1. Reservation in Services/Posts in the Government and Public Sector Undertaking to be filled up by the direct recruitment or promotion.
    2. Relaxation of maximum age limit for direct recruitment and posts to be filled up by promotion.
    3. Concessions in recruitment, examination fees, etc.
    4. A separate interviews for SC/ST candidates for direct recruitment.
    5. Relaxation of qualification, experience and other criteria for appointment.
    6. Travelling allowance for attending written test and interviews for recruitment.
    7. Extension of zone for consideration for promotions to SC/ST employees.
    8. Reservation in general residential accommodation.
    9. Provisions in the Central Civil Services (Conduct) rules against harassment of SC/ST employees.
    10. Reservation in dealership of PSUs products, and concessions in conditions related to dealership.
15. Institutional Safeguards–
    1. Establishment of National Commission for Scheduled Castes and Scheduled Tribes with purpose and functions as delineated under Article 338 of the Constitution.
    2. National Commission for Safai Karamcharis.
    3. Establishment of Committee of Parliament on the Welfare of SC/ST to examine the representation of SCs/STs in services and to make suitable recommendation for improvements.
    4. Establishment of National Scheduled Caste Finance and Development Corporation, National Safai Karamcharis Finance and Development Corporations and Dr Ambedkar Foundation.
    5. Provision of Liasion Officers and Special Cells to assist them to monitor and ensure the proper implementation of concessions for SCs and STs.

16. Surya Narayan Chaudhary v. State of Rajasthan, A.I.R. 1989. Raj. 99. (J. S. Verma C.J. Raj. H.C.)
17. See Madhu Dandvate, 'The Rape of Justice in Bhanwari Case'. *The Times of India*, (Lack. ed.) 7.2.1996, p. 6.
18. (In) V.T. Patil, Studies in Ambedkar, Devika Publications, Delhi 1995, pp. 15-38 at p. 37.
19. "Constitution Day After", The Indian Express 3.12.2015, p. 10.
20. The status of S.C.B.Cs is little better then SCs/STs. But, in Central class I services, in spite of just double population, the percentage of SCBCs is less then SCs/STs. And therefore, the whole social reservation has been covered in the book.
21. "Unequal Justice to Professional Courses" (in) Indian Law- Dynamic Dimensions of the Abstract. Universal Law Publishing, New Delhi 2012, pp. 418- 420 at p. 418s.

Chapter - 2

Problems of Discrimination

2.1 The Problem in Retrospect: Phoenix raising head from Ashes Again and Again

Compensatory discrimination is the state devised policy to boost to extent the historically deprived, persecuted and discriminated classes. It is an attempt to dilute the ill impact of men created evil to snatch away from such classes the right to equality, live with human dignity and justice.

The act of deprivation, persecution and hostile discrimination is the product of betrayal of men of the trust reposed by God in them. God created man in the last of the process of creation. He created man out of clay in his own image and bestowed on him the privilege to utilise all the creatures, plants etc. He created woman out of the bones of the man. Thus, man and woman were made of the same thing. God made the man rational and possessed with discretion (vivek). Discretion is very pure and pious concept with faculty to discern what is just and what is unjust and what is right and what is wrong. God mandated man to procreate and treat woman virtuously with love and affection. Since all men and women are creation of the same God, a natural affinity was bestowed on them to live with mutual understanding and respect. To love God meant to love all the creatures in general and all the human beings in particular. Live and let others live was the message of the Almighty God. The sense of otherness was the keynote of all the human actions. The clear message of Bible is: "Love thy neighbour as thyself." A truly religious man or woman adhere this principle in letter and spirit. For some the whole world is neighbourhood. To be good and to do good to others is psalm of the life. Mother Teresa rightly says:

> "Life can offer a happiness
> That cannot be turned into grief.

Giving Joy to another
Is a joy beyond belief."

This is the message of Dharma (religion). The Great Hindi poet very aptly enunciates: There is no dharma like protection of the interest of others. (Parahita Saris Dharam Nahi Bhai – Tulasidas). Dharma is the most secular word of the world. It comes from Sanskrit root "dhri" meaning to hold together. Man forget manavadharma taught by God to them. The evil started with the world. Rationality went off. Selfish motive began to reign. Exploitation of men started for personal gain. The psychological evil sense of superiority over others became dominant. Prejudices developed. Some created privileges for themselves and put others in disadvantages. Discrimination started. Some became fortunate others became unfortunate. Be it U.S.A., be it India or be it elsewhere, the policy of segregation started. The present day's dominant scholar Ronald M. Dworkin rightly comments, "Segregation treats Blacks differently and history shows that the seeds of the different treatment lies in prejudice."[1] The intelligent dominant class persons began to philosophise it and in order to gave their practices legitimacy declared such acts as the will of God. They used to say, "Segregation was God's will that everyone had right to live with his own people." The great philosopher Plato too gave legitimacy to class division: conceding all people brothers as creation of the same God, he justified social arrangements. He believed in natural inequality. Plato said in his Republic: "you in this city are all brothers but God as he was fashioning you, put gold in those who are capable of ruling, hence they are deserving the most reverence. He put silver in the auxiliaries, and iron and copper in the farmers and the other craftsmen."[2] In Platonic scheme some were born to rule and others to be ruled. He also molded the definition of justice: "to mind one's business and not to be meddlesome is justice."[3] He also warned "there is an oracle that the city shall perish when it is guarded by iron or copper."[4] Platonic arrangement can be compared with Hindu Varna Vyavastha – Brahmins coming from the mouth of Paramapursh – Brahman, Kshatriyas from arms, Vaishyas from thigh and Shudras from feet. The mandate of Manuvadi arrangement being obedience to Swadharma and not interfere with the dharma of the other varnas. Slavery or dasa pratha was justified by some of the great thinkers like Aristotle and Indian sages. Aristotle thought that slavery was natural: some were born slave and condition of slavery was both beneficial and just. But experiencing the pitiable condition, ill-treatment, slaves being treated as chattel, he appeared amenable to reasons. He accepted it is easy to see that those who hold the opposite view (i.e. condemn slavery) are also in a way correct.

The discrimination deprived certain classes the status of equality. Contrary to the nature that men were born equal, inequality began to take root under institutional protection including the judicial one. In ***Dread Scott v. Sanford***[5], Chief Justice Roger Taney declared that at the time when the Constitution of the United States was adopted, Negroes were regarded as persons of inferior status, not as citizens. Though the Stoic philosophers were of firm view that men were essentially equal and that discrimination between them on account of sex, class, race or nationality were unjust and contrary to the law of nature[6], Chief Justice Roger Taney struck down the Missouri Compromise because the Court thought that slave owners had constitutionally protected rights in their slaves.[7] It goes without saying that the Supreme Court could not read the wind blowing against slavery. Edgar Bodenheimer very pertinently remarks, "If the same Court, in the famous **Dread Scott** decision had recognised the strength of the anti-slavery sentiments in many parts of the country instead of taking the extreme view that the institution of slavery was sacrosanct, the civil war might conceivably have been avoided.[8] A just order can be established only in a just society which the American society was lacking. Dworkin remarks that "classification that usually cause disadvantage to groups like Black or Jews or Women or homo-sexuals, that have historically been the target of prejudice."[9]

The dominant group prejudices led to construct preconceived duality of good or bad between whites and blacks and men and women.

Table 2.1: Male – Female dualism[10]

Male (Full of virtues)	*Female (Full of vices)*
Rational	Irrational
Active	Passive
Thought	Feeling
Reason	Emotion
Culture	Nature
Power	Sensitivity
Objectivity	Subjectivity
Abstract	Conceptualised

The preconceived, prejudiced and ill intentioned generalisation about women prevails in all the societies. Take some examples from the Indian outlook. Tulsi pronounces "Nari Sahaj Jad Agya" (a woman is by nature stupid) or what he puts in the mouth of the great knowledgeable scholar Ravana – They rightly observe in regard to the character of a woman that eight evils ever abide in her heart:[11] (1) recklessness ; (2) mendacity; (3) fickleness; (4) deceit; (5) timidity; (6) indiscretion; (7) impurity, and (8) callousness.

Like Men and Women dualism prevails in the case of unscientific dualism between White and Black images.

Table 2.2: Black and White Images[12]

White Image	*Black Image*
Industrious	Lazy
Intelligent	Unintelligent
Moral	Immoral
Knowledgeable	Ignorant
Enabling Culture	Disabling Culture
Responsible	Shiftness
Virtuous/ pious	Lascivious
Law-Abiding	Criminal

The Indian condition is not better.

The great Hindi poet Tulsi putting in the mouth of guilt conscious Sea (Samudra) equates Sudras with drum, rustic, beast and woman and pronounces that they all deserve instructions (Tadna) / beating.[13] The American White-Black images may be seen in the cultural discourse in India.

Like American White-Black dualism, we can find cultural discourse opposites in Upper Caste perception of dalits and Dalits own perception about themselves.

The white-black dualism and comment upon that holds equal good in Indian context of the graded society. It has been nicely been pointed out in reference to United States that the attitude of superiority – inferiority gave birth to discontentment. And by and by people's growing sense became that "racial segregation was wrong in principle, because it was incompatible with decency to treat one race as inherently inferior to another."[15] That is reason why Dworkin condemns racial discrimination by exposing inherent illogicity in its practice. To quote Dworkin "racial discrimination that

Table 2.3: Cultural discourse[14]

Dominant Caste's Perception of Dalits	***Dalit Perception about themselves***
Dirty-Filthy Fellows	Capable- But no opportunities
Thieves / Robbers	Hardworking
Cunning	Honest
Lazy- kamchor	Assertive
Useless- Good for nothing	Straight forward / less cunning
Gluttons – petu, khau	Culturally talented
Loose morals	Sensitive Emotional
Dishonest	Self-sacrificing
Quarrelsome – Disunity	Sagacious – good judgment
Ungrateful	Collective

disadvantages blacks is unjust, not because people cannot choose their race, but because that discrimination expresses prejudice."[16]

The other vulnerable and victims of prejudices of society have been women. The position of women during the nineteenth century was in many respects, comparable to that of blacks under the pre-civil War codes[17]. Even the Judiciary was not far behind. Bradley J. as late as 1973, observed in ***Bradwell v. Illinois***[18] that, "Man is or should be, women's protector or defender… The paramount destiny and mission of woman are to fulfill the noble and benign offer of wife and mother. This is the law of creator."[19] Manusmriti speaks the same language of dependence of a woman on father, husband and son as per her age. Much verse prejudicial utterance is "Jimi Swantantra Bhaye Bigarahi Naree" or "Sahaj Apawan Naree"[20]. So long as human prejudices did not prevail women enjoyed equal status with men during the Vedic period and girls like boys underwent Upanayan ceremony. But, patriarchal superiority through Samhitas, Brahmanas, Upanishads, Dharamsutras and Smritis degraded women to the status of Shudras. It is totally unfounded, irrational and unproved. To quote Justice V.R. Krishna Iyer, "to exaggerate the biological factor is masculine strategies to keep the woman down."[21] To quote him, 'It is blasphemy to brand women as nitwits, incompetent and most tough enough for hard and heavy tasks. They can win laurels in any sector. Given training, they can be pilots and cosmonauts, fighting squads and intellectual groups, not merely dainty dolls at home and dubious recruits to beauty parlour."[22] If we look at the Indian social structure, taboos and mores prevailing in the Indian society, all women are not equally degraded and exploited. The intermixed social status of men and women in Indian society (still prevalent in interior village community) is as, follows:

Table 2.4

Brahmins	(revered as Baba (grand father)
Wives of Brahmins	(revered as Matwa / Panditine)
Kshatriyas	(Respected as Thakur Saheb / Babu Saheb)
Wives of Kshatriyas	(Respected as Thakurine)
Vaishyas	(Respected Seth Ji)
Wives of Vaishyas	(Respected as Sethani Ji)
Shudras other than SCs/STs	(Though looked upon by three Upper Castes, but respected by S.Cs/S.Ts.)
Wives of Shudras other than SCs/STs	(---- do -----)
SCs/STs	(Look upon by all and inhere utter inferiority in themselves)
Wives of SCs/ STs	(Most deplorable, hated / neglected and vulnerable, abject sexual violence)

Though even the women of upper castes had been bracketed to the status of Shudras, they have better hope of progress, dignity and equality in the changing scenario than the depressed classes. **First**, the women of the higher castes have not suffered that much indignity as the Shudra's. **Second**, now the awakening has mitigated the difference between the girl and the boy. **Third**, in all the examinations the girls are excelling the boys. The result of 2015 UPSC shows that women secured top four ranks.[23] Days are not far away when they will not only succeed in compelling others to feel their presence, but they will also excel the boys in every walk of life. **Fourth**, from 2017 women will serve as pilot and even in fighting crew. In spite of this happy and inspiring trend the social more and people's outlook towards women is not substantially changing. Increasing cases of rape, dowry death and atrocities tell the awful stories and a separate study on the line indicated is need of the hour. Here we confine to observe that women have been victim of prejudices and the women in the form of P.Ms., administrators and intellectuals like Bruntland moulding the thinking of the whole world about Our Common Future have proved that they are in no way inferior to men and the Indian Supreme Court has put innovative interpretation of the equality clause to assert equality of women in employment.[24] But, the gender prejudices are so deep-rooted that they have not gone forever. A separate independent study on gender discrimination and efforts towards gender justice is needed and therefore this aspect of discrimination based on deep-rooted prejudices has not been touched any more in the present book. The present book relates and is confined to social justice through social reservation – reservation for negroes in United States and SCs/STs and SEBCs in India. In both the countries in spite of many governmental affirmative actions and preferential treatments in favour of the depressed, despised and disprivileged people, discrimination and persecution based superiority-interiority complexes and deeply-rooted prejudicial social mores are raising heads from time to time in new and new ways like phoenix from ashes.

The ensuring study presents an in-depth account of a vital gap in legal and political commitment and social mores resulting into continuum discrimination.

2.2. Race and Caste Based Discrimination in US and India: A Story of Continuum Prejudice: Primordial to Present

Discrimination has been a world-wide phenomenon. It has more intimate connection with the British dominance in different parts of the world.[25] Once upon a time it was said that the sun does not set in the British imperialism. So was the story of discrimination with aboriginal and indigenous people somewhere like Australia and with people brought from other countries for the economic purposes like the United States. In Australia, Britishers created a myth of ***terra nullius***[26] with a motive to deprive the original and indigenous people of their status and rights and adult suffrage could be extended to the indigenous people only in 1962. In 1992, in ***Mabo(2) v. Queensland***[27] the highest Court of the land could break the common law doctrine based on unjust discrimination in the enjoyment of civil and political rights and "declared that" the Merian people were entitled as against the whole world to possession, occupation, use and enjoyment of the lands of the Murry Islands." Aboriginals had been denied voting rights for long on prejudicial assessment that, "aboriginals have not intelligence, interest and capacity to vote."[28] The position and bargaining in first nations occupied by Britishers viz. the United States, Canada and Newzealand was a shed better as some agreement with aboriginals was arrived at.

The position of discrimination in the United States and the India has been of a special significance. In the United States, Black Negroes were caught and brought to that country from the African continent. African Americans were slave from the day one. White-Black division started on the basis of colour and race. In India, Dasas were not brought and enslaved from outside. They were either the original inhabitants or degraded persons of the same Aryan community known as Shudras and later untouchables. **First,** Both in U.S. and India the origin appears to be based on colour. In the United States it was evident, has been evident and is continuing to be evident that British settlers in America are Whites and African – Americans are Blacks popularly known as Negroes. In India there are two views. According Mahabharata there were no distinct castes and classes of men in **Kritayuga**.[29] Bhrigu says that only few Brahmanas were first created by the great Brahman.[30] But, later on the view came to be expressed that FOUR divisions of mankind came into being – Brahmana, Kshatriya, Vaisya and Shudra. Bhrigu narrated the origin of varna to Bharadwaj according to colour/complexion. The complexion of Brahmana was White (sita), that of Kshatriya red (Lohita), that of Vaisya yellow (pitah)[31] and that of Shudra black (asitah). The etymological meaning of **Varna** is colour. Thus, Brahmanas stood at the pinnacle with White colour and Shudras at the lowest with black complexion. But, in between the White and Black stood two others – Kshatriyas with red colour and Vaishya with yellow colour. But this distinction could not work well as Bharadwaj himself challenged the basis of division according to colour. It was said that there are endless varieties of men and colour. Any way Shudras were destined to act as the servant of the other three Varnas[32] known as dwija. **Second**, both in U.S. and in India, be it negroes or Shudras were excluded from the mainstream of the society. They were deprived of the status of human being. They were treated like Chattlea thing to be possessed and disposed of. In America slaves were marketable commodity. They did not have even right to person. Even their children were property of their masters like animals begetting calves etc. In India too the untouchable dasas enjoyed no status. They were equated with animals. Slaves had no property. Property of a slave belonged to his master.[33] The Chandala like a domestic pig, a cock, a dog was to feed on refuse and filth.[34] The Chandala was relegated to the cremation grounds and lived on men's refuse.[35] The Chandala were declared to be moving burial. **Third**, both in U.S. and India, blacks and shudras were deprived of learning. In India, situation was still worse. Shastric mandate to pour heated gloss into the years of Chandala who had heard Vedas or cut his tongue who had enchanted mantras was too iniquitous and inhuman. The story of beheading Shambook for his Tapsya and excelling in Vedas and cutting of thumb of Eklabya for excelling in archery tell- their own story of hostile discrimination and contempt for merit in society. **Fourth**, both in U.S. and India, the ulterior purpose was to deprive despised classes of money and wealth and secure wealth for the privileged classes. In U.S.A., slavery and Jim Crow contributed to the widening of gap between Negroes and White people's wealth. In India, Homo Hierarchicus resulted into exploitation and deprivation of depressed people and converged with Homo Economicus. **Fifth,** both in U.S. and in India, prejudices ran continuously. Some concessions or reforms were rendered meaningless due to social prejudices and tacit support of the governmental agencies. In U.S.A., inspite of great civil war and enactment of 13th, 14th and 15th Amendments to the Constitution, equality was denied to negroes on one pretext or the other and found culmination in Judicial stamp of 'separate but equal' doctrine in ***Plessy v. Fergusan***[36]. In India, no revolutionary attempt was made which could be equated with abolition of Slavery in U.S.A. That was reason why Jyotiba Phule wrote in his famous writing Gulamgiri[37] addresses dedication to:

> The good people of the United States
> As a token admiration for their
> Sublime disinterested and
> Self sacrificing devotion
> In the cause of Negro Slavery; and with
> An earnest desire, that my countrymen
> May take their noble example as their guide
> In the emancipation of their Sudra Brethren
> From the trammels of Brahmin thraldom.[38]

In India, too reformative measures adopted by Chhatrapati Sahu Ji Maharaj and attempt towards the education of the down-trodden Harijans was not taken in proper way by upper caste people. There have been certain dissimilarities in the U.S. and the Indian society in relation to the emancipation of negroes and depressed and untouchables in India. **First**, American society had and still has to deal with the problem of a negligible size of American Negores who are in identified minority number. Indian society has to deal with majority of the people who had been discriminated, persecuted and deprived at the hands of a handful upper class dominant people. **Second,** in U.S. Negroes had been a well knit unit putting concerted efforts and ready for sacrifices for the community cause. In India, depressed had been disunited, scattered and themselves victim of hierarchical Hindu society suffering from superiority –inferiority complex among themselves. Consequent to it the Negroes as well as well intentioned their supporter Whites paid heavy price of emancipation from discriminatory degradation. Thus, slavery ended as the result of a war in which more than 600,000 people lost their lives.[39] The champion of the abolition move President Abraham Lincoln was shot at and so was the fate of President Johnson who had issued an executive order on affirmative action in 1965 and Martin Luther King Jr. who played vital role in getting the Civil Rights Act, 1964 passed. In India, no such bold positive action was undertaken nor prejudices reached to that grave situation trenching with the blood of noble souls. **Third**, in U.S.A., extreme prejudicial discrimination took place in the form of Jim crow system leaving blacks without" legal protection against even most oppressive laws; Tulsa, Oklahoma race riot in 1921, the Rosewood, Florida massacre of 1923 and the thousand of wrongful protections and lynching and dozen of riots that took place throughout the country in the period from Reconstruction to the Civil Rights era.[40] But, the subsequent administration realised the excesses and discrimination committed which resulted into apologies.

- President William J. Clinton during his African visit in 1998 discussing the horror of slavery admitted that European Americans received the fruits of the slave trade and "we were wrong in that" and he tendered apology for slavery. When he visited Goree Island.[41]

  In 2003 President George W. Bush visited Africa expressed the view – "at this place, liberty and life were stolen and sold. Human beings were delivered and sorted, and weighed and branded with the marks of commercial enterprises, and loaded as cargo on a voyage without return. One of the largest migrations of history was also one of the greatest crimes of history."
- House of Representatives, on Jan. 6, 1999 in H.R. 40, 106th Congress, Ist Session acknowledged the fundamental injustice, cruelty, brutality and inhumanity of slavery in the United States and the 13 American Colonies between 1619 and 1865. It constituted Commission to make recommendations for appropriate remedies.
- United States Senate apology for Failure to Pass Anti-Lynching Legislation, 109th Congress, Ist Session made clear that at least 4, 742 people, predominantly African-American, were reported lynched in the United States between 1882 and 1968 and

99 per cent of all perpetrators of lynching escaped from punishment by State or local officials. The Senate resolved – that the Senate –

(1) "apologises to the victims of lynching for the lynching for the failure of the Senate to enact anti-lynching legislation.

(2) expresses the deepest sympathies and most solemn regrets of the Senate to the descendants of victims of lynching, the ancestors of whom were deprived of life, human dignity and the constitutional protections accorded all citizens of the United States; and

(3) remembers the history of lynching, to ensure that these tragedies will be neither forgotten nor repeated."

Pope Francis apologised with a sense of culpa for sins and crimes of the Catholic Church against the indigenous peoples during the colonial conquest of America. In July, 2015 itself during his tour to South America, he noted that Latin American Church leaders in the past had acknowledged that "grave sins were committed against the native peoples of America in the name of God." Earlier in 1992, St. Paul-II had apologised to the continent's indigenous for the "pain and suffering" caused during 500 years of the Church's presence in America. But Francis, going further, did so with 'regret'.

Report of Nicole Winfield from Santa Cruz, Bolivia, July, 10 (2015) expressed well the genuine remorse on part of Pope Francis and reciprocity on the part of addressees. Says, the report-

> "I would also say, and here I wish to be quite clear, as was St. John Paul II: I humbly ask forgiveness, not only for the offences of the church herself, but also for crimes committed against the native peoples during the so-called conquest of America," he said to applause from the crowd.

Then deviating from his prepared script, he added: "I also want for us to remember the thousands and thousands of priests who strongly opposed the logic of the sword with the power of the cross. There was sin, and it was plentiful. But we never apologised, so I now ask for forgiveness. But where there was sin, and there was plenty of sing, there was also an abundant grace increased by the men who defended indigenous peoples."

Francis's apology was met with wild applause from the indigenous and other grass-roots groups gathered for a world summit of popular movements whose fight against injustice and social inequality has been championed by the pope.

"We accept the apologies. What more can we expect from a man like Pope Francis ?" Said Adolfo Chavez, a leader of a lowlands indigenous group. "It's time to turn the page and pitch in to start anew. We indigenous were never lesser beings." AP (The Indian Express (Chandigarh) 11.7.2015 p. 12, See also Pope and Promise, Frontline, Aug. 21, 2015 pp. 64-66.

Indian society or government or Legislatures or priests have never shown a sense of remorse, apology and contrition for tragic and prejudicial discriminatory treatment with depressed classes in general and untouchables in particular. Bapu felt it. He inspired people to repent for that. But, of no avail. It has become fashionable in political circle to issue empty commitment to do justice with all and save secularism at any cost.

Fourth, Indian social structure is peculiar and different from other countries including U.S.A. In U.S., Negroes are different from Whites. In India, depressed people are part and parcel of the dominant Hindu society. In U.S., affirmative actions are not the problematic as majority has to discriminate against itself and only minor adjustment has to be done against the minority of seats. In India, a handful of privileged class has to ensure justice to the majority of the people and number of seats affected by affirmative action may be sizeable – not few but many to be adjusted within the upper limit of 50 per cent.

Explaining the peculiar position of Caste ridden Indian hierarchical society, Nobel Laureate Amartya Sen observes: "All countries in the world have inequalities of various kinds. India, however, has a unique cocktail lethal divisions and disparities. Few countries have to contend with such extreme inequalities in so many dimensions including large economic inequalities as well as major disparities of caste, class and gender. Caste has a peculiar role in India that separates it out from the rest of the world. Many countries, to be sure, have had in the past (and to some extent even right now) caste-like institutions that place people in confined boxes. But, India seems to be quite unique both in terms of the centrality of caste hierarchies and in terms of their continuing hold in the society (despite a great many pieces of legislation and outlawing any practice of caste discrimination). And caste stratification often reinforces class inequality, giving it resilience that is harder to conquer."[42]

Fifth, In America, Negroes have been suppressed, discriminated in all walks of life, but on defense front they have been united and have fought for the country including Vietnam War. In India, persecution of common people had created a wall of hatred and apathy between the ruling class and the common people. As Marx making remark on the future result of British rule in India said, "How was English supremacy established in

India ? A country not only divided between the Mohammedan and Hindu, but between tribe and tribe; between caste and caste; a society whose framework was based on a sort of equilibrium resulting from a general repulsion and constitutional exclusiveness between all its members. Such a country and such a society, were they not the predestined prey of conquest ?"[43]

Kisan Fago Bansode draws a picture of Hindu Nation as follow:

Look, Look All People
    This is my Hindu Nation.
Divided at its root
    A Jungle of divisions
Honour for enmity
    This is my Hindu Nation.
Nowhere in the world
    Such segregation as here
Caste at birth
    This is my Hindu nation
High place to the Brahmans,
    Low to all others.[44]

Gangadhar Pantawane, a Dalit Journal Editor says, 'To me, Dalit is not a caste. He is a man exploited by the social and economic traditions of the country.'[45]

The Indian caste system has been responsible for invader's easy invasion. To quote Justice Kuldip Singh, "This country remained under shackles of slavery for over one thousand years. The reason for our inability to fight the foreign rule was the social degenerations of India because of the caste system. To rule this country was not necessary to divide the people, the caste system conveyed the message, "Divided we are – come and rule us."[46]

Sixth, One very noticeable difference between the U.S. and India may be discern in judicial outlook to tackle the problem of social inequality through preferential treatment. In the United States the Supreme Court evolved the principle of indication of source in favour of negroes.[47] On the other hand, the judiciary in India searched the indication of source principle to deprive the depressed of their claims and help persons other than SCs/STs[48] or other reserved category and augment the cause of unreserved category.[49]

Seventh, Since the Constitution of India was framed in mid-twentieth century with experiences of Nazi race extremism, horror of two World Wars, the dawn of human rights movement through United Nations and Universal Declaration of Human Rights, 1948 many a safeguards were undertaken in it to prohibit discrimination based on religion, race, caste, sex, place of birth etc. along with the requirement of positive action of preferential treatment, it took lead and as Marc Galanter points out the United States took inspiration for affirmative action. But, in practice America has taken some lead through diversity theory which India has to follow.

Eighth, India has added dimension of the concept of fifth Varna – Antyaj, outcastes, untouchable, Panchamas and pollution was thought to be basis for exclusiveness. 'Harijans pollute' was the bold statement coming from caste-Hindus. No doubt they did menial jobs, they ate meat of dead animals, but the moot question is: was there any option for them ? Dr Ambedkar very aptly points out:

> Nobody would like to eat rotten meat, if fresh meat is available. Untouchables eat rotten meat, not because they like it.
>
> Untouchables eat rotten meat, because nothing else is available, So may they remain alive.
>
> They have no means of livelihood, all businesses are closed for them…Untouchables eat rotten meat because Hindus have given to them no respectable means of livelihood."[50]

Dr Ambedkar very well exposes the social mind set in his poem Problem of Discrimination:

> An untouchable Leader is said Untouchable leader
>
> A Brahmin leader is not said A Brahmin Leader
>
> He is said to be a great Indian Leader.
>
> So is the case of doctor, singer, wrestler etc. This discrimination is born of Hindu thinking that qualified untouchable too are degraded and nicknamed.

Dr Ambedkar also pointed out how all dirty jobs are get done by untouchables and Hindus are given high salary posts. Civil rights peoples government, equal opportunity, equal rights have no meaning for depressed people and this segregation makes untouchable poor and vulnerable and unable to progress.

The United States also remains a country deeply infected by racism[51] W. Harwood Burns narrates how Kansas Legislature discriminated in punishment of Whites and Negroes for the crime of rape with a White woman. The White rapist could be convicted up to five years imprisonment while "the penalty for a black man convicted of the same offence was castration, the costs of the procedure to be rendered by the desexed."[52] Even the liberal Northerners in America had design behind liberation of Blacks. To quote W. Harwood Burns, "Even in the so-called Free states there was ample borrowing from the statutory schemes of the slavocracy to enforce a social (White) view of the black person's rightful station in life. Thus, northern states systematically resorted to legislative devices to impose their collective view on the lives of "free" blacks, restricting them in employment, education, the franchise, legal personality and public accommodation."[53]

Ninth, Both in U.S. and in India, racial or caste discrimination had dual effect. **First**, it deprived despised people of equality and allowed ill treatment. Abolition of slavery in America was ineffectuated by Jim Crow approval and states began to systematically codify separation of races during 1880s. The culmination point reached in ***Plessy v. Ferguson***.[54] W. Haywood Burns comments in this case "separate but equal" was approved as the law of the land, and the seal of approval of the nation's highest Court was placed upon our own American brand of apartheid."[55] In India untouchables were not allowed to wear the clean clothes, to put roof on the house, to send their Children to school, to purchase land etc. In 'Hindus and War of Public Conscious' Dr Ambedkar narrated how Hindus feel ill if untouchable ladies used to wear ornaments of gold and silver, fetch water from well etc., though such acts were not against Hindus. **Second**, it has enormously served the purpose and interest of the dominant class. In America, Whites captured all economic resources and ousted Negroes from business and sources of earning. In India, even during British regime monopoly in the field of education was continued and in the time of Jotiba Phule, Brahmin opposition to the education of the lower castes was prominent. Atishudras/untouchables could not even dream of education.[56] The philosophy of higher classes liberal leaders like Raja Ram Mohan Roy and government policymakers was that educating the Upper classes would filter downwards. The Britishers too allied with upper Caste strategy. Report of the Director of Education for the year 1857-58 read: "Education and civilisation may descends from the higher to the inferior classes and so communicated may impart new vigour to the community; but they will never ascend from the lower classes to those above them; they can only, if imparted solely to the lower classes, lead to general convulsion of which foreigner would be the first victim."[57] The conduct of upper caste students with a Mahar student is eye-opener. They could not tolerate his presence in the class even though he sat at the last on a different bench. Their reaction was: "yes, but there is matting on the floor, and it transmits pollution. We Brahmans are now all polluted and must wash away the defilement before we eat."[58] Ultimately the Mahar student withdrew himself from the class. The conduct of Brahmin teacher too was not good with despised class. A Brahmin teacher Pantoji had one cane and clods in the class. When Rev. Adam White inquired, his reply was: "I use my cane in the class of caste boys. If I struck the Mahar pollution from the outcaste boy would come along with the stick and the whole body would be polluted. So when the Mahar boy is stupid, I just take a clod and let fly at him, and when I miss I take another."[59] The accumulated effect of neglect of education to Dalits and caste consideration resulted into capture of economic position. K. S. Chalam pointed out that the **dvija** castes of Brahmin, Kshatriya and Vaishya have always remained in higher echelons of economic power and Dalits on the lower rung.[60] Even during the post-independence Nehruvian era opportunities created by the public sector were systematically grabbed by the educated **dvija**. Periyar E.U.R. was prompted to comment on bank nationalisation, "bank nationalisation is bank Brahmanisation."[61]

A comparative study of U.S. and Indian socio-economic scenario reveals that in spite of some inherent differences in the two systems one thing is common and that is the continued prejudicial treatment of Whites and dominant caste people with the despised Negroes in U.S. and depressed people in India. It is but natural that there is human urge for respect for equal treatment and human desire to be free from domination of others. And the sense of injustice revolts against whatever is unequal by caprice. What for Negroes in the United State or SCs, STs and OBCs in India have been craving is their right to live with human dignity without discrimination and humiliation. Their urge, passion and genuine concern are to sit on equal footing with Whites and dominant classes. Martin Luther King, Jr. dreamt that "one day..sons of the former slaves and the sons of former slave owners will be able to sit down together at the table of brotherhood." And, similar was the dream of Dr B.R. Ambedkar in India.

The famous speech of Dr Martin Luther King Jr., on the occasion of the Lincoln Memorial in Washington D.C., on 28 August, 1963 communicates many a things – continued ill-treatment of Negros in spite of the abolition of slavery and earnest desire of brotherhood. King's 'I have a Dream' is produced below:

> **"Five score years ago, a great American in whose symbolic shadow we stand signed the Emancipation Proclamation. This momentous decree came as a great beacon light of hope to millions of Negro slaves who had been seared in the flames of withering injustice. It came as a joyous daybreak to end the long night of captivity.**
>
> But, one hundred years later, we must face the tragic fact that the Negro is still not free. One hundred years later, the life of the Negro is still sadly crippled by the manacles of segregation and the chains of discrimination.
>
> One hundred years later, the Negro lives on a lonely island of poverty in a vast ocean of material prosperity. One hundred years later, the Negro is still languishing in the corners of American society and finds himself an exile in his own land. So we have come here today to dramatise an appalling condition.
>
> In a sense we have come to our nation's capital to cash a check. When the architects of our republic wrote the magnificent words of the Constitution and the Declaration of Independence, they were signing a promissory note to which every American was to fall heir. The note was a promise that all men would be guaranteed the inalienable rights of life, liberty, and the pursuit of happiness. It is obvious today that America has defaulted on this promissory note insofar as her citizens of color are concerned. Instead of honoring this sacred obligation, America has given the Negro people a bad check which has come back marked 'insufficient funds'. But, we refuse to believe that the bank of justice is bankrupt. We refuse to believe that there are insufficient funds in the great vaults of opportunity of this nation. So we have come to cash this check – a check (as spelt there) that will give us upon demand the riches of freedom and the security of justice. We have come to this hallowed spot to remind America of the fierce urgency now. This is no time to engage in the luxury of cooling off or take the tranquillising drug of gradualism. Now is the time to rise from the dark and desolate valley of segregation to the sunlit path of racial justice. Now is the time to open the doors of opportunity to all of God's children. Now is the time to lift our nation from the quicksand of racial injustice to the solid rock of brotherhood."

The reality of life is that slavery was abolished, segregation was abolished but racists and racism has not disappeared. On political and legal levels they have gone but on social level they survive. The Kerner

Commission's Report of 1967 indicting American social system giving rise to racism, said: "This is our basic conclusion that our nation is moving towards two societies, one black, one white, separate and unequal." Due to the fast moving world scenario, human rights assertion and all efforts to end discrimination. America has also changed but in spite of a black adoring Presidency for two terms, the American mind set appears to be the same as it was one and half century earlier when Jefferson's Notes on the State of Virginia asserted that free blacks were "pests" on society[62] or what a south Carolina Judge had uttered in ***Morton v. Thompson*** (S.C., 1854)" a free African population is a curse to any country."[63]

Nearly half a century earlier on March 7, 1965 when 600 blackmen and women attempted to cross a bridge in Selma were brutally attacked by police. The incident has been recorded as "**bloody Sunday**". Nothing has changed in twenty first century when a Negro (Black) President is in office for the second term. In the month of November December 2014 a white policeman killed by shooting an unarmed blackman Michael Brown in Ferguson (Missouri). In another case Eric Garner, a blackmen in New York was strangulated (chokehold) by a White police man. What added fuel to fire was the verdict of Grand Jury of Whitemen in both cases acquitting the white policemen. A million dollar question is: Whether American Justice system is colour-blind in dealing with cases of lives of the black people? Are not these instances of colour-conscious denial of justice to blackmen? The comment of chairman, Central Washington Coalition for Social Justice under Caption, "U.S. Justice Not Colour Blind" is most opportune. U.S. is under racial stress and the above two cases within 10 days have exposed U.S.'s vulnerability to racial division.[64] R. K. Raghvan, former director of Central Bureau of Investigation commented under Caption, "Black City, White Police, and Brown" that the shooting in Ferguson and its violent aftermath shows that policing divorced from the realities of social inequality can be dangerous.[65] The comment of the Chairman, Washington State Network for Human Rights speaks truth: 'Electing a Black as President of the Country was supposed to have reduced confrontation between blacks and whites. However, nothing has happened ?"[66] The World view column of The Hindu from David Brooks, New York Times News Service rightly expresses "The nature of racism has changed; there has been a migration away from prejudice based on genetics to prejudice based on class."[67] The U.S. is celebrating 150th anniversary of the abolition of slavery but racial acts of terrorism at Charleston and killing of unarmed blacks by white police men at Ferguson and Baltimore and ensuring resentment, reactions and violence prove that the roots of races is very deep like the roots of casteism in India and there is no hope for its withering away near future.

The world is moving round. India sails on the same boat. But incidents have surfaced due to social mind set and caste prejudices against the Scheduled Classes persons. A survey of 42,000 households across the country conducted by the National Council of Applied Economic Research (NCAER) revealed that 1 in 4 i.e. 25 per cent Indians admit (in reality figure may be more) to practicing untouchability.[68] There is hardly a day which does carry any news of rape, exploitation, misbehaviour, beating and sometimes even killing of some despised Scheduled Caste person. To cite a few.

Indian News Service 26.8.2014 – Dalit 'beaten up, lock in Kernel.'[69] The Indian Express dated 17.11.2014 published news Mahadalit boy burnt to death in Bihar[70]. In Mohanpur, Rohtas a 15 year old SC boy was burnt to death after his goat had eaten the paddy crop of an upper caste man. Earlier in Bihar six Dalit women had been raped by three high caste men in Bhojpur and 150 dalit had been forced to flee a village in Gaya after member of their community was killed in September, 2014.[71]

The Hindu 19.3.2015 – Dalit youth assaulted, urinated on.

During a temple festival a castemen gang attacked a youngman of Kuravar community employed as a Ratter in Bangalore.

Indian Express 20.3.2015 – Dalit Youth 'forced' to attend 'peace meeting' with men who attacked him.[72]

The Indian Express 8.9.2014 – Dalit face 'boycott' after landlords announce fine on those hiring them.[73]

- The bone of contention is 6.5 acres of land in the village, which is reserved for Dalits.
- On Loudspeaker landowners in Sangrur (Namol village) announced anyone who hired Dalit to work in their fields would be fined Rs 10,000.
- Dalit boy thrashed for taking plate from 'non-dalit' stack.[74]
- Two dalit infants of three year and nine months old were burnt alive by Rajputs in village Sunpeth in Faridabad, Haryana on 20.10.2015.[75]

What is more damaging is that during the first week of Feb. 2015 (Friday) the apex Court bench consisting of Justices M.B. Lokur and 4 Lalit refused to any order restraining social boycott of dalits by high caste people. In violence hit Mirchpur village in Haryana high caste people declared to boycott and not allow to give any work to dalits. The Court showed its helpness. Declaring the judicial hands off the social justice bench said; what is solution to end the social boycott ? The Courts cannot say that end the social boycott of dalits. It would be an ineffective order." The situation arose when an old dalit man and his physically challenged daughter were killed by dominant Jat Community members.[76]

One moot question is: Have SCs no fundamental right to bread, means of livelihood and safe shelter in this country ? What is meaning of freedom for the SC community ? What is significance of fundamental rights for them ? Have courts not issued orders in anticipation of not being effectively complied with ? Have not Courts order completion of national highway in certain area within stipulated time ? Have not they ordered non-burning paddy-roots in Punjab and Haryana which has been observed only in being broken ? Have not courts felt the need of continuing mandamus in view of non-compliance of their orders ?

Result is obvious. The National news page of The Hindu dated 5.6.2015 first column[77] read: facing Social Boycott

Dalit families want to relocate

- 13 families in a Maharashtra village live in constant fear of attack.

Reason ?

On April 28, the Dalits took out a procession to mark the birth day anniversary of Baba Saheb Ambedkar, where songs dedicated to the Dalit icon were played. A few upper caste youths objected to it and demanded to play the songs on Shivaji Maharaj. They desecrated the image of Dr Ambedkar, abused Dalit women. An F.I.R. was filed which furiated upper castes to call for a social boycott. In the village out of the population of 1500 people only 13 households belong to Dalits – 11 Buddhist Mahar and two of the Mang Community. Upper castes people asked –

- Dalits not to drink water from public taps;
- Not to gaze their cattle in village
- Shopkeepers not to sell groceries to Dalits.

Families of Dalits were living in fear of a possible attack by upper castes. They expressed desire before the D.M. to shift somewhere safer.

On 15.8.2015 Dalit were taking procession – temple car in Seshasamuthiran village of Tamil Nadu's Villupuram district through Vanniyars Upper Caste area on police permission. Vanniyar caste people who had population of 3000 as against 400 Dalits set 10 dalit huts on fire and hurt 15 people including S.P. and 6 other police men.[78] This is happening inspite of Article 25 of the Constitution.

The Times of India (Varanasi) 13.06.2015 p. 1 news read –Clash over Rs 4: Two Dalit youth Shot Three injured. The Indian Express new read: "Brahmins and Dalits Clash over Rs 4 in Allahabad two killed."[79]

Such incidences are happening after 68 years of our Independence with assurance to wipe every tear from every eye and when all major political parties are busy to celebrate and take the political benefit of the name of Dr Ambedkar. In 1991, the author had dedicated the book on Reservation Policy and Practice in India: A Means to an End to –

> Millions of those who have been
>
> Victim of the System of Graded Inequality
>
> Gradation and Degradation
>
> And, Gigentic cold-blooded Repression
>
> And, who have been lamenting since long:
>
> Hush My Child: don't cry, my treasure;
>
> Weeping in vain,
>
> For the enemy will never
>
> Understand our pain.
>
> For the Ocean has its limits
>
> Prisons have their Walls around.
>
> But our suffering and our torment
>
> Have no limit and no bound.[80]

Nothing has changed. Now we realise half a century earlier song by a Joker turned Headmaster Mr Udai Bhan Singh. In 1963, Chairman, District Board Deoria had organised a function, Dr Sitaram was the Chief Guest. Mr Udai Bhan Singh presented his item on request to say something addressing "Dr Saheb". He in tone of a famous filmi song sang – Centuries before, Harijan was chamar.

He is still today and will remain tomorrow. (Sadiyon Se Pahale Harijan Chamar tha, Ajbhi hai aur kal bhi Rahega"). Dr Sitaram smilingly responded – well said: they are not tapping well the sources and opportunities. But, one may find spirit, mind set and thinking of the society about SCs. The unconscious prejudices and bias finds expressions hither and thither. The incidence of Union Minister General V.K. Singh's utterance on 21.10.2015 in context of burning alive two dalit infants by Rajputs by setting fire in Faridabad, Haryana crossed all the limits of cultured society. Mr Singh uttered (exonerating Central government from any responsibility) for everything…like if somebody throws a stone at dog, then the Central Government is responsible…it is not like that (To her cheez per, Ki Jo wahan per usne pathar mar diya kutte pe, to sarkar jimmewar hai, aisa nahi hai).[81] A study reported in The Indian express dated 20.5.2015 shows that less than eight per cent SCs in Maharashtra get education quota benefit. Tata Institute of Social Sciences (TISS) nationwide survey reveals 67 per cent SCs say they missed benefit due to administrative problems – non-cooperation of school or colleges and apathy among the officials in charge.[82] After many decades of enforcement of equality, abolition of untouchability and drum beating of social-justice on 6.6.2015 a startling news appeared – Dalit groom becomes first to ride horse in Raj village. How it happened is also very interesting.

The marriage procession of Dalit Anil Raijner (22), who became first Dalit groom of village Pathredi (Rajasthan) passed through caste settlements while 125 policemen guarded it in the presence of top police and district administration officers.[83]

Gradation, degeneration and deprivation has created the bread problem. The Hindu reporting (by ArtiDhar) dated 16.3.2015 read: 'Rajnat' girls unable to quit flesh trade – Survey finds socio-cultural and economic reasons for this situation.

It has rightly been exposed by Karoline Davis Head of Gender and Development Division of World Vision that "commercial sexual exploitation of girls for financial benefit is a contemporary form of slavery."

The mindset and savarna centric media both in U.S. and in India have discouraged Dalit or black authorities to speak frankly on any issue. Media exposed, highlighted a criticised the views expressed by President Sri K. R. Narayanan through file-noting that the claims of the qualified SCs, STs, OBCs and Women also be taken care of while recommending the names for appointments to the higher judiciary. On the occasion of 50th anniversary commemoration of "Bloody Sunday" or on recent killings of two unarmed blacks by white policemen President Barak Obama could not use his position as President to speak on racial issues. Still he was routinely been painted as "an angry blackman" and an unpatriotic one.[84]

In a nutshell, both U.S. and India are still currently equally race and caste conscious society and the suggestions of Ronald M. Dworkin holds equal good in relation to India. He points out that it is the goal of affirmative action, "to reduce the degree to which American society is over-all a racially conscious society."[85] That is reason why Tribe assesses 'affirmative action' in context of 'Dismantling the House That Racism Built'[86] and suggestion comes that such programme is "an effective way of attacking a national problem."[87] So is the case of India. It is a caste conscious hierarchical society suffering badly with caste-prejudices. Hidden caste prejudices survive Article 17 abolishing untouchability. That is reason why Interim Constitution of Nepal 2007 barred any demonstration of superiority or inferiority of any person or a group of person belonging to any caste, tribe or origin, such demonstrations are seen as linked to the practice of untouchability. In May 2015 a peculiar caste bias case was seen in a marriage advertisement. Padma Iyer, mother of gay rights activist Harrish Iyer put advertisement that read. Seeking 25-40, well placed, animal loving, vegetarian groom for my son 36, 5′11" who works with an N.G.O. caste no bar (though Iyer preferred). The Hindu column Perspective: Prejudice disguised as politeness dated May 30, 2015, p. 7 exposed purity line with comment caste as a form of hierarchical bias is still a factor in Indian marriage alliances in newer form and vocabulary. The said study of Suryakant Waghmore gives many instances of advertisements showing caste preference with note "S.C. S.T. please excuse."[88]

Deep prejudices run in the vein of our society. The great Indian monk Swami Vivekananda stated that, "we refuse entirely to identify ourselves with 'do not touch me'. That is not Hinduism. It is in none of our books. It is an orthodox superstition which had interfered with the national life along the line."[89] So was said by P.B. Gajendragadkar, C.J. in ***Shastri Yagnapurudas Ji v. Muldas Bhudardas Vaishya***.[90] The great social justice adherer Chief Justice held, "untouchability is founded by superstition, ignorance, complete misunderstanding of the true teachings of Hindu religion." The impact of such superstitions and misunderstanding is ongoing process. In ***State of Karnataka v. Appa Balu Ingale***[91], the respondent had restrained a group of Harijans on gun point from taking water from a newly dug-up bore well on the ground that they were untouchables. The trial court and appellate court had sentenced under Section 4 of Protection of Civil Rights Act, 1955. But in revision the High Court upset it. In appeal a division bench of the Supreme Court allowed the appeal, set aside the High Court decision and upheld restored the decision of Additional Sessions Judge dated Sept. 5, 1980. The Supreme Court decision was pronounced by Kuldip Singh, J.. In his concurring judgment, supplementing Kuldip Singh, J., Ramaswamy, J. went into "sociological and constitutional angulations at great length. He referred to a number of empirical study conducted by sociologists[92], reasons for vulnerability of Dalits to oppression and cited many pre-and post-independence examples of deep-rooted pre-judicial behaviour of caste people with even Scheduled Caste prominent position holders. To say:

- Dr Ambedkar having been the victim of this cruel practice and suffered ignomy of throwing of files by a peon at his face while he was Military Secretary to Maharaja of Baroda.[93]
- Dr Ambedkar's being beaten up for staying incognito as a paying guest in a Parse Inn (though Parsee do not believe in casteism).[94]
- In Feb. 1978, when a leader no less than the Deputy Prime Minister of Free India, Shri Jagjivan Ram unveiled the Statue of Sampurnanand at Varanasi, it was believed to have been defiled and was purified ceremoniously with water brought from Ganges with all religious fervor.[95]
- At a dinner hosted by the Speaker of Rajasthan Legislative Assembly in honour of the Chief Minister, Shri Jagannath Pahadia, the wife of the Speaker trembled to serve food to the C.M. thinking to have been polluted.[96]
- A highly educated and well off son of a Union Minister entered into inter-caste marriage, the bride's father, whose annual income was not equal to a month's salary of the manager of the boy, i.e. even of humble means, neither celebrated the marriage nor visited her house, nor even permitted her to visit his house.[97]
- On October, 30, 1978, the Doctor in Government Hospital in Munger did not admit a Sweeper Dalit woman, who was struggling for life.[98]
- A Dalit Judge in a North Indian High Court could not secure a house and had to get posted to another place whereat he had abode.[99]
- A Judge in a South Indian High Court did not touch even water in the houses of Dalit or backward class Judges.[100]
- Even in Delhi (Cosmopolitan City), the Capital of the Country, in 1991 a Dalit officer had to vacate a rented house due to practice of untouchability.[101]

The learned Judge cited incidents of mass murder at Belchi in North and Taundur in South, gang rapes of Dalit women and arson of their huts and other incidents of "the relentless practice of untouchability, let alone, humiliations to countless Dalits which are every day routine."[102] He found truth in Dr Ambedkar's writing that 'untouchables are born and die as untouchable's and scorn and scoff is carried from birth to graveyard.[103]

The message is clear: political democracy cannot successfully flourish unless social democracy is nurtured on the trinity of liberty, equality and fraternity and justice–social, economic and political becomes reality for all.

References

1. Ronald M. Dworkin, Law's Empire. Cambrige, Mass: Harvard University Press, 1986, p. 384.
2. The Republic, BK III, p. 415.
3. *Ibid.* Book V, p. 473.
4. *Ibid.* Book III, p. 415.
5. 60 U.S. 393 (1856)
6. Jurist Florentinus observed, "Slavery is an institution of Jus gentium by which contrary to nature, one man is made the property of another," Digest I–5, 4, p. 60 U.S. 393 (1856).
7. 60 U.S. 393 (1856).
8. Bodenheimer, Jurisprudence : The Philosophy and Method of Law, 1974, pp. 371-372.
9. Law's empire. Cambrige, Mass: Harvard University Press. 1986, p. 386.
10. Oslen, Feminism and Critical Legal Theory : American Perspective' (1990) 18, International Journal of Sociology 199 at pp. 200-201.
11. Lankakanda (Ramacharitmanas) 15 AB 1,2
12. Kimberle Crenshaw, "Race Reform And Retrenchment : Transformation and Legitimation (in) Anti- Discriminatgion Law" (1988) 101, Harvard Law Review, 1331.
13. Ramacharitmanas, Sundara Kanda, 58 : 3.
14. Based on the works of discussion about the reconstruction, of Dalits in six Indian States.Prakash Louis, Political sociology of Dalit Assertion, Gyan Publishing House, New Delhi, (2003A) A, p. 79.
15. Ronald M. Dworkin, The Law's Empire, p. 388.
16. *Ibid.* p. 393.
17. Wollstonecraft, M., A Vindication of the Rights of Women (London, Dent, 1929) p. 587.
18. 16 Wall 141 (1973).
19. *Ibid.*
20. Tulsidas, Ramcharitmanas.
21. Human Rights and The Law, Vedpal Law House, 1986 p. 41.
22. *Ibid.*
23. The Hindu. July 5, 2015 p. 9 (UPSC : Women Secured Top Four Ranks).
24. See, Government of A.P. v. P.B. Vijay Kumar [preferential treatment in Jobs reading articles 15(3) and 16 together].
25. Tanjutek, The 500 Years Curse 1492-1992, PT. PaCodana Indoexim Abadi. Singapore (1998). In this book Tanjutek gives account racial curse practiced by Britishers in AAA World (Africa, Arab and Asia Nations World).

26. Britishers claimed that Australia was no man's land (vacant). They occupied for the first time.
27. (1992) 175 CLR 1.
28. Issac-Issacs Opposed voting rights to aboriginals on that plea.
29. MahaVana 149, 18.
30. Maha Shanti, 188, 1-17.
31. Nilkantha explains : "Sitah (White) = Sattva-gunah; Lohitah = rajogunah; Pitakah = rajas-tamo-vyamisrah; asitah (black) – tamo-gunah.
32. Pandharinath H. Prabhu, Hindu Social Organisation – A Study in Socio-Psychological and Ideological Foundations, Popular Prakashan Bombay, 1995, (Reprint) p. 299.
33. Manu VIII 416.
34. Narada 138-140.
35. Dumond, Louis, Homo Hierarchicus : The Caste system and its implications, (1970) New Delhi; Vikas, p. 52.
36. 163 U.S. 537 (1896).
37. Phule, Jotirao (1873) Slavery (in) Selected Writings of JotiraoPhule, G.P. Deshpande (ed.) New Delhi : Left Word Books pp. 25-46.
38. *Ibid.* p. 25.
39. Alfred L. Brophy, Reparations : Prog and Con, Oxp. Univ. Press, 2006 p. 20.
40. *Ibid.* p. 12.
41. Ann Scales, Clinton, in Senegal, Revisits Slavery's Horrors Emotional End to Historic Trip, Boston GlobA2, April 3, 1998.
42. Jean Dreze and Amartya Sen, "An Uncertain Glory –India and its Contradictions," 'Allen Lane – Penguin Books 2013. Chapter 8 –The Grip of Inequality, pp. 213-242 at p. 213.
43. A. B. Bardhan, 'Caste-class Situation in India' (in) K.L. Sharma (ed.) Caste and Class in India, Rawat Publications. Jaipur 1944 (Reprint, 2005), p. 405.
44. Mulkraj Anand Eleanor Zelliot (ed.)An Anthropology of Dalit Literature, Gyan Publishing House, New Delhi, 1992 p. 6.
45. *Ibid.* p. 11.
46. Indra Sawhney v. Union of India, 1992 SCC (L & S) Supp. 1 at p. 176 (para 337).
47. Regent of the University of Caligfornia v. Alan Bakke 438 U.S. 265 (1978) (Powell J.)
48. In Jagdish Rai v. State of Haryana A.I.R. 1977 P. and H. 56, the losing petitioner was herself a Scheduled Caste.
49. The principle of indication of source was evolved by the Supreme Court in D.N. Chanchala v. State of Mysore A.I.R. 1971 S.C. 1762 to reservation in favour of beneficiaries other than SC/STs and OBCs. It was adopted in a number of subsequent cases to serve the interest of beneficiaries outside social reservation group e.g. Pradeep Jain v. Union of India (1984) 3 SCC 654, Jagdish Saran v. Union of India (1980) 3 SCC 768. A.I.R. 1980 S.C. 820; Pradeep Jain v. Union

of India (1984) 3 SCCC 654; Dinesh Kumar (I) v. Motilal Nehru Medical College, Allahabad (1985) 3 SCC 22; Dinesh Kumar (II) v. Motilal Nehru Medical College, Allahabad (1986) 3 SCCC 727. Saurabh Chaudhari (I) v. Union of India (2003) 11 SCC 146; Saurabh Chaudhuri (II) v. Union of India (2004) 5 SCC 618.

50. The Revolt of the Untouchables.
51. Problem of Discrimination.
52. W. Haywood Burns, 'Race Discrimination : Law And Race in America' (in) David Kairy (ed.) The Politics of Law – A Progressive Critique, Pantheon Book, New York, 1982, p. 89.
53. *Ibid.* p. 91. A book newly published by Daria Roithmayr exposes white men's design behind Black's sympathetic treatment. See his book, "Reproducing Racism: How Every day Choices Lock in White Advantage, New York: Ny-u Press, 2014.
54. 163 U.S. 537 (1896).
55. W. Haywood Burns supra f.n. 52, p. 92.
56. Dhananjay Keer, Mahatma Jotiba Phooley – Father of the Indian Social Revolution, Bombay Popular Prakashan (1979) 52, 115. *Ibid.*
57. Report of the Director of Education for the year 1857-58, pp. 10-111.
58. Dhananjay Keer, Mahatma Jotiba Phooley – The Father of the Indian Social Revolution, Bombay popular Prakashan, 1979, p. 55.
59. Report of Director of education for the year 1857-58 pp. 315-316.
60. K.S. Chalam, Caste Based Reservations and Human Development in India, Sage Publications, 2007, p. 29.
61. *Ibid.*
62. Melvin I. Urofsky Paul Finkelman, "A March of Liberty – A Constitutional History of the United States, Vol. I, second ed. 2002 p. 362.
63. *Ibid.*
64. See Dr. Munish Kumar Raizada's views in Daily Post, 8.12.2014, p. 8.
65. R.K. Raghavan, Black City, White Police, and Brown, The Hindu 27.12.2014, p. 9 (Comment Column).
66. Swarajsingh 'Towards race war'. As late as on July 13, Sandra Bland, 28, died in police custody after she was pulled over for a trivial traffic violation. She had been active in the Black Lives Matter Movement. He voice was silenced in police custody, see, Frontline Aug. 21, 2015 column. Guilty as hell. pp. 62-63.
67. David Brooks, 'Class Prejudice resurgent', The Hindu, Dec. 3, 2014. See, Nissim Manna Thukkaren 'Fetters of Hate' The Hindu Magazine 5.7.2015 p. 1.
68. The Indian Express, 29.11.2014, pp. 1 and 2.
69. The Indian Express 26.8.2014, p. 5.
70. The Indian Express 17.11.2014, p. 6.
71. *Ibid.*
72. The Indian Express, 20.3.2015, p. 2.
73. The Indian Express, 8.9.2014, p. 3.

74. The Indian Express 4.10.2015, p. 5. At Rajkiya Ucch- Madhyamik Vidyalaya in Jodhpur during mid-day meal a 12 year Dalit student picked up a plate from a stack meant for non-Dalit students made cry and Hemant Jat, a teacher thrashed him for that and the dalit boy had to be hospitalised.
75. The Times of India 21.10.2015, p. 1.
76. The Times of India, "Can't end social boycott of dalits by Judicial Order : S.C." 21.2.2015 p. 8.
77. The Hindu 5.6.2015, p. 9.
78. The Indian Express 17.8.2015, p. 5.
79. Indian Express 13.06.2015, p. 1.
80. Anirudh Prasad, Reservation Policy in India Deep and Deep Publications, New Delhi, 1991. This book was cited by Hon'ble Justice R.M. Sahai in famous Mandal Case i.e. Indra Sawhney v. Union of India (1992) SCC (L & S) 1. (para 567 and 574)
81. "Throw Stones at dog, blame Govt ? V.K. Singh's remarks Kick up a storm". The Indian Express 22.10.2015, pp. 1 and 2.
82. The Indian Express, 20.5.2015, p. 7.
83. The Times of India 6.6.2015, p. 9.
84. The Indian Express, "Obama's Country" 11.3.2015, p. 10.
85. Michael Sandel, "Liberalism and the Claims of Community : The Case of Affirmative Action". (in) Marshal Cohen (ed.) Ronald Dworkin & Contemporary Jurisprudence, Duckworth (1983) pp. 227-237.
86. Lawrence H. Tribe, Constitutional Choices – Chapter Fourteen, 'Dismantling the House That Racism Built : Assessing "Affirmative Action" pp. 221-245 and f.n. pp. 412-421.
87. Michael Sandel, p. 235.
88. Surya Kant Waghmore, Prejudice disguised as Politeness, The Hindu 30.5.2015, p. 7.
89. The Complete Works of Vivekananda.
90. A.I.R. 1966 S.C. 1119 : (1966) 3 S.C.R. 242.
91. 1995 Supp. (4) SCC 469.
92. Dilip K. Basu and Richard Sission (ed) Social and Economic Development in India – A Assessment, Sage Publication, New Delhi (1960), S.R. Kakde, Scheduled Castes and National Integration (1990). G. R. Gupta (ed) Main Currents in Indian Society and Cohesion and Conflict in Modern India, Vol. 3; Dr Dinesh Khosla, Myth and Reality of the Protection of Civil Rights Law, Hindustan Publishing Corporation India, Delhi (1987); and Biswa B. Chatterjee, Shiv Swarth Singh and Dharamraj Yadav, Impact of Social Legislation on Social Change, The Minerva Associaties Publication, (1971).
93. Ingale Case, 1995 Sup. (4) SCC 469 at p. 478.
94. *Ibid.*
95. *Ibid* p. 479.
96. *Ibid.*

97. *Ibid.*
98. *Ibid*, p. 480.
99. *Ibid.*
100. *Ibid.*
101. *Ibid.* Citing 21st Report of SC and ST Commission, p. 165.
102. *Ibid.*
103. *Ibid.*

Chapter - 3

Compensatory Discrimination/ Preferential Treatment: What, Why and How Long?

3.1 Compensatory Discrimination/Preferential Treatment

3.1.1 What?

'Compensatory discrimination' is the expression which became popular in legal circle since the scholarly and in-depth study of the Indian attempt to handle the problem of the historically deprived group through American 'civil rights' lenses of Marc Galanter, a Fullbright Scholar. His book under caption, "Competing Equalities – Law and the Backward Classes in India" was published in 1984, after the experience of more than three decade functioning of the Indian Constitution with policies to safeguard the interest of the historically disadvantaged sections of the population. The writer himself tried to provide justification for the use of the terms 'Compensatory discrimination'. Are the two expressions – Compensatory Discrimination and Preferential Treatment interchangeable and sufficient to provide justification for the Indian problems of the caste-ridden society and their constitutional solution, are themselves subject of thorough study. The Constitution of India enshrined provisions dealing with the special provisions, reservations and preferential treatment from the very first date of its commencement. America experienced need of such provisions with the start of 1960s i.e. after one hundred and seventy years of that Constitution. America has history of "Affirmative Action". The scholars not so happy with such actions termed such governmental policy declaration as 'reverse discrimination'. Marc Galanter was well aware of contrast between the two expressions. In India, different expressions like "special treatment", "concessions", "privileges", "special provisions", or "preferential treatment" were in coin. In addition two more uses of the expressions came before him – one was "Protective Discrimination" which was used by Professor C.H. Alexandrowictz in his famous book 'Constitutional Development in India, 1957'[1], and second was 'Compensatory Discrimination' used by Professor Parmanand Singh in one of his articles published in Journal of the Indian Law Institute, New Delhi.[2] Galanter accepts "special treatment", accurate but finds defect in it as it omits "any reference to the principles that animate the policies and distinguish them from other distributive themes".[3] Likewise "protective discrimination is found to have" a parentalistic and static quality; it suggests a one way flow of beneficence and lacks any implication that it is a policy of change Galanter prefers 'Compensatory discrimination'.[4] But, he is also conscious of its drawbacks. The preference is due reasons that "by using discrimination it does not blink at the fact that some are left out, that we are dealing with something more than a benign process of inclusion. At least where scarce resources are distributed, it employees a principle of selection that is akin to the old discrimination. But, the purpose is different; it is not exclusion and relegation but inclusion and recompense both for historic deprivations and to offset present handicaps. And it carries an implication that discrimination will cease when compensatory treatment has remedied these conditions."[5]

But, Marc Galanter is conscious of the incompleteness of 'Compensatory discrimination' to cover all the ways to provide benefit to the deprived and socially persecuted persons in India.[6] That is reason why Galanter has used certain more expressions as synonyms and abbreviated forms, such as "preference policy" or "preference."[7] The term compensatory discrimination is not only inappropriate and incomplete, though preferable, it has a connotation which is value loaded and not neutral. The protagonists of reverse discrimination in America like Goldman and compensatory discrimination in India like Parmanand Singh have some inclination towards formal equality and meritarian value preferences. The very word discrimination is not a happy one and has variety of connotations. According to the International Encyclopaedia of Sociology reads: "Discrimination is the denial of opportunities and rights to certain groups on the basis of race, sex, ethnicity, age or disability." In a common parlance it simply connotes prejudice transformed into action. It may be of four categories.

1. Intentional individual discrimination. This refers to isolated act of discrimination performed by an individual on the basis of personal prejudice.

2. Unintentional individual discrimination, which is an insolated act of discrimination performed unconsciously by an individual.
3. Intentional institutional discrimination occurs when discrimination is based on the personal prejudices of the members of an institution.
4. Unintentional institutional discrimination that is part of routine behaviour of an institution that has unknowingly incorporated prejudicial practices into its operating procedures."[8]

To some extent affirmative action programmes may correct such discrimination. In India, discrimination is caste-based and unfortunately in post-Constitution period economic development is based on upper and lower caste – development at the upper end and stagnation at the bottom.[9] The net impact of caste discrimination is that it leads "to move disadvantage, dispossession, dehumanisation and degradation and maintains and reinforces social segregation and exclusion".[10] Caste in India is institutionalised form of discrimination and dehumanisation. Compensatory discrimination does not intend to do anything to the affected class.

There are many terms used to explain the special governmental actions to do away with the injustices done with the Negroes in America and Dalits in India.

3.1.1.1 Affirmative Action

'Affirmative action' is a term associated with the United States positive acts done for the amelioration of the racially deprived Negroes. It was originated in Wagner Act of 1935 indicating discrimination by employers against trade union member employees. But it came in more popular use in 1960s following the school desegregation of Schools in post ***Brown v. Board of Education***[11] demolishing the myth of 'separate but equal' and declaring in effect that, "separate can never be equal". Segregation disappeared but racists and racism had not disappeared. Affirmative Action is directly related to Title VII of the Civil Rights Act of 1965 and a series of executive orders between 1965 and 1971. Signing the Act, President Johnson explained the purpose of the Act being that "those who are equal before God shall now also be equal in the polling booths, in the classrooms, in the factories and in hotels and restaurants and movie theatres, and other places that provide service to the public."[12] The sound foundation was laid in the famous speech of President Lyndon Johnson in 1965 wherein he made clear, "you do not take a person who, for years, has been hobbled by chains, bring him to the starting line in a race and then say, 'you are free to compete with others'. It is not enough just to open the gates of opportunity. All our citizens must have the ability to walk through those gates". The executive order of government was summarised by Edwards Shils as follow:

"Universities were informed that for each category of employee in the university it would be necessary to specify rates of remuneration and number in each category by "racial breakdown, i.e. Negroe, oriental, American Indian, Spanish surnamed – Americans...."

This had to be accompanied by an "affirmative action programme which specifically and succinctly identifies problem areas by division, department location and job classification, and includes more specific recommendations and plans for overcoming them". The "Affirmative Action", must "include specific goals and objectives by divisions, department, job classification including target completion dates on both long and short ranges as the particulars case may indicate. Analytical provision should be made for evaluating recruitment methods and sources: the total number of candidates interview, job offers made, the numbers hired with the number of minority group persons interviewed, made job offers and hired."[13]

"Affirmative action is very comprehensive to cover the situation of discrimination to representation. That is reason why Daniel Sabbagh defines affirmative action to encompass any measure that allocate goods – such as admission into selective universities or professional schools, jobs, promotions, public contracts, business loans, and rights to buy, sell or use land and other natural resources – through a process that takes into account individual membership in designated groups, for the purpose of increasing the proportion of members of those groups in the relevant labour force, entrepreneurial class, or student population, where they are currently under-represented as a result of past oppression by State authorities and/or presented societal discrimination."[14]

Both in American and in India, affirmative action takes a moral force from the corrective justice ideal. It may take different shapes through positive discrimination or preferential treatment. It consists of measures that grant advantage to the members of designated groups in the final decision over the allocation of scare goods through compulsory quotas, tie-break rules, aspirational goals and targets.[15]

In America, Affirmative action is very popular. In India, compensatory discrimination, which is searched as substitute for that is used only in academic writings, that is to say, Marc Galanter[16], Parmanand Singh[17], Dr Buxi and U.G.C. curriculum prescribing a subject of study[18]. Justices prefer to use mostly affirmative action. In famous Mandal case, [19] the terms affirmative action, reverse discrimination, protective benefits, positive measures, positive discrimination, benign discrimination, ameliorative measures and special provisions have been used interchangeably. Hon'ble Justices accepted affirmative action or positive discrimination as part of equalising measures under Arts. 14, 15(1), 16(1), 29(2) and 38(2) with a view to do away inequality. But, the majority and minority judges used different terms. Among the dissenting justices, Justices (Dr) T. K. Thommen and R.M. Sahai used the term affirmative action and reverse discrimination. Their analysis was akin to the interpretation of affirmative action given by the American Supreme Court and some of academicians like Alan H. Goldman. Goldman has summarised the acceptability and unacceptability reverse discrimination. That is to say, reverse discrimination is admissible as "widespread use of preferential policy as a means to compensate past injustice and create equality of opportunity for the chronically deprived."[20] However, reverse discrimination as preferential treatment was "unjustified when directed indiscriminately towards members of groups defined only by race or sex."[21] R. M. Sahi J. observed, "Ethical Justification for reverse discrimination or protective benefits or ameliorative measures emanates from the moral of compensating such class or group for the past injustices inflicted or it and for promoting social values."[22] But, he preferred constraints on such measures. **First**, it cannot be prolonged. In his opinion it would be a mockery of 'protective discrimination' to argue that since disadvantaged people were kept excluded for hundred years the compensation by way of protective benefits should continue for hundred years.[23] **Second**, the social utility of preferential treatment "extended to the disadvantage and weaker section should not be pushed too far on what happened in the past without looking to present."[24] **Third**, reverse discrimination or preferential treatment must qualify reasonable classification test pertinent Constitutional purpose of compensation or social justice.[25] Justice T.K. Thommen accepted affirmative action programme of protective measures for uplifting of identified disadvantaged groups.[26] He pointed out that reservation is part of affirmative action and "while reservation is a remedy for historical discrimination and its continuing ill-effects, other affirmative action programmes are intended to redress discrimination of all kinds, whether current or historical."[27] But Justice Thommen like Justice Sahai expressed the view that affirmative action has to satisfy the test of valid classification based on an intelligible differentia i.e. reasonable nexus between classes of person chosen for affirmative action measures and classes of citizens excluded from such measures.[28] Thommen J. preferred very restricted scope of reservational mode of doing justice to the disadvantaged groups.

First, treating reservation prima facie as the very antithesis of a free and open selection, the learned judge observed: "It is a discriminatory exclusion of the disfavoured classes of meritorious candidates. Reservation which excludes from consideration of all those persons falling outside the specially favoured groups, irrespective of merits and qualifications, is much more positive and drastic a discrimination – albeit to achieve the same end of qualitative equality – but unless strictly narrowly tailored to a compelling constitutional mandate, it is unlikely to qualify as a benign discrimination."[29]

Second, maintaining a difference between reservational way of affirmative action programmes and other (short of reservation) affirmative action programmes, Justice Thommen pointed out that "backwardness by itself is not sufficient to warrant reservation."[30] Thomen J. explained:

> "What qualifies for reservation is backwardness which is the result of identified past discrimination and which is comparable to that of the Scheduled Castes and the Scheduled Tribes. Reservation is a remedial action specially addressed to the ill-effects stemming from historical discrimination. To ignore this vital distinction between affirmative action short of reservation and reservation by a predetermined quota as a remedy for past inequities is to ignore the special characteristic of the Constitutional grant of power specifically addressed to the constitutionally recognised backwardness."[31]

Thirdly, Justice Thommen pointed out that affirmative action' should not be viewed as merely retributive or giving over emphasis to its compensatory aspects. The learned judge warned that to do so and "widen the scope of reservation beyond minority of posts or seats is to practice excessive and invidious reverse discrimination.[32]

Fourth, Thommen J. pointed out that, 'affirmative action must find justification in the removal of disadvantages and not in their imposition."[33]

Among the majority judges in Mandal Case Justice Ratnavel Pandian and P.B. Sawant were more vocal on the point. Pandian J. used the terms 'special preferences', 'compensatory treatment' 'preferential treatment.'[34] Justice Sawant used the term 'positive measures'. Thus, he pointed out, "the trinity of the goals of the Constitution, viz. socialism, secularism and democracy cannot be realised unless all sections of the society participate in the State power equally, irrespective of their caste, community, race, religion and sex and all discriminations in the sparing of the State power made on those grounds are eliminated by positive measures."[35] He agreed with American judicial opinion that the reservation or affirmative action may be undertaken to remove the "persisting or present and continuing effects of past discrimination." He pointed out that India is more in need of such measures due to its special conditions. He pointed out, "What applies to American society applies ***ex propria vigore*** to our society. The discrimination in our society is more chronic and is continuing effects more discernible and disastrous. Unlike in America, in all pervasive discrimination here is against a vast majority."[36] The majority decision of B.P. Jeevan Reddy J. (speaking) for himself and M.H. Kania, C.J. and M.N. Venkatachaliah, A.M. Ahmadi JJ.) bluntly refused to confine preferential treatment to American affirmative action. Jeevan Reddy J. ruled, "We are afraid we may not be able to fit these provisions into this kind of compartmentalisation in the context and scheme of our constitutional provisions." The majority judgment very elaborately discussed the issue in context of our Constitution: Said, the court:

> "By now, it is well settled that reservations in educational institutions and other walks of life can be provided under Article 15(4) just as reservations can be provided in services under Article 16(4). If so, it would not be correct to confine Article 15(4) to programmes of positive action alone. Article 15(4) is wider than Article 16(4) inasmuch as several kinds of positive action programmes can also be evolved and implemented thereunder (in addition to reservations) to improve the conditions of SEBCs, Scheduled Castes and Scheduled Tribes, whereas Article 16(4) speaks only of one type of remedial measure, namely, reservation of appointments/ posts. But, it may not be entirely right to say that Article 15(4) is a provision envisaging programmes of positive action. Indeed, even programmes of positive action may sometimes involve a degree of discrimination. For example, if a special residential school is established for Scheduled Tribes or Scheduled Castes at State expense, it is a discrimination against other students, upon whose education a far lesser amount is being spent by the State. Or for that matter, take the very American cases – Fullilove[37] or Metro Broacasting[38] – can it be said that they do not involve any discrimination? They do. It is another matter that such discrimination is not unconstitutional for the reason that it is designed to achieve an important government objective."

A similar trend was discernible between the dissenting and majority judges in ***Ashok Kumar Thakur v. Union of India***.[39] Chief Justice K.G. Balakrishnan used positive measures and pointed out that reservation is one of the many tools that are used to preserve and promote the essence of equality, so that disadvantaged groups can be brought to the forefront of the civil life."[40] Chief Justice Balakrishnan noticed the basic distinction between the American and the Indian constitutional set up i.e. in America affirmative action programme is based on administrative orders and has no constitutional status in India positive measures have the constitutional sanctity. Consequently, he refused to borrow the American Supreme Court's principles[41] such as "suspect legislation", 'strict scrutiny' and 'compelling State necessity' in interpretation of reservation or other affirmative action contemplated under Article 15(5) of the Constitution.

Likewise the other majority decision of Justice Arijit Pasayat (for himself and Justice C.K. Thakker) discussed and distinguished American scenario and the judicial view on narrow tailoring, strict scrutiny etc. from the Indian scenario as "the provisions of the American Constitution in the United States relating to formal equality concept do not appear to have operated from the beginning of the American Constitution."[42] On the other hand, Indian Constitution started with such provisions. What is more objectionable in America is quota. But, preferential treatment is not objected to. It was pointed out in the Constitutionality of Preferential Treatment For Minority Applicants to Professional Schools:[43] It would be a sad day indeed, were America to become a quota-ridden society, with each identifiable minority assigned proportional representation in every desirable walk of life. But, that is not the rational for programmes of preferential treatment, "the acid test of their justification will be their efficacy in eliminating the need for any racial or ethnic preferences at all." It is to be noted that Indian Constitution itself provides for preferential treatment including reservation. Pasayat J. ruled that "the strict scrutiny test is not applicable and indepth scrutiny has to be made to decide the constitutionality or otherwise of the statute."[44]

The dissenting judge Dalveer Bhandari J. was inclined to find similarity between the American and Indian scenario on thinking that "of the classification on which there is case law, the one that most closely resembles caste is race." This is because both are immulable traits. They are used by the powerful, or those seeking power, to justify oppression. "Racism and casteism have long haunted both nations."[45] Citing different American decisions on the point to scrutinise affirmative action as suspect classification, rational basis test, strict scrutiny, compelling state interest he favoured guidance from those cases. Though Bhandari J. accepted that, "of course Indian courts have not accepted the principles of narrow tailoring and strict scrutiny"[46] still he was inclined to test the 93rd Amendment on careful scrutiny.

Raveendran J. agreed with Chief Justice Balakrishnan, Pasayat and C.K. Thakker JJ. He preferred temporary use of affirmative action.

The Indian courts have preferred preferential treatment in comparison to what American courts have thought of affirmative action. They have also avoided use of compensatory discrimination coined by Marc Galanter. It is so because Indian Constitution provides solid ground for preferential treatment and also is view of the fact that in America there are handful of disadvantaged and persecuted, in India it is majority – SCs, STs and SEBCs which need getting rid of persecution and amelioration from disadvantaged status at hand of minority of the privileged class.

3.1.1.2 Allied Concepts

In addition to the compensatory discrimination and affirmation action, many expressions have been used to clarify the different facets of preferential treatment. Thus,

Protective discrimination: It indicates a policy which aims at protection of the interests of those who have been oppressed for ages and therefore, at present are not in a position to compete with the privileged section of the society.

Reverse Discrimination: The special privileges or protective discrimination is termed by some scholars as reverse discrimination, as it involves favourable treatment to disadvantaged and leaving aside privileged. It is used mostly by those who do not approve the wider range of preferential treatment to the deprived sections.

Positive Discrimination: Eradication of the present institutionalised effect of the past discrimination through positive state steps awarding preferential treatment in favour of certain identified weaker section of society leaving aside those who are privileged.

Reservation: It is one of the mechanisms of the special treatment, as a social policy of the State to implement quota system to ensure the participation of the traditionally neglected section of the people.

Silent, Untellable and pernicious discrimination: This is reality in Indian society. But no writer or court takes it seriously. Merit is shattered at the hands prevalent untold reservational discrimination whereby on the basis of caste prejudices, class interest, money consideration the meritorious disprivileged are discriminated and open posts are filled by less meritorious candidates coming from the privileged class. The author had coined the term 'destructive discrimination' in his book on, "Reservation Policy and Practice in India – A Means to an End."

Compensatory Justice: Justice with the disadvantaged classes through preferential treatment programmes so as to compensate for wrong done to them in past and their vulnerable position at the present.

Benign Discrimination: The compassionate preferential treatment measures with a view to eliminate the continued effects of past segregation, discrimination and exploitation.

Reparatory Justice: Reparatory Justice aims at racial justice and racial harmony. It put emphasis on part harms and provides for correcting it. The programme believes in corrective justice. Thus, reparation aims at programmes that "are justified on the basis of past harm and that are also designed to assess and correct"[47] that harm and/or improve the lives of victims into the future. Reparation has four features: "(1) a focus on the past to account for the present; (2) a focus on the present to reveal the continuing existence of race-based discrimination; (3) an accounting of the past harms or injuries that have not been compensated; and (4) a challenge to society to devise ways to respond as a whole to the uncompensated harm identified in the past."[48] Reparation theory was born out of Critical Race Theory. With decline of Affirmative action through Judicial back tracking allowing it to serve the compelling governmental interest focusing 'narrowly tailoring' the Critical Race Study got momentum by the mid 1980s. The plea of Vincene Verdun is, "Because society perpetuated and benefited from the institution of slavery, all of society must pay."[49] As is America so is India on race/caste ridden society and complexes. India is a shed better as it has constitutional basis for amelioration and reparation for disadvantaged. Expressing the same idea of reparation through compensatory Justice Krishna Iyer J. observed in Thomas case:[50]

"The distinction would seem to be between handicaps imposed accidently by nature and those resulting from societal arrangements such as caste structures and group suppression. Society being in such a broad sense responsible for these latter conditions, it also has the duty to regard them as relevant differences among men and to compensate for them whenever they operate to prevent equal access to basic, minimal advantages enjoyed by other citizens."

Clear and more specific provision regarding positive action is incorporated in Section 15(2) of the Canadian Charter of Rights and freedoms. Section 15(1) incorporates non-discrimination principle. But clause (2) provides that clause (1) "does not preclude any law, program or activity that has as its object the amelioration of conditions of disadvantaged individuals or groups including those that are disadvantaged because of race, national or ethnic origin, colour, religion, sex, age or mental or physical disability."

Preferential treatment: The original Indian Constitution contribution – preferential treatment vide Articles 15(4), 46, 330-343, now 243-D, 243T and Fifth and Sixth Schedules, is the expression preferable to other alternates. It is all embracing exhaustive and an expression of wide connotation. **First,** it includes reservation as well as all possible positive efforts/steps for improving the competitive ability of deprived sections of the Indian society along with measures giving some weightage with a view to neutralise the lower scores of socially handicapped, disadvantages and compelled to bear the stresses and strains of the disadvantages of backward class- SCs/STs and OBCs and **secondly**, in addition to the wide range of state help to backward classes, the expression preferential treatment is a neutral term.[51]

3.1.2 Why?

There is old adage 'rich men rule the law, law grinds the poor'. Both in U.S. and in India society degraded some people with help of institutionalised protection. American Jim Crow, klu klau klan and legislative and judicial pronouncement relegated Negroes to the status of commodity. Emancipation came but they are struggling still for survival and right to live with human dignity. They cry for justice, equality, fraternity and good life. India too has experimented with Dalits who crave for bread. A very heart, touching impact of Indian caste-ridden hierarchical society is painted by a Dalit poet in the following words:

> Life is a myth, world is a myth
> Everything really always a struggle
> A vain struggle, never ending struggle
> We struggle, always for survival
> You for your life, life of comfort
> Wealth and power, Leisure and Pleasure,
> Thinking stupidly, these are Developments !
> You keep running, without stopping ever !
> While we struggle, work and plough
> Sow and Reap, Create and Produce
> Everything just, for a slice of Bread
> To keep the soul and bodies together !
> Always a struggle, never ending struggle !
> You are struggling, for Butter to Butter
> The Bread you have stolen from us !

A vain struggle ! Never ending struggle !
-so wrote a Dalit Poet in 1985.[52]

Compensatory discrimination is helping state hand to raise the fallen, degraded, despised and persecuted depressed classes people who cannot stand on their own in the struggle of life or contribute in the nation building. In view of the social movement towards emancipation, wind of change blowing in different parts of the world and more specifically Universal Declaration of Human Rights, 1948 and other human rights commitment, no society can afford to continue to discriminate certain people and keep them under bondage. When societal obligation to give dignity, liberation and respectful life to such unfortunate people through State agencies is discharged, it invites resistance, challenges and efforts to frustrate such move. Statusquoist enjoying privileges do not allow easily to materialise the move of the welfare states.

In the above backdrop many justifications have been proffered: Such justifications relate to the broad categories of legitimacy, equity and difference. Legitimacy relates to the confidence of the people in Parliament, Government and judiciary that they have to serve the whole citizenry not only few people. Equity is about realising the abilities of all members of the society. Difference relates to involve different segment of society in administration and decision-making process i.e. to encourage diversity with new definition of merit giving place to diversity.

1. Compensatory discrimination is needed to ensure justice to the people who are disprivileged, deprived and bewildered. The move appears to be from ***homo hierarchicus to homo equitas***. In his celebrated book, 'The Discovery of India'[53], Pt. Jawahar Lal Nehru noted that, "the spirit of the age is in favour of equality, though practice denies it almost everywhere"[54] Compensatory discrimination has an aspect of compensatory justice to those who had been and are still the victim of deprivation. Justice – social, economic and political to all citizens of the country is the signature tune of our Constitution. Our tryst with destiny started with vow to remove every tear from every eye. Compensatory discrimination aims to equalitarian justice through enforcing equality in result; it aims at corrective justice by correcting the social disbalances due to deprivation of some disprivileged and persecuted little men of the society and it ensures distributive justice by ensuring distribution of national resources among the disadvantaged section of the society.

Compensatory discrimination gives functional meaning to equalitarian justice which requires that among the equals law shall be equal and shall be equally administered. If it is pressed too far and unequals are treated equally in justice may ensue. The requirement of justice is that equalising measures should be resorted to make unequal disadvantaged to come on the equal plane. Thus, the unequals are required to invite unequal treatment. P. B. Sawant J. made it clear in Mandal Case that to bring about equality between the unequals, it is necessary to adopt positive measures to abolish inequality.[55] Compensatory discrimination measures may be taken in the form of reservation and also the measures other than reservation. Thommen J. made clear in Mandal Case that "while reservation is a remedy for historical discrimination and its continuing ill-effect, other affirmative action programmes are intended to redress discrimination of all kinds, whether current or historical."[56] Pandian J. in the same case observed that, "certain social groups who are inherently unequal and who have fallen victim of societal discrimination require compensatory treatment."[57]

Justice R. M. Sahai viewed the compensatory measures from the point of the view of morals. Abstract equality is neither theme nor philosophy of our Constitution. Real equality through practical means is the call of the time. "Atoning for the past injustices on backward classes through constitutional mechanism was morality raised to a legal plane."[58] The element of distributive justice was perceived by Thommen J. when he observed, "affirmative action is not merely compensatory justice, which it is, but it is also distributive justice to ensure that community resources are more equitably and justly shared among all classes of citizens."[59]

2. Compensatory discrimination serves a great national cause through ameliorating the condition of the disadvantaged people. In context of the United States the great jurist Ronald M. Dworkin has observed, "Affirmative action is justified, not because those who are given preference are entitled to an advantage, whether in compensation for past discrimination or for any other reason, but simply because helping them is now effective way of attacking a national problem."[60] A large chunk of population cannot be left to remain dissatisfied. T. R. Curr rightly comments, "deprivation leads people to frustration and the great frustration the greater the quantity of aggression against the source of frustration"[61] It is common human nature. Discrimination, deprivation, exclusion and exploitation are endemic to every society. They lead to frustration, anger and aggression.[62] Compensatory discrimination measures divert the energy of disadvantaged section with positive effect. Thus, "affirmative action promotes maximum well being for the society as a whole and strengthens forces of national integration and general economic prosperity."[63] The great Indian Judge who sponsor the cause of workers and social justice, Mr Justice Gajendra Gadkar

observed in his historical pronouncement in Balaji case[64] that, "When Article 15(4) refers to the special provision for the advancement of certain classes or Scheduled Castes or Scheduled Tribes, it must not be ignored that the provision which is authorised to be made is a special provision, it is not a provision which is exclusive in character, so that in looking after the advancement of those classes, the State would be justified in ignoring altogether the advancement of the rest of the society. It is because the interests of the society at large would be served by promoting the advancement of the weaker elements in the society that Article 15(4) authorises special provision to be made."[65] (emphasis added)

3. Compensatory discrimination is a weapon to fulfil the mission of casteless and classless Indian society. The realist and justice oriented approach both in India and the United States repudiate the charge of race-caste accentuation. In America anti-affirmative actionists argue that affirmative actions aim to achieve "a racially conscious society divided into racial and ethnic groups, each entitled as a group of some proportionable share of resources, careers or opportunities."[66] Ronald Dworkin terms this approach as perverse. He points out "American society is currently a racially conscious society; this is the inevitable and evident consequence of a history of slavery, repression and prejudice."[67] Dworkin rightly remarks that racially explicit criteria used affirmative action aims to increase the number of some races in certain professions, but their long run goal is "to reduce the degree to which American society is overall a racially conscious society."[68] He refutes the charge that affirmative action programme are designed to produce a balkanised America and illustrates how the ***Brown v. Board of Education*** succeeded in 'reforming the racially consciousness of American society by racially neutral means.[69] Dworkin argues for sympathetic attitude towards affirmative actions and not to forbid such programmes on certain ill conceived/ mindless maxim, like the maxim that it can not be right to fight fire with fire or that the end cannot justify the means.[70] He concludes that the affirmative programmes are intended to decrease the importance of race in the United States in the long run.[71] The first Backward Classes Commission appointed by the Union popularly known as Kaka Kalelkar Commission identified socially and educationally backward classes on the basis of Caste on any analogy thorn by thorn. Though under extraneous pressure he took U-turn and lamented that it would have been better had the Commission chosen criteria other than caste. Karnataka Backward Classes Commission headed by L. G. Havanur recognised that in India "caste has come to stay" and therefore, "Constitution suggests recognition of castes for their equalisation."[72] In Mandal Case in his concurring judgment

P. B. Sawant J. rejected the argument that the adoption of caste as a factor for identifying backwardness would perpetuate casteism.[73] He pointed out that, "one of the most damaging and perpetuating social consequence of the caste system has been the discrimination suffered by certain castes and communities as such castes and communities. The result has been that these castes and communities as a whole continued to remain as backward class."[74] Keeping in view the core reality of the Indian society Justice Sawant observed:

> "If, therefore, an affirmative action is to be taken to give them the special advantage envisaged by Article 16(4), it must be given to them because they belong to such discriminated castes. It is not possible to redress the balance in their favour on any other basis. A different basis would perpetuate the *status quo* and therefore, the caste system instead of eliminating it."[75]

The learned Judge further clarified:

> "On the other hand, by giving the discriminated caste groups the benefits in question, discrimination would in course of time be eliminated and along with it the casteism.[76] (emphasis added).

Some of the academicians too have expressed the view that caste conscious compensatory discrimination will lead to caste consciousness elimination. Thus, Louis Dumont observed, "the road of the abolition of caste-system in India is likely to lie in the caste action."[77] Rajni Kothari expressed the view that, "if you wants to bring casteism to an end, provide more reservations for backward classes."[78] The senior advocate of the Supreme Court of India Ram Jethmalani pointed out that "reservations do not perpetuate caste. They destroy its ugly manifestation."[79]

So far as Courts' decisions are concerned the opinion of Judges differ. Minority/dissenting judges both in Mandal Case[80] and Ashok Kumar Thakur case[81] expressed the view that the vision and mission of the framers was to establish a casteless and classless society and they expressed apprehension that reservation will perpetuate casteism. It is disputable on facts. Many scholars/sociologist share the view that the framers object was of have a plural society and not classless society.[82] The concurring Judge in Ashok Kumar Thakur shared the reality that, "the Constitution does not specifically prescribe a casteless society nor tries to abolish caste. But, by barring discrimination in the name of caste and by providing for affirmative action Constitution seeks to remove the difference in status on the basis of caste. When the differences in the status among castes are removed, all castes will become equal. That will be the beginning for a casteless egalitarian society."[83]

4. Compensatory discrimination programmes corrects the wrong and therefore, there is no intellectually inconsistency. As Richard Wasserstrom pointed the opposition which preferential treatment programmes face is said to involve intellectual inconsistency. That is to say, the very idea of such programmes is initiated put an end to discriminatory practices made under considerations of race, gender and caste. But the basis such programmes lies in considerations of race, sex and caste. Wasserstrom disputes it and defends preferential treatment on the rationality that the two vitally differ. In the former case the action discriminated against blacks as a part of the larger social universe which systematically maintained a net work of institutions which unjustifiably concentrated power, authority and goods in the hands of whites which systematically cognised blacks to subordinate position in society.[84] It is obvious that discrimination in later case though based on race and caste is with good intention to help the disadvantaged. Dealing with compensatory discrimination with reference to India Marc Galanter contrasted preferential treatment which involved race-based discrimination by way of exclusion or inclusion of certain disadvantaged people and observed: "the purpose of discriminating on a compensatory basis is not exclusion and relegation but inclusion and recompense both for historic deprivations and to offset the present handicaps."[85]

5. Compensatory discrimination is justified as a discharge of social obligation. It is the society which failed to protect the disadvantaged class from the exploitation of the privileged class. It supported the evil acts of such exploiters through social and legal institutions. In U.S.A. not only individual but different organ of the state allowed exploitation. So has been the case in India. The opponent of societal responsibility argue that "the one who have a right to compensation are those who have personally been injured by discrimination and who have not yet been able to overcome this injury."[86] They argue that the governmental preferential hiring and admission policies give an advantage in competition for jobs or places in educational institutions to the members of particular groups.[87] Paul W. Taylor gives a befitting answer to individualist argumentators. He, says:

> "When an injustice has been committed to a group compensation or reparation must be made to that group. Group rights to compensation are not rights against wrong doers but against society as a whole. The obligation to offer such benefits to the group as a whole is an obligation that falls on society in general, not on any particular person. For it is

society that through its established social practice brought upon itself the obligation."[88]

It is common knowledge that in America Negroes and in India untouchables as a group were put in disadvantaged and exploited position by dominant groups. They became perpetual underclass and exploited and exploiter became perpetual exploiting class accumulating plenty. To redress it, the redistribution is required. As Fish views, "this redistribution may be rooted in a theory of compensation – blacks as a group were put in that position by others and the redistributive measures are owed to the groups as a form of compensation. The debt would be viewed as owed by society once again viewed as collectivity."[89] Applying the American analogy in relation to worst of Dalits Marc Galanter concedes the usefulness of 'compensatory discrimination' to offset disadvantages that are concentrated and cumulative.

6. Compensatory discriminations is India part of the national commitment to ensure justice to all including SCs, STs and OBCs. Article 46 reads: "The State shall promote with special care the educational and economic interests of the weaker sections of the people, and in particular, of the Scheduled Castes and the Scheduled Tribes, and shall protect them from social injustice and all forms of exploitation." In ***Balaji v. State of Mysore***[90], Justice Gajendra Gadkar gave due credence to this Article emphasising the need of a balance of interests between recipients of the benefits of Article 46 and rest of the society. In ***Keshavananda Bharati v. State of Kerala***[91] the Supreme Court conceded the liberal implementation of SCs and STs rights under Article 46 vis-à-vis Articles 15 and 16. Finding failing of State commitment towards disadvantaged people clause (2) was inserted in Article 38 vide The Constitution 44th Amendment Act, 1978 which reads, "The State shall in particular, strive to minimise the inequalities in income, and endeavour to eliminate inequalities in status, facilities and opportunities, not only among individuals but also amongst groups of people residing in different areas or engaged in different vocations."

7. Compensatory discrimination through reservation tries to ensure participation of different segments of the Indian society. Gandhi Ji's dream was to ensure it. He wished, "— the main objective is obvious and it is to gain independence, not for the literate and the rich in India, but for the dumb millions. I shall work for an India in which the poorest shall feel that it is their country, in whose making they have an effective voice, an India in which there shall be no high class and low class of people."[92] Swami Vivekananda also pointed out that: "if there is inequality in nature, still

there must be equal chance for all 0 or if greater for some and less for others – the weaker should be given more chance than the strong."[93]

When V. P. Singh implemented reservation scheme recommended by Mandal Commission he expressed the view that he knew only one per cent of population is involved in services and 27 per cent of that one per cent was not substantial but his design was: "Now the bid by the deprived sections is not for mere jobs or any other benefits of power, but to operate the levers of power itself."[94] It reminds us of Dr B. R. Ambedkar's view that reservation is a tool to get participation in administration. Reservation is a medium to get proportionate share in power.[95]

V. P. Singh's aim was to bring transformation in Indian Society. Mandal Commission was conscious of substantially chronic under-representation of disadvantaged socially and educationally backward classes and the spirit behind the Report was, "of full participation of such classes in the governance of society". Report of the Mandal Commission read: "The chief merit of reservation is not that it will introduce egalitarianism among OBCs when the rest of the Indian society is seized by all sorts of inequalities. But reservation will certainly erode the hold of higher castes on the services and enable OBCs in general to have a sense of participation in running the affairs of their country." This idea of participation in governance of the country was also pointed out by Justice P. B. Sawant in Mandal case. Justice Sawant observed:

> "The goals of the Constitution cannot be realised unless all sections of the society participate in the state power equally irrespective of their caste, community, race, religion and sex and all discriminations in the sharing of the state power made on those grounds are eliminated by positive measures."[96]
>
> The learned judge arrived at conclusion that –
>
> "The purpose of keeping reservations even in favour of socially and educationally backward classes under clause (4) (of Article 16), is not to alleviate poverty, but to give it an adequate share in power."[97]

The majority judgment in Mandal case pronounced by B. P. Jeevan Reddy J. (on behalf of himself and M.H. Kania C.J. and M. N. Venkatachaliah and A.M. Ahmadi JJ.) also made clear that –

> "The objective behind the Article 16(4) is empowerment of the deprived backward communities –to give them a share in the administrative apparatus in the governance of the country."[98]

What would be benefit of participation of different segment of society? The answer is obvious. It will ensure objectivity, transparency and sensitivity towards common peoples problem.

8. Compensatory discrimination gives new meaning to the merit. The greatest judge of the early twenty first century Lord Bingham has rightly pointed out that 'the term merit is not self-defining.' It directs attention to proven, professional achievement as a necessary condition, but also enables account to be taken of wider considerations, including the virtue of gender and ethnic diversity.[99] In India there is paucity of disadvantaged peoples participation in decision-making process. In order to attract confidence of all sections in administration compensatory discrimination has greater value.

9. In peculiar circumstances of India where merit has become misnomer and social reservation is converted into – 1. SCs/STs, 2. OBCs and 3. GC for upper caste only and appointing less meritorious in General category and relegating brilliant and more meritorious all round first class careerists to the reserved category protective/compensatory discrimination through, reservation has special justification for protection of merit otherwise all posts will be filled in by mediocre upper caste through untellable hidden reservation.

Compensatory Discrimination/Preferential Treatment

3.1.3 How Long ?

There has been a heated debate among legal luminaries, honourable Justices, politicians and different sections of society as to duration of the preferential treatment measures. Some think it is a self-liquidating process. Others think that its perpetuation is unavoidable in view of the lack of honest implementation of preferential treatment policies. The fate of 10 years limit of Article 334(2) is clear example.[100] In his dissenting opinion Dalveer Bhandari J. pointed out in ***Ashok Kumar Thakur v. Union of India***[101] that it is consistent with our constitutional goal of achieving a classless/casteless society that a time-limit be set. But he expressed his helpness to do so.[102] In his own words, "I am bound by Sawhney (I)[103] and believe that only a larger bench could make such a ruling." There was unanimity on the point that an act is not invalid merely because no time-limit is prescribed for caste-based reservation. Raveendran, J. in his concurring decision preferred periodic review and no unnecessary prolongation. To quote him, "—Preferably there should be a review after ten years to take note of the change of circumstances. A genuine measure of reservation may not be open to challenge when made. But during a period of time, if the reservation is continued in spite of achieving the object of reservation, the law which was valid when made, may become invalid."[104] Raveendran J. further made clear that any provision for reservation is a temporary crutch. Such crutch by unnecessary prolonged use, should not become a permanent liability.[105] Judiciary has expressed opinion about the continuance or otherwise of compensatory discrimination/ preferential measures adopted by the government. In **Mandal case** Justice R.M. Sahai pointed out that – the Constitution makers did not "restrict the period of its continuance as was done for Anglo-Indian by Article 336 as an enlightened and progressive State a responsible government of a welfare country must decide itself periodically on prevalent social and economic conditions and not on political consideration or extraneous compulsion if the protective umbrella has to be kept opened, for whom and for how long."[106]

The problem of continuing the affirmative action/ preferential treatment has agitated even the judicial mind. In ***Grutter v. University of Michigan***[107] Justice O Connor wished to put time-limit on race-conscious action. She suggested twenty-five years. The Indian judiciary has also sparked some thinking on that line. In ***Akhil Bharatiya Soshit Karamachari Sangh (Rly). V. Union of India***[108] Justice V. R. Krishna Iyer hinted at non-perpetuation of reservational way to do justice with the backward segment of the society. He appeared to disfavour reservation for long for backwards other than SCs and STs "To lend immortality to the reservation policy", said Iyer J., 'is to defeat its **raison d'etre**, to politicise this provision for communal support and party ends is to subvert the solemn undertaking under Article 16(1), to castify reservation even beyond the dismal groups of backward most people, euphemistically described as SC and ST is to run a grave constitutional risk."[109] Justice S. Ranganathan in one of extra judicial writing disfavoured continuation of reservation for long. Said, justice Ranganathan, "while certain types of reservations are necessary in principle, in some cases and for sometime, there cannot be reservations of all types, for all cases and for all times."[110] Some of the judges of the Supreme Court in ***K.C. Vasanth Kumar v. State of Karnataka***[111] hinted at the necessity of removing of the reservation scheme by the end of twentieth century.

Chief Justice Chandrachud conceded fifteen years concession to SCs and STs and suggested that reservation to them should continue upto 2000 without means test. In his opinion 50 years time since the commencement of the Constitution would be a period reasonably long for the upper crust of the oppressed classes to overcome the baneful effects of social oppression, isolation and humiliation. Thereafter, economic test was to be made applicable to SCs and STs too. He also suggested periodic review of five year or so of the policy of reservation in employment, education and legislative institutions.[112]

The issue of continuity of reservational compensatory discrimination/ affirmative action is getting momentum both in U.S.A. and India. The abolitionist argue very emotively that Constitution is race/colour-blind and casteless and classless society is its mission. Reservational affirmative action is curse. The moot question is: has the social more in India changed. Are Negroes and Dalits enjoying status equal to whites and caste-people ? If affirmative action plan are withdrawn is there any guarantee that the brilliant and more meritorious of depressed classes will get berth in merit pool ? A Dalit poet has pointed very correct picture and has given befitting justification for continuation of affirmative action programmes (reservation).

Oh caste hindoos, you are satans !
You are nothing but the devils !
You are embodiment of all evils !
What else can we say ? Why not ?
You abhor, flout, loathe and revile us
You disregard, neglect, look down at us
You denigrate, despise, deride, detest, hate, slight and spurn us
You only have contempt, disdain and scorn for us
You are antagonistic, prejudiced and biased against us
You always discriminate, exploit, marginalise and suppress us
You are hundred percent unfair, unjust and dishonest while dealing with us
You are phoney
You are always deceptive, dubious, subversive and treacherous
You are a fake, fraud, hoax and a thief
You are a trickster
You are a hypocrite and oppressor
In short, you cannot be trusted
You are only an aggressor
You are a cruel criminal exploiter
You are cold-blooded vengeful venomous vindictive savage fanatic
None can ever trust you
No one can believe or have faith in you

One way or the other, you will appropriate everything for yourselves,
Defraud us and leave us bleeding badly
We can never trust you, your Governments, your Police, your
Administrations, your Lawyers, your judges, your Press and your media
We can never, therefore, believe you or accept your promises
We cannot ever trust your teachers and have faith in their teachings
We are different !
We have a separate identity ?
We are a separate people, separate race and a separate Nation
We have always been a separate society
Hence we want our shares and dues separately always and everywhere.
The moment we fall in our resolve, and believe you, trust you, or leave things to happened on their own, we are doomed, sunk, and will be dead and gone.
Therefore the Reservation !
Reservation in every sphere !
And every walk of life !

To this it may be added –

Reservation will continue
In services as well as in education
As is continued in the Legislatures
Without any hitch and hesitation.

Reason

Remove reservation, representation will fall
Hidden untellable reservation will capture all
Ideology, philosophy will not work
Unless social economic discriminations shirk
Equality on paper or slogan breeds no fruit
Only equality in reality and of result suit.
Reservation is not cause but way to minimise the effect
Need is to remove graded and degraded social defect
Reservation in heart, and discrimination must decay
Cause is removed, effect will itself wither away.

The warning of Justice Ratnavel Pandian in his concurring judgment in **Mandal case** is a very pertinent reminder:

"No one can be permitted to invoke, the Constitution either as a sword for an offence or as a shield for anticipatory defence, in the sense that no one under the guise of interpreting the Constitution can cause irreversible injustice and irredeemable inequalities to any section of the people or can protect, those unethically claiming unquestionable dynastic monopoly over the constitutional benefits."[113]

What is most disturbing is that personal preferences, hunches and ideologies overshadow the constitutional reality. Even many anti-reservationists and well-red men, argue that reservation was made only as a temporary measure, that is to say, for ten years.[114] Even some of the Hon'ble justices express the similar view and work on that line. To quote Justice Dalveer Bhandari, "Caste-based reservation was initially a temporary measure that was to last for ten years. The original Framers considered caste-based reservation a necessary evil. Thus, they limited it in time. Extending this time-limit has only exacerbated casteism."[115] This conclusion is based on major premise that the framers intended to establish a casteless and classless society and then conclusion is derived that reservation perpetuates, rather encourages casteism and delays the achievement of the mission of casteless and classless Indian society.[116] The fact is otherwise. Only representation of SCs and STs in the representative bodies Parliament and State Legislatures was aimed to be for 10 years duration vide Article 334 (which itself is being extended every 10 years, at present upto 70). Neither Article 16(4) says anything about time limit nor Article 15(4) inserted in 1951 by the Provisional Parliament i.e. the Constituent Assembly itself performing that function. Article 15(4) specifically mentions SEBCs in addition to SCs and STs and Article 16(4) intends to cover all –SCs, STs and SEBCs within the purview of backward classes. It is also doubtful if Framers intended to a establish casteless society or a plural society ? How long is a big magical bond ? Can remedy be removed even if discrimination, deprivation, persecution etc. persist ? Will appointments be honestly done according to merit, if reservation is done away and the five first class division holder OBCs or SCs will find berth in services in General Category in preference to mediocre caste persons ? Will it not bring the position to square one i.e. situation of no participation or scant participation of 85 per cent population in governance of the country ?

References

1. Constitutional Developments in India, Bombay: Oxford Univ. Press, 1957.
2. "Equal opportunity" and "Compensatory Discrimination" : Constitutional Policy and Judicial Control." 18 Journal of the Indian Law Institute 1976 pp. 300-319.
3. Marc Galanter, Competing Equalities, Oxf. Univ. Press. 1984, p. 2.
4. *Ibid.*
5. *Ibid.* pp. 2-3.
6. "The drawback of the term – apart from its being ten syllables –is that it draws attention away from the non-discrimination and general welfare themes in these policies. If this name would be inappropriate in the settling where the element of historical compensation is less prominent, it does seem to fit the Indian situation better than other candidates." *Ibid.* p. 3.
7. *Ibid.*
8. Prakash Louis, Political Sociology of Dalit Assertion, Gyan Publishing House, New Delhi, 2003, pp. 37-38.
9. Marc Galanter, "The Compensatory, Discrimination. Theme in the Indian commitment to Human Rights" (in) Upendra Buxi (ed.) The Right to be Human, Lancer International, p. 82.
10. Prakash Louis, supra, pp. 38-39.
11. 343, U.S. 483.
12. Stanislav Kondrashov, Martin Luther King, Novooti Press, Agency Publishing House. Moscow, 1988.
13. Edward Shils, "Editorial", Minerva (April, 1971), p. 165.
14. Daniel Sabbagh, Affirmative Action (in) Michael Rosenfeld, Andras Sajo (ed.) Oxford Hnadbook of Comparative Constitutional Law (2012) Paperback ed. 2013 pp. 1124-1141 at p. 1124.
15. *Ibid.* p. 1126.
16. Marc Galanter, Competing Equalities, Oxf. Univ. Press, 1984, p. 2.
17. 18 JILI 1976, pp. 300-319.
18. Report of the Curriculum development Centre in Law, Vol.II, U.G.C., New Delhi, 1992 (prescribing Hons. Course paper Compensatory Discrimination) 033 pp. 177-179.
19. Indra Sawhney v. Union of India, 1992 SCC (L & S) Supp. 1., Ashok Kumar Thakur v. Union of India (2008) 6 SCC 1.
20. Allan H. Goldman, Justice And Reverse Discrimination, Princeton Univ. Press, 1979, p. 233.
21. *Ibid.* p. 231.
22. Indra Sawhney v. Union of India 1992 SCC (L. & S) Supp. 1, para 596 (Sahai J.).
23. *Ibid.*
24. *Ibid.*
25. *Ibid.* para 599 (ii) read with para 615.

26. *Ibid.* para 261 (Thommen J.).
27. *Ibid.* para 323 ((14).
28. *Ibid.* para 323 (15)
29. *Ibid* para 294 and 311.
30. *Ibid* para 294.
31. *Ibid.*
32. *Ibid.* para 320.
33. *Ibid* para 322.
34. *Ibid* paras 146, 155.
35. *Ibid.* para 416.
36. *Ibid* para 419.
37. H. Earl Fullilove v. Philip M. Khutznick, 448 : 65 L Ed 2d 902 (1980).
38. Metro Broadcasting Inc. v. federal Communications Commission, 58 IW 5053.
39. (2008) 6 SCC 1.
40. *Ibid.* p. 446 (para 6).
41. The Supreme Court of America evolved certain principles to cut the scope of affirmative action in Regents of the University of California v. Allan Bakke 438 U.S. 265. (1978); Grutter v. Bollinger 539 U.S. 306 (2003) and Parents involved in Community Schools v. Seattle School District 127 S ct. 2738 (2007).
42. *Ibid.* p. 548 (para 273).
43. 58 Chicago Bar Rec. 282, 293 (May-June 1977).
44. Ashok Kumar Thakur p. 626 (para 358 (10)).
45. *Ibid.* p. 683 (para 554).
46. *Ibid.* p. 682 (para 552).
47. Alfred L. Brophy, Reparation : Pro &Con, Oxf. Univ. Press, 2006, p. 9.
48. Charles J. Ogletree, The Current Repration Debates, 36 UC. Davis L. Reu 1051,1055 (2003).
49. Vincene Verdun, If the Shore Fits, Wear it : An analysis of Reparations to African Americans, 67 Tul. L. Rev. 597 (1993) at p. 638.
50. State of Kerala v. N.M. Thomas A.I.R. 1976 S.C. 490 = (1976) 2 SCC 310.
51. Professor U.R. Rai, Fundamental Rights and Their Enforcement, PHI Learning Limited, New Delhi, 2011 p. 594.
52. Cited from Rakesh K. Sinha, Dalits And Human Rights, Mohit Publications, New Delhi, 2010, p. 190.
53. Jawahar Lal Nehru, The Discovery of India, Asia Publishing House, 1961.
54. *Ibid.* p. 521
55. Mandal Case 1992 SCC (L& S). Supp. 1 (para 415) (Sawant J.).
56. *Ibid.* para 323 (14) (Thommen J.).
57. *Ibid.* para 146.
58. *Ibid.* para 596 and 616. (R. M. Sahai J.).
59. *Ibid.* para 321.

60. Ronald M. Dworkin, "Why Bakke Has No Case", New York Review of Books, 24, no. 18 (Nov., 1977), p. 12.
61. T. R. Curr, Why Men Rebel ? Princeton University Press, Princeton, 1970, p. 7.
62. Prakash Louis, Political Sociology of Dalit Assertion, Gyan Publishing House, New Delhi, 2003, p. 125.
63. Mandal Case (para 321, Thommen J.).
64. M. R. Balaji v. State of Mysore A.I.R. 1963 S.C. 649 = (1963) Supp. 1 SCR 439.
65. *Ibid.* at p. 467.
66. Ronald Dworkin, A Matter of Principle, Clarendon Press, Oxford, 1986 p. 294.
67. *Ibid.*
68. *Ibid.*
69. A Matter of Principle Clarendon Press, Oxford, 1986 p. 295.
70. *Ibid.* p. 297.
71. *Ibid.*
72. Report, Government of Karnatka (1975) Vol. I. part I, pp. 98-99.
73. Mandal Case, p. 228 (para 450).
74. *Ibid.*
75. *Ibid.*
76. *Ibid.*
77. Louis Dumont, Homo Hierarchicus, Granada Publishing Ltd., Londoln, 1972, p. 27.
78. National Herald, December, 1989.
79. Mandal Revisited, Indian Bar Review, Vol. 17 & 18 (1991) 393 at p. 396.
80. (1992) SCC (L& S) Supp. 1.
81. (2008) 6 SCC 1.
82. G. S. Ghurye, Caste And Race in India, Popular Prakashan, Bombay (2008 reprint) Chapter 14, A Casteless Society or a Plural society ? pp. 404-460.
83. *Ibid.* p. 717 (para 666).
84. Richard Wasserstrom, 'A Defence of Programmes of Preferential Treatment' (in) Jan. Narvason (ed.) Moral Issues (1983) p. 394.
85. Marc Galanter, Competing Equalities : Law and the Backward Classes in India, (Delhi : Oxf. Univer.Press, 1984 (with new Preface), p. 3.
86. James M. Nickel, Preferential Policies in Hiring and Admissions : A Jurisprudential Approach, 75 Columbia Law Review, p. 534 (1975).
87. *Ibid.*
88. Reverse Discrimination and Compensatory Justice, 33 Analysis (1973), p. 177.
89. 'Groups and the Equal Protection Clause', p. 27.
90. A.I.R. 1963 S.C. 649.
91. (1973) 4 SCC 225.
92. Gandhi, "India of My Dreams", (Navjivan : 1947), p. 6.

93. Swami Vivekananda : Quoted from B.N. Ganguli, Concept of Equality (Simla: Indian Institutes of Advanced Study, 1975), p. 124.

94. V. P. Singh's Lecture at Harvard on "Power And Equality : Changing Grammar of Indian Politics".

95. See, Dr Amitabh Nagrade, Reservation A Matter of Participation, "The reservation is the right of participation in education, services and politics etc." S. K. Biswas, Dr Ambedkar on Reservation, Manbodh Agency, Calcutta, 1992, pp. 16-17.

96. Indra Sawhney v. Union of India (1992) SCC (L & S) Supp. 1.

97. *Ibid.* para 492.

98. *Ibid.* para 694.

99. Lord Bingham.

100. 334. Reservation of seats and special representation to cease after (sixty years). Subs. By the Constitution (Seventy-Ninth Amendment) Act, 1999, S. 2, for "fifty years" (w.e.f. 25.1.2000). Originally it read "ten years" which was substituted by "twenty years" by the Constitution (Eighth Amendment) Act, 1959, by "thirty years" by the Constitution (Twenty-third Amendment) Act, 1969, by "forty years" by the Constitution (Forty-fifth Amendment) Act, 1980 and "fifty years" by the Constitution (Sixty-second Amendment) Act,1989. Notwithstanding anything in the foregoing provisions of this Part, the provisions of this Constitution relating to-

    (a) the reservation of seats for the Scheduled Castes and the Scheduled Tribes in the House of the People and in the Legislative Assemblies on the States; and

    (b) the representation of the Anglo-Indian community in the House of the People and in the Legislative Assemblies of the states by nomination.

    Shall cease to have effect on the expiration of a period of [sixty years] from the commencement of this Constitution.

    Provided that nothing in this article shall affect any representation in the House of the People or in the Legislative Assembly of a State until the dissolution of the then existing House or Assembly, as the case may be.

101. Ashok Kumar Thakur v. Union of India (2008) 6 SCC 1.

102. *Ibid.* p. 704 (para 625) (Dalveer Bhandari J.).

103. (1992) Supp. (3) SCC 217.

104. Ashok Kumar Thakur, p. 711. (para 651, Raveendran J.).

105. *Ibid.* p. 717 (para 666).

106. Indra Sawhney v. Union ofIndia 1992 SCC (L & S) Supp. 1. P. 286 (para 564).

107. 539 U.S. 306 (2003). Madam Justice O. Connor observed : "race-conscious admission policy must be limited in time — all governmental use of race must have a logical and point We expect that 25 years from now the use of racial preferences will no longer be necessary to further the interest approved today." *Ibid,* pp. 342-343.

108. (1981) 1SCC 246.

109. *Ibid.* at p. 264.

110. S. Ranganathan, Constitution of India – Five Decades, Bharat Law House, 1999 at p. 312.
111. K.C. Vasanth Kumar v. State of Kernataka A.I.R. 1985 S.C. 1495 at p. 1499.
112. *Ibid.*
113. Indra Sawhney v. Union of India 1992 SCC (L & S) Supp. 1 at p. 70 (para 24) (Pandian J.).
114. Latest to express this view is Indira Hirway, Director & Professor of Economics at the Centre For Development Alternatives, Ahmedabad, See 'Rethinking Reservations And Development', The Hindu, 31.8.2015, p. 10.
115. Ashok Kumar Thakur v. Union of India (2008) 6 SCC 1 at p. 684 (para 558).
116. *Ibid.*

Chapter - 4

Vision of the Framers of the Indian Constitution

4.1 To Establish a Casteless Or A Plural Society?

The Constitution of India is said to be a foremost social document. The foremost objective of the Constitution is to forge the unity and integrity of the nation through ensuring Justice–social, economic and political to all its citizens and liberty of thought, expression, belief, faith and worship; equality of status and opportunity; and promoting among them all fraternity assuring dignity of the individual. Equality, liberty and fraternity within the framework of our sovereign, socialist, secular, democratic republic is the spirit of the Constitution.

At interpretational level two points of view emerge –one view is that the framers project to achieve the constitutional objectives by establishing a casteless society and the other view is that the framers', project was to accomplish the constitutional goal through the effective plural society.

The status quoist plea is that the objective of the Constitution is to establish a casteless society so as to forge the integrative forces and avoid fissiparous tendencies. They place main emphasis on the provisions of the Constitution enshrined in Articles 15(1) and (2); 16(2); 29(2) and 325 which prohibit discrimination, disability or ineligibility on grounds only of religion, race, caste etc.[1] The real objective was to be achieved through social transformation.

The most celebrated, authoritative and off-cited book by our Apex Court – Granville Austin's Indian Constitution: Cornerstone of a Nation[2] presents three revolutions – political, social and economic. Social revolution meant 'to get (India) out of the medievalism based on birth, religion, custom and community and reconstruct her social structure on modern foundations of law, individual merit and secular education.'[3] Most of the writings of the legal scholars in India dwell upon this theory and work on syllogistic study, that is to say, the objective of the Constitution is to establish casteless society. Any programme based on caste is violative of the constitutional mandate and therefore, illegal. A detail study would be proffered a head. But, a few instances are given here to indicate extremism. A noted Constitutional law expert and senior advocate Mr Nani A Palkhivala published a two parts article in the Times of India (November 24 and 25, 1992) only after a week of the famous Mandal Case pronouncement on 16.11.1992. Mandal Case-I expressed Palkhivala's outburst, 'S.C. Verdict will Cleave Nation'. Reacting on Mr V. P. Singh, the former P.M.'s assertion of satisfaction to die in peace after implementing the long-awaited reservational Justice to OBCs through Mandal Commission, Mr Palkhivala said, "I am sure Mr V.P. Singh was sincere when he said that, after the Supreme Court judgment in the Mandal case he could die in peace. But, his policy has ensured that the national will not live in peace. The poisonous weed of casteism has been replanted, where it will trouble us a thousand years, each age will have to reconsider it."[4] Palkhivala was also not generous to the Supreme Court decision. Commenting on the verdict he said, "By ensuring a fresh lease of life to the canker of casteism for a long and indefinite future the judgment fractures the nation and disregards the basic structure of the Constitution".[5] In his opinion:

> "The decision would revitalise casteism, cleave the nation into two- forward and backward – and open up new vistas for internecine conflict and fissiparous forces, and backwardness a vested interest'. It will undo whatever has been achieved since independence, towards crafting a unified, integrated nation".[6]
>
> Why so ? His answer was that the basic structure of the Constitution envisages "a cohesive, unified and casteless society in which casteism, testified and ossified for centuries, should become merely the dust on the shelf of Indian history."[7]

Palkhivala's view was based on preconceived status quoist notions that castelessness is the basic structure of the Constitution. It is not factually correct as none of the honourable judges in eleven judgments of thirteen judges bench evolving basic structure theory in ***Kesavananda Bharati v. State of Kerala***[8] said so. Had caste consciousness disapeared from Indian society which Mandal case revived ? India had been caste ridden society with hierarchical structure, it is so and there is no semblance of its disappearance still in near future. Diversity is the special trait of the Indian society and unity in diversity is the speciality of the Indian culture.

Capture of all privileges through services by a few and permanent deprivation of many can not be the intendment of the founding fathers who promised to wipe tear from every eye. Thus, Palkhivala's major premise that India had become casteless society by 1990 is refutable, unsustainable and devoid of any reality.

On the other hand, the argument to establish India as a casteless society has been disputed by those who view that framers project was to achieve unity of the country by strengthening the pluralist society of India through satisfying the deprived section of the society. The framers did not abolish caste. They abolished untouchability. The tree was left intact. Only the fruit was plucked. Article 17 reads, "Untouchability" is abolished and its practice in any form is forbidden. The enforcement of any disability arising out of Untouchability shall be an offence punishable in accordance with law." The scheme and provisions of the Constitution as well as judicial pronouncements led the well known sociologist G.S. Ghurye to conclude that they are quite lending clearly the Indian society towards becoming a "plural society".[9] Mr Mohamed Ismail Sahib, member, Constituent Assembly while participating in discussion on reservation issue under Draft Article 10(3) (present Article 16(4) made categorically clear:

> "When we speak of reservations and rights and privileges the bogey of communalism is being raised. Sir, communalism does not come in because people want their rights. When people find that they are not adequately represented, they rightly feel that they must have due representation and then such demand comes up. It comes because of their non-representation in the services and because of their discontent. When such discontent is removed, the unity of hearts come in. It is the unity of hearts and not any attempt at a physical unity that will do good to the country and to the people. The difference will be there, but there must be harmony and that is what we all really and that harmony can be brought about only creating contentment amongst the people. And reservation in service is one of the measure we can adopt to bring about contentment among the people. You can then say to the people, "Look here you have your proper share in the services and you have nothing to complain." When people themselves find that they are given as good an opportunity as others, harmony will be there and the so-called communalism will not come in at all."[10]

The learned member further added –

> "There are countries which have followed the procedure which I am advocating and quite effectively, they have eliminated communalism.

Therefore, I say that one of the ways of removing disharmony and producing harmony is to make provision for the people's representation in the services and to make them feel that they have got a real share and an effective share in the governance of the country."[11]

4.2 Views Surfaced during Constituent Assembly

The present provision dealing with reservation in public employment is the improvement upon the recommendation of the adhoc committee made by Ambedkar – Munshi formula. Sub Committee on Minorities had recommended affirmative assertion of equality of opportunity in services adjusting the claims of minorities to special representation in the services. Advisory Committee discussed the matter with the recommendations of the Minorities Sub-Committee on April 21, 1947. Dr K.M. Munshi suggested compromistic view that the general principle regarding equality of opportunity to all must be asserted in affirmative and exception in favour of backward communities should be provided by incorporating a separate sub-clause to that effect.[12] Dr Munshi expressed the opinion of Sub-Committee making observation that, "the sub-committee feel that we must put the positive right first and then put in the negative clause otherwise it will be a dead letter. Some reservation was to be conceded for minority. K.M. Pannikar argued practice of some Provinces giving preference to certain sections of the people. Rajagopalachari felt that in absence of some reservation in favour of the people there may be all round resentment. Ad hoc committee was appointed to look into the matter which recommended that, "Nothing herein contained shall prevent State from making provision for reservations in favour of classes not adequately represented in the public services."[13]

Dr B. R. Ambedkar suggested deletion of all the words after reservation and in their place insertion of words, "in public services in favour of classes as may be prescribed by the State."[14] He pleaded that retention of words, "not adequately represented" could lead to judicial interpretation by opening challenge into Courts against the government decisions. Dr K.M. Munshi suggested a compromistic formula to retain the spirit of the recommendation of the Ad hoc Committee and meet out Dr Ambedkar's apprehension by accepting, "Classes which in the opinion of the State are not adequately represented."[15] At the stage of preparing the Draft Constitution by the Drafting Committee one important modification was made by the Chairman, Drafting Committee by substituting expressions "in favour of any backward class of citizens."[16]

Thus, Clause (3) of Article 10 [Clause (4) of Article 16 of the present Constitution] prepared by the Drafting Committee read "Nothing in this Article shall prevent the State from making any provision for the reservation of appointments or posts in favour any backward class of citizens who, in the opinion of the State, are not adequately represented in the services under the State."

Draft provision was circulated for eliciting opinion. R. R. Diwakar and S.V. Krishnamoorthy Rao proposed the addition of the expressions, "economically or culturally" before the word backward.[17] Sir B.N. Rau commented on it that though there was no great objection in doing so, such addition was unnecessary.[18] T. A. Ramalingam Chettiar elicited the opinion to drop the word 'backward' from clause (3) of Article 10.[19] To this the answer / clarification of Sir B.N. Rau was that it would expand the scope of the clause as it would be open to a State to reserve posts in favour of any class of citizens who were not adequately represented in the Services.[20] One view elicited by an advocate from Calcutta (now Kolkata) was to limit the period of reservation for fifteen years so as to put a check on growth of a vested interest in backwardness.[21]

Clause (3) of Article 10 came up for consideration before the Constituent Assembly on 30.11.1948. The following different set of views based on upbringing and inhered feelings came to the fore.

4.2.1 Status quoist-cum-Idealist points of view: Complete deletion of Clause (3) to the Draft Article 10.

Loknath Mishra suggested deletion of Clause (3) on plea that it was unnecessary as it has two flaws – *first,* it would put a premium on backwardness and inefficiency, and, *second,* it was not a fundamental right of any citizen to claim state employment on consideration other than merit.[22] Shri Damodar Swarup Seth (United Provinces: General) moved deletion of Clause (3). The reasons proffered were: (I) reservation of posts or appointments in services for the backward classes means the very negation of efficiency and good government; (ii) no satisfactory criteria to ascertain backward classes; (iii) if retained, it would give rise to casteism and favouritism which is inconsistent with the idea of a secular State. Mr Seth favoured necessary facilities and concession to backward classes for improving their educational qualifications and raise general level of their uplift.[23] Posing full faith in impartiality of the Public Service Commission to recruit personnel on merit consideration, Mr Seth emphatically argued that, "no concession whatever should be allowed to any class on the plea that the some happens to be backward."[24] Mr Seth's view was quite idealist, though the impartiality of P.S.C. was disputed by the Scheduled Castes' members (discussed a head). Dr Seth was also unaware of the repercussion of his view which would put premium on status quoism and alienation of a sizeable number of Indian citizenry from the governance of the country and deprivation of participation in administration of the State affairs.

4.2.2 Temporary phase of reservation: No clear view on the Point:

Pandit Hriday Nath Kunjru (United Provinces: General) though agreed with the need of the protection of the interests of those who were unable to lookafter themselves without aid, wanted to put time limit of ten years on such concessions. In his view Clause (3) would read, "Nothing in this article shall, during a period of ten years after the commencement of this Constitution, prevent the State from making any reservation of posts in favour of any backward class of citizens who…etc." Pt. Kunjru found several difficulties in continuing reservational safeguards for long; **First**, the expression backward was not defined which would lead to courts interpretation;[25] **second**, reservation should not be left for indefinite period because it was not desirable in the interest of both backward classes and the State. He preferred periodic review;[26] **third**, he wanted to make reservation in service on par with reservation in legislatures i.e. for ten years. He also thought that it could encourage fissiparous tendencies and he wished that country might fully integrated if reservation is done away after 10 years.[27] He himself was apprehensive that his amendment would not find favour with Dr Ambedkar.[28] Dr Ambedkar did not respond in that measure which Pandit Kunjru thought but other honourable members from the Schedule Caste gave befitting answers. Shri Chandrika Ram (Bihar: General) lamented that backward class has not been given reservation in Legislatures, that is, neither in the Assemblies nor in the councils. He pleaded, [29] "Just as we have provided reservations for the Harijans in Services, in Assemblies and in Councils, it would be proper on our part to make similar provision for backward classes also."[30] He also saw the lack of reservation of backward class in Legislatures as denial of equal opportunity.[31] Mr Shantanu Kumar Dass (Orissa: General) supported Chandrika Ram by pleading that "there should be reservation in services and elections."[32] Mr T. Channiah was very vocal and categorical as to impractibility of equality assurance within ten years. He pointedly argued: "I am really sorry that the honourable Pandit Kunjru should have felt that the backward class should be given this opportunity only for a period of 10 years. Sir, I want this reservation for 150 years which has been the period during which opportunities have been denied to them."[33] Shri Shantanu Kumar Dass tauntingly pooh poohed the idea of 10 years plea of

Pandit Kunjru. He said: "It has been said that reservation should be kept for ten years. Why only for ten years ? If we get equal rights within two years all would be on the same level after that period and there would be no need for reservations. With these I support the article."[34] Mr Mohamed Ismail Sahib too opposed Pandit Kunjru time-bound reservation for 10 years. He said:

> "Sir, the measure or yardstick in any such matter should not be the period of time. The backwardness of the people is the result of conditions which have been persisting and in existence for several centuries and ages, and these will not die off easily. So measure really should be the steps that are being taken to liquidate that backward condition, and should be the forwardness of the people which has resulted as a consequence of those steps. Therefore, when these people advance and have come forward as much as any other community in the land then these reservations would automatically disappear."
>
> He emphasised:
>
> "I feel no period need be stipulated at all for this purpose. That period might be less than ten years; or it may be more than ten years according to the backwardness persists or disappears".[35]

4.2.3 Widening Scope of Reservation

Mr Aziz Ahmad Khan (United Provinces: Muslim) proposed that "in clause (3) of Article 10 the word "backward" be omitted. He reminded that insertion of "backward" was after thought, as it was thought unnecessary by Minority Committee Report to include the word "backward". He also found contradiction between Article 10(3) and Articles 296 and 299 of the draft Constitution. If backward meant only educationally and culturally backward then minorities would be kept outside. Result being that "State services are monopolised by one particular class, then others might think that their existence has been ignored.[36] It would create unpleasantness in the country. In order to make provision in consonance with the Minority Committee report and remove apprehension of isolation in the mind of minorities he made strong plea for deletion of the word, "backward". He concluded: "To my mind if the word "backward" is deleted, then the hand of the Government will be strengthened in such a way that it will enable the Government from time to time to make adequate arrangements in case the claims of any particular group are overlooked in public services."[37] Some other members supported omission the word "backward", as the scope of the word was likely to be misconstrued. Mr Mohamed Ismail Sahib (Madras: Muslim) expressed the view that "if one reads the clause without this word, then one can quite clearly and easily understand its meaning. But, when the word "backward" is inserted, it obscures the meaning a great deal. Keeping in mind the specific meaning of the word 'backward' in Madras, he apprehended that minorities like Muslim, Christians and the Scheduled Caste would be excluded from the purview of the reservation clause."[38] He requested that mover of the motion should remove atleast the word "backward" and "make it clear to the House that here, when the clause speaks of reservation, it means also minorities, who stand in need of such reservations."[39]

4.2.4 Substitution of the word 'backward' by Scheduled Caste or Depressed Class

With a view to protect the Scheduled Castes interest in better way a number of hon'ble members of the Constituent Assembly preferred the substitution of the word 'backward' by the Scheduled Caste. R.M. Nalavade (Bombay: General) argued that the words "backward classes" are so vague that they could be interpreted in such a way so as to include so many classes which are even educationally advanced.[40] He argued that if words "Scheduled Castes" might have been used it would have been easier for the depressed classes to get adequate representation in the services. Dr Dharam Prakash argued that the expression "backward classes" was vague and supported the amendment that the words "backward classes" should be substituted by the words, "Scheduled castes or depressed class" because they have a definite meaning.[41] Some members wished that benefit of reservation should be assured only to them. Their bent of mind was Scheduled Caste versus other backwards. The substitution of scheduled caste would have ousted other backward classes. There was atleast one member who did find merit in insertion of the words "backward classes" putting no threat to the interest of the Scheduled Castes, Shri H.J. Khandekar supported Article 10(3), congratulated the member of drafting committee who inserted the word 'backward' and pointed out "If this word 'backward' had not been here, the purpose of the Scheduled Caste would not have been served as it should be."[42]

4.2.5 Retention of Backward Classes: Different points of view

One view has just been discussed above how H.J. Khandekar preferred retention of backward classes as a means to secure Schedule Caste interest in better way. Shri Ari Bhadur Gurung pleaded for the inclusion of Gurkhas in backward class as they were socially and educationally backward and had served the country by their army services.[43] Reading Article 10 and 296 together Pandit Kunjru made lear that "though it is word 'minority' that is used in Article 296 and the expression 'backward classes' is used in Article 10(3), it seems to be that in fairness to the country protection can be granted to any class, whether you call it a backward class or a minority only on the ground that it is backward and if left to itself, would be unable to protect its interest."[44] It was only Shri Chandrika Ram (Bihar: general) who whole heartedly and boldly stood for support of Article 10(3).[45] So was the case of T. Channiah who preferred retention of the word 'backward' so that Clauses (1) and (2) of Article 10 would not be rendered null and void.[46]

4.2.6 Defence of 'Reservation' as Such

Reservation was defended by a number of Hon'ble members on different Counts. First, Shri R.M. Nalavade (Bombay: General) supported reservation on ground that in Provinces even if depressed classes are educated and qualified, they are not given chances of employment under the Provincial Governments. He thought that now Schedule Castes had no fear in view of the constitutional provisions for chances in employment. Dr Dharm Prakash[47] defended reservation in view of administrative machinery guided by provincial, communal and caste considerations instead of being guided by merit and merit alone. Shri P. Kakkan (Madras: General) supported reservation on the same count that Harijan did not get appointment or promotion in government services.[48] Shri V.I. Muniswamy Pidlay defended reservation on account of justice to the depressed. He pointed out, "Sir, some honourable Members feel that reservation is not necessary. I think this is unwholesome thinking because so long as communal canker remains in the body politic, I feel there will be communities coming up for reservation; but the case of the Scheduled Caste is not pleaded on a matter of communalism, because they have been left in lurch and due to their lack of social, economic and educational advancement for years and decades it is necessary, and I also feel that their case must be presented in this House vehemently, so that we get justice at all times."[49] Shri Shantanu Kumar Dass (Orissa: General) was more vocal. He cited example of advertisements in Railway and Postal Departments where apprentice are selected and contenders coming from distance are ignored. He pointed out minority – Harijan, Muslims and Christians fear that "without reservation it would not be able to gain seats in elections or employment in services."[50] He also contested the claim of Seth Damodar Swarup as to no need for reservations in view of the impartiality of Public Service Commission. To quote Mr Dass, 'Candidates appear at its examination and many of those who qualify appear in the lists, yet when there is a chance of filling posts those who have not even appeared at the examination are taken in. How does it happen? It happens because such people have a strong backing which enables them to get selected." Shri H. J. Khandekar expressed his experience that in provinces well qualified Scheduled Caste persons do not get opportunity and fair treatment in the services.[51]

4.2.7 Munshi – Ambedkar Defence of Reservation to Backward Classes and Clarifications

Dr K. M. Munshi clarified and assured the Scheduled Castes members that the use of expression 'backward classes' in no way will curtail their rights or privileges or opportunities. Backward class definitely includes the Scheduled Caste. He pointed out that the non-scheduled caste persons had been in forefront to save the interests of the Scheduled Castes. Dr Munshi made clear that when the generic term backward is read with draft Article 301 is perfectly clear that –

> "the word "backward" signifies that class of people – does not matter whether you call them untouchables or touchables, belonging to this community or that, - a class of people who are so backward that special protection is required in the services and I see no reason why any member should be apprehensive of regard to the word "backward."[52]

Dr Munshi further elaborated 'backward' class in light of experience of Madras and Bombay Provinces. It meant and included, "not only Scheduled Castes and Scheduled Tribes but also other backward classes who are economically, educationally and socially backward".[53]

Dr B. R. Ambedkar, Chairman Drafting Committee did two jobs at the last. **First**, he answered the three objections of Shri T.T. Krishnamachari: (i) constitution being produced as a paradise for lawyers; (ii) whether rule of reservation was justiciable; and (iii) who is a reasonable man and who is a prudent man. Dr Ambedkar answered that all Constitutions involve judicial interpretation and no country has ever produced a Constitution which has not been paradise for lawyers – to say United States, Canada and other countries.[54] He also pointed out that he personally felt that the reservation issue would be a justiciable issue. He also pointed out that the words, "reasonable persons and prudent persons" have well defined meaning under many statutes like transfer of Property Act and others.[55]

Second, Dr Ambedkar also clarified the meaning of a backward community and giving due credence to the local government said, "a backward community is a community which is backward in the opinion of the Government."[56]

Third, Dr Ambedkar tried to satisfy the hon'ble members by reconciliatory mission and in that light to interpret the use of the expression 'backward'. The exchange of views among members revealed three points of view which needed reconciliation:[57] **first**, there shall be equality of opportunity for all citizens, (ii) if the first principle is to be operative in its fullest extent, there ought to be no reservations of any sort for any class or community at all – all qualified to be put on equal footing so far as the public service is concerned; and the third and massive opinion, "that although theoretically it is good to have the principle that there shall be equality of opportunity, there must be at the same time a provision made for the entry of certain communities which have so far been outside the administration."[58] The Drafting Committee adopted a formula which would reconcile the three points of view: "**firstly**, that thee shall be equality of opportunity, **secondly,** that there shall be reservations in favour of certain communities which have not so far had a "proper took-in" so to say into the administration."[59] Article 10(3) was the best formula to reconcile with generic principle in clause (1) of Article 10.

Fourth, a proper balance between clause (1) and (3) of Article 10 was preferred by suggesting reservation of seats to be confined to minority of the seats. Dr Ambedkar gave an example of absurd reservation. He said:

"Let me give an illustration. Supposing, for instance, reservations were made for a community or a collection of communities, the total of which come to something like 70 per cent of the total posts under the State and only 30 per cent are retained as the unreserved. Could any body say that reservation of 30 per cent as open to general competition would be satisfactory from the point of view of giving effect to the first principle, namely, that there shall be equality of opportunity ? It cannot be in my judgment. Therefore, the seats to be reserved, if the reservation is to be consistent with sub-clause (1) of Article 10, must be confined to a minority of seats."[60]

Fifth, Dr Ambedkar pointed out "the signification of the word 'backward' used in Article 10(3). He made clear, if we have to safeguard two things, namely, the principle of equality of opportunity and at the same time satisfy the demand of communities which have not had so far representation in the State, then, I am sure that they will agree that unless you use some such qualifying phrase as "backward" the exception made in favour of reservation will ultimately eat up the rule altogether."[61]

The issue of the Scheduled Castes and Tribes was discussed as part of minority. By all the idea that the Scheduled Castes[62] and Tribes and to some extent Anglo-Indians needed special concession and treatment was appreciated and conceded. Minorities also showed good gesture and their co-operative and nationalistic approach led to give up their claim for reservation.[63] Even for the SCs, STs and Anglo-Indians the representation/ reservation in Legislatures was conceded for a temporary period of ten years inspite of the personal feelings of Dr Ambedkar to continue it for a longer period. So far services were concerned no reservation was conceded to any minority and that was on their own initiative. Thus, the classless society's initiative taken by Raj Kumari Amrit Kaur: (i) privileges and safeguards really weaken those who demand them, (ii) any thing in the nature of privileges for any special class or section of society was wrong in principle, and when it was given on the ground of religion, it was doubly wrong, for all religions stood for the brotherhood of man and none for separatism; (iii) such reservations and special privileges would militate against the declared objective of the Indian Union, which was to establish a classless society and (iv) Special privileges and protection would lead to the fragmentation of the Indian nation,[64] got the credence and patriotic, emotive and nationalistic appeal of Sardar Vallabh Bhai Patel had magic effect on minorities including Muslims. Discussion, persuation and appeal brought quite transformation in attitude of minorities – the development starting from reservation in services, Cabinet, Legislature on communal line, but ended in sacrificing all claims in the national interest.[65] Letter of Sardar Patel addressed to the President, Constituent Assembly of India on 11th May, 1949 sufficiently made clear that in view of vastly changed circumstances, it was no longer appropriate in the context of free India and of present conditions that there should be reservation for Muslims, Christians, Sikhs or any other religious minority. Although the abolition of separate electorates had removed much of the poison from the body politic, the reservation of seats for religious communities, it was felt, did lead to certain degree of separation and was to that extent contrary to the conception of a secular democratic state." Certain members of the Constituent Assembly like Dr H.C. Mookerjee, Mr Tajmul Hussain, Shri Lakshmi Kanta Maitra and some others had given noticed of resolutions recommending that "there should be no reservation of seats in the Legislature for any community in India. But, Shri V.I. Muniswami gave notice for amendment to the effect to exclude the Scheduled Castes from the purview of the same resolutions. On May 11, 1947 the following Resolution was passed:

> "That the system of reservation for minorities other than Scheduled Castes in Legislatures be abolished."

The other exclusion from Resolutions were representation of Tribals in the Legislatures and recommendations made by the North East Frontier

(Assam) Tribal and excluded Areas Sub Committee; representation of Anglo-Indian in the Legislature.[66]

As has been discussed earlier certain classes of Sikhs were included in the Scheduled Castes.

Still one issue was left and that was the issue of backward classes. The issue of backward class was first dealt with reference to the minorities. The draft Constitution prepared by the Drafting Committee dealt with the issue of different kinds of reservations and concessions conceded to minorities including the appointment of the Commission by the President of India to enquire into the conditions of the socially and educationally backward classes.[67] Since the idea of reservation to minorities as such was abandoned in the final draft of the Constitution which emerged after due deliberations in the Constituent Assembly, Part XIV was adopted. It dealt with Special Provisions Relating to certain classes consisting of Articles 330-342 dealing with safeguards to SCs, STs, and SEBCs. In addition Article 275 conceded grants-in-aid of revenues out of the Consolidated Fund of India to states for the purpose of promoting the welfare of the Scheduled Tribes in the State or raising the level of administration of the Scheduled areas therein of that of the administration of the rest of the areas of that State[68] and to the State of Assam for the same purpose[69] and to autonomous state of Assam[70] for the same object. Schedule Fifth deals with the administration and control of Scheduled Areas and Scheduled Tribes and the Sixth Schedule deals with provisions as to administration of Tribal Areas in Assam, Meghalaya, Tripura and Mizoram.

The issues is: Was caste consideration totally buried by the framers of the Constitution ? What is Scheduled Caste ? The outcome of framers effort was definition of the "Scheduled castes" given in Article 366 (24) which reads to mean, "such caste, races, or tribes or parts of or groups within such castes, races or tribes as are deemed under Article 341 to be the Scheduled Castes for the purpose of the Constitution." Article 341 again enables the President to make public notification specifying castes, races or tribes or parts of or groups within castes, races or tribes to be Scheduled Caste for the purpose of the Constitution. So is the case with tribes or tribal communities forming part of the scheduled tribes (definition given in Article 366 (25) to be read with Article 342). What about backwards ? No clear definition was given in the Constitution. The Constituent Assembly debates show that framers had a flexible idea of backward classes. Even the deprived and poor classes of religions based on the principle of non-gradation and equality – Muslims, Sikhs, Christians were intended to be included in the backward class. "Backward" was rather residuary class to include all destitudes, depressed, undeveloped, deprived, weak and meek class of Hindu, Sikh, Muslim and Christian. The provisions of Article 15(4), 16(4) and 46 make clear that the intendment of the framers was to establish a plural society with mission to satisfy all the sections of society so as to contribute towards the nation-building collectively. It leads to genuine conclusion that our Constitution is both caste-blind and caste-conscious. The aim is to bring all in the mainstream of national life.

4.3 Vision of the Constitution: Colour-Caste Blindness or Both Colour-Caste Blindness and Colour-Caste Consciousness ?

Everything is influx in India. The parody is that SEBCs' problem, during Constituent Assembly Debates, started in context minorities. In post-Constitution period it was minimised to Hindu, as Hindu believe in hierarchical caste system and minorities – Muslim, Sikh and Christians do not Equality and denial of equality to depressed/backward classes formed the basis for determination of backward classes. Since Muslims or Christians do not believe in caste-based inequality, persecution, deprivation etc. the backward among them had been left out. To be fair to the first Socially and Educationally Backward Class Commission (Kaka Kalelkar Commission) lamented that due to lack caste system and hierarchical status amongst Muslims and Christians backward among them had not been taken care of. And, IInd SEBC Commission took care of that. It is also hard reality of the Indian Society that vices of Hindu fractured society and caste conscious persecution has spread over the Muslims, Christians and Sikh too. To quote hon'ble Mr Justice S. Ratnavel Pandian in famous ***Indra Sawhney v. Union of India*** (popularly known as Mandal case)[71] "it is said that caste-system is unknown to other communities such as Muslims, Christians, Sikhs, Jews, Parsis, Jains etc. in whose respective religion, the caste system is not recognised and permitted. But in practice, it can not be irrefutably asserted that Islam, Christianity, Sikhism are all completely immune from casteism."[72] He gave example Andhra Pradesh and Tamil Nadu.[73] So did Sawant J. in the same case.[74] Sawant J. made clear that "almost all followers of the non-Hindu religions except those of Zoroastrianism, are converts from Hindu religion, and in the new religion they carried with them there castes as well. It is unnatural to expect that the social prejudices and biases, and the notions and feelings of superiority and inferiority, nurtured for centuries together, would disappear by a mere change of religion."[75] That is reason why Dr Ambedkar, the then Law Minister in the course of debate in Parliament on the intendment of Article 16(4) expressed his views that "backward classes are nothing but collection of certain castes". It is most significant that Dr Ambedkar was not only Law Minister, he was Chairman,

Drafting Committee. He had the authorship of adding the expression backward class which was not in the original report of Advisory Committee. He defended the addition of the 'backward class' in the Constituent Assembly.

Not only backward class problems but also the issue of the Scheduled castes were discussed alongwith minority problems. The "Scheduled castes" was the part of the consideration of the Sub-Committee on Minorities into three groups.

A. Population less than half per cent in the Indian Dominion, omitting the Indian States

1. Anglo-Indians
2. Parsees
3. Plains tribesmen in Assam

B. Population not More Than one and half per cent

4. Indian Christians
5. Sikhs

C. Population Exceeding one and half per cent

6. Muslims
7. Schedule Castes

The Scheduled Castes was part of the Hindu society. In famous Gandhian assertion they were part and parcel of the Hindu society. But, for the purposes of their issues, problems and assertive claims they were treated minority having more than one and half per cent population in British India (their population in the Indian states excepted). At last stage the concession and reservations for minorities as such was dropped. That is reason why Part XII of Draft Constitution prepared by the Constitutional Advisor and Part XIV of the Draft Constitution dealing with Special Provisions Relating to Minorities were abandoned and present Part XVI under caption Special Provisions Relating to Certain classes was adopted. The expression certain classes included the Scheduled Castes, the Scheduled Tribes, the Anglo-Indian Communities and backward classes. As has been discussed earlier the Scheduled Castes defined and determined [Article 366 (24) and Article 341] have got not rid of Caste and races. They display role in identification in 1950 and are expected to play role in inclusion in or exclusion from the list of Scheduled are under Article 341(2) by the Parliament.

Thus, the Caste consciousness was not totally absent from the consideration of reservational issue by the Constitution makers. Even the most celebrated decision of ***M.R. Balaji v. State of Mysore***[76] the unanimous Supreme Court could not totally ignore caste in determination of the Socially and Educationally backward classes. To quote Gajendragadkar J., "in dealing with in question as to whether any class of citizen is socially backward or not, it may not be irrelevant to consider the Caste of the said group of citizens."[77] What the Court did not approve was that Caste could not sole or dominant criterion for determination of backwardness. If the entire Caste or majority is socially and educationally backward why it can not be classified as backward or Caste cannot become class ? Actually the Supreme Court approved Caste as class in the above referred contingency in ***State of A.P. v. U.S. Balram***[78]. In ***P. Rajendran v. State of Madras***[79], the Supreme Court ruled that Caste is also a class and if the Caste as a whole is socially and educationally backward reservation can be made for that Caste on that ground. In ***A. Periakaruppan v. State of T.N.***[80], the Supreme Court asserted that a Caste has always been recognised as a class.

Even First Backward Classes Commission was honest and candid enough to speak the hard realities of the Indian society. The Commission observed:

> "We tried to avoid Caste but we find it difficult to ignore caste in the present prevailing conditions. We wish it were easy to dissociate Caste from social backwardness at the present juncture. In modern time anybody can take any profession. The Brahmin taking to tailoring does not become a tailor by caste, nor is his social status lowered as a Brahmin. A Brahmin may be seller of boots and shoes, and yet his social status is not lowered thereby. Social backwardness, therefore, is not today due to the particular profession of a person, but we cannot escape Caste in considering the social backwardness in India."[81] ——————————————————————"All this goes to prove that socially backwardness is mainly based on racial, tribal, Caste and denominational differences."[82]

One of Constitutional law jurisprudent of repute, candidly accepts despite the majority view in **Thomas**[83] that the Scheduled Castes did not constitute a caste category in the traditional sense, the hard fact is that they are classified on the basis of caste and religion.[84]

In ***K.C. Vasanth Kumar v. State of Karnataka***[85] the Supreme Court was specially requested to determine criteria for determination of the backward classes. No final conclusion was arrived at O. Chinnappa Reddy J. recognising the fusion of social status and economic power, observed that in rural society they are too interwoven that, "one may without hesitation, say that if poverty be the cause, caste is the primary index of social backwardness, so that social backwardness is often readily identifiable with reference to a person's caste."[86] The learned Judge exclaimed, "So sadly and oppressively deep-rooted is Caste in our country that it has cut across even the barriers of religion."[87] In the same case Hon'ble Mr Justice Venkataramiah echoed the same spirit when he said, "an examination of question in the background of the Indian social conditions shows that the expression 'backward classes' used in the Constitution referred only to those who were born in particular castes or who belonged of particular races or tribes or religious minorities which were backward."

It makes clear that the framers were not quite oblivious of caste. Thus, in context of peculiar hierarchical structure the talk of colour-caste blindedness is to shut eyes to the real problems.

The theory of "colour blind" mission of the framers is the first step or only one side of the coin. We know that the hostile discrimination were based on colour consciousness both in U.S.A. and in India. In both the societies some were conceded as superior and others as inferior on the basis of race/colour of caste. In U.S.A. blacks – African Americans and Whites met different treatments. The basis was not genuine, rational, well-conceived or approved on the test of righteousness. Whites in the United States had constructed dualism so as to create an atmosphere of White superiority and Black inferiority. As has been discussed in Chapter one all the good and impressive images like industrious, intelligent, moral, knowledgeable, enabling culture, responsible, virtuous/pious and law-abiding has been put in account of the whites and all the deplorable traits and images like lazy, unintelligent, immoral, ignorant, disabiling culture, shiftness, lascivious and criminals have been relegated in the accounts of blacks.

So has been the case in India. The upper caste, especially Brahmin were treated to be learned, virtuous, cultured, right thinking and Scheduled Castes/low born were treated as ignorant, deviant, thief/criminals.

In America, the Black-Negroes were deprived of liberty, property and even family life and were treated as chattels. So was the case in India. Shudras could not keep money what they owned was the property of his master. Though there was variation in the name- in U.S.A., It was slavery, in India it was the institution bondedness to serve the upper caste, but both served the same purpose of deprivation, persecution and lack of property and initiative on the part of Negroes and Shudras. All the institutions worked with colour consciousness to make negroes destitute, humiliated by hostile discrimination. In America, legislature, executive and judiciary all contributed to the injury of Negroes. The Supreme Court of America in ***Dread Scott v. Sanford***[88] was well aware of changes in public opinion of the civilised world. But, was swayed by preconceived colour conscious of the American Society. Chief Justice Roger Taney held that at the time when the Constitution of United States was adopted Negroes were regarded as **persons of inferior status**, not as citizens. Thus, they could have no right to sue in the Federal Courts. The learned Chief Justice declared the philosophy to shut eye to the developments inside or outside the country. His presumption prevailed. He proclaimed: "No one, we presume, supposes, that any change in public opinion or feeling, in relation to this unfortunate race, in the civilised nations of Europe or in this country, should induce the Court to give to the words of the Constitution a more liberal construction in their favour than they were intended to bear when the instrument was framed and adopted."[89] It goes without saying that the conservative approach of the Court is not in consonance with the famous Marshallian prophetic assertion that Court should not forget that it is the Constitution which they are expounding and which has to endure for ages solving many crises.[90] The same status quoist, conservative and preconceived notion of judiciary continued after four decades in ***Holmer Adolf Plessy v. Joh H. Ferguson***[91] inspite of the enactment of 13th Amendment to the American Constitution ending slavery and involuntary servitude and XIVth Amendment enforcing equality and equal protection of law. In the instant case the constitutionality of the statute passed by the State of Louisiana passed in 1890 was challenged on account of the violation of the equality clause of the 14th Amendment, 1968. The statute provided for separate compartment in Railways for Negroes and Whites. Plessy, a Negro was prosecuted for trying to travel in the compartment meant for Whites. The Learned Judge Brown who spoke for majority of the Court did not find any violation of thirteenth Amendment. He said, "A statute which implies merely a legal distinction between the white and coloured races – a distinction which is founded in the colour of the two races and which must always exist so long as white men are distinguished from the other race by colour- has no tendency to destroy the legal equality of the two races or re-establish a State of involuntary servitude." As regards the 14th Amendment the Learned Judge gave a peculiar interpretation so as to perpetuate colour-consciousness. "The object of the amendment", said, Brown J. was, "undoubtedly to enforce the equality of the two races before the law, but in the nature of things it could not have been intended to abolish distinctions based upon colour, or to enforce social, as distinguished from political, equality, or a commingling of the two races upon terms unsatisfactory to either."[92] The learned Judge poured colour-consciousness to justify the colour-conscious statutory discrimination. Said, Justice Brown, "Laws permitting and even requiring their separation in places where they are liable to be brought into contact do not necessarily imply the inferiority of either race to the other, and have been generally, if not universally recognised as within the competency of the state."[93] Brown J. cited common instance of separate schools for Whites and Negroes. Thus, the colour-race consciousness led to evolve the doctrine of 'separate, but equal' nicely to negate equality among Whites and Blacks.

In backdrop of the above colour-conscious evil, in his strong dissent Justice Harlan pleaded for 'Colour-blind' constitutional philosophy. He gave a most befitting answer to colour-conscious contention of Justice Brown i.e. "if the civil and political rights of both races be equal, one can not be inferior to the other civilly or politically. If one race is inferior to the other socially, the Constitution of the United States cannot put them upon the same plane...".

Harlan J. started with equality premise and said that in respect of civil right, the Constitution of the United States "does not permit any public authority to know the race of those entitled to be protected in the enjoyment of such rights. He interpreted 13th and 14th amendment with the same spirit. Harlan J. took help of 15th Amendment Said, Justice Harlan, "finally, and to the end that no citizen should be denied, on account of his race, the privilege of participating in the political control of this country, it was declared by the 15th Amendment that"[94] the rights of citizens of the United States to vote shall not be denied or abridged by the United States or by any state on account of race, colour or previous condition of servitude." Such move were widely acclaimed by the world community and "they removed the race line from our governmental system..."[95] Justice Harlan then observed the constitutional philosophy as to "colour-race blindness" so as to ensure justice to the persecuted and deprived blacks by putting them on par with Whites. He called spade and spade: "The White race deems itself to be the dominant race in this country. And so it is, in prestige, in achievements, in education, in wealth and in power. So, I doubt not that it will continue to be for all time, if it remains true to its great heritage and holds fast to the principles of constitutional liberty. But in view of the Constitution, in the eye of the law, there is in this country no superior, dominant, ruling class of citizens. There is no caste here. Our Constitution is colour-blind, and neither knows nor tolerates classes among citizens. In respect of civil rights, all citizens are equal before the law. The humblest is the peer of the most powerful. The law regards man as man, and takes no account of his surroundings or of his colour when his civil rights as guaranteed by the supreme law of the land are involved."[96]

Harlan J. lamented: "It is, therefore, to be regretted that this highest tribunal, the final expositor of the fundamental law of the land, has reached the conclusion that it is competent for a state to regulate the enjoyment by citizens of their rights solely upon the basis of race. In the view of Harlan J. such colour conscious move are bound to arouse race hate and will perpetuate a feeling of distrust between the races and encourage tendency to treat coloured citizens so inferior and degraded that they cannot be allowed to sit in public coaches occupied by White citizens.

It took again nearly, six decades period to answer Justice Brown segregation in school on the ground of separate but equal. Thus, in ***Brown v. Board of Education of Topeka***[97] the Supreme Court of America was confronted with the question: Does segregation of children in public schools solely on the basis of race, even though physical facilities and other 'tangible' factors may be equal, deprive the children of the minority group of equal opportunities ? The nine Judge bench unanimously said: "We believe that this does." Delivering the judgment of the unanimous Court Warren C.J. observed: Segregation of White and coloured children in public schools has a detrimental effect upon the coloured children. The impact is greater when it has the sanction of the law ; for the policy of separating the races is usually interpreted as denoting the inferiority of the negro group. A sense of inferiority affects the motivation of a child to learn. Segregation with the sanction of law, therefore, has a tendency to [retard] the educational and mental development of negro children and to deprive them of some of the benefits they would receive a racial [ly] integrated school system." The Court demolished the doctrine of 'separate but equal' in public schools declaring separate educational facilities as inherently unequal.

This was the first phase of equalitarian Justice demanding equal treatment among Whites and Negroes. With a view to ensure Justice to deprived and depressed classes colour-caste-race consciousness is done away through anti-discrimination laws throughout the world.

Afterwards the second phase starts. The fact is that the non-discrimination may result into the perpetuation of injustice to negroes unless some helping hands of the government come forward. Some affirmative programme or action to favour such dejected, rejected and bewildered class is must. And the new theory of equalisational Justice starts. Equality in law does not work well when the equality of result is viewed and it requires some positive action to equalise. To quote Lester Ward, an American sociologist. "Justice consists in the enforcement by society of an artificial equality in social conditions which are naturally unequal."[98] It is required that in inherently unequal society broadly based on past treatment on prejudices equalisation opportunity needs deliberate educational scheme aimed at equalising intelligence among the members of the upper and lower classes in society. He argues that "intelligence is unrelated to class origin and depended strongly on environmental factors, especially on access to all available sources of information and on opening up to all persons the heritage of the past wisdom and the treasure of present knowledge." This idea of equality of outcome requires colour consciousness to help the negroes in America. Appreciating this requirement in ***United States v. Jefferson county Board of Education***[99] it was pointed out that, "Our Constitution is both colour blind and colour conscious. To avoid conflict with the equal protection clause, a classification that denies a benefit, causes harm or imposes a burden must not be based on race. In that sense the constitution is colour-blind. But, the Constitution is colour conscious, to prevent discrimination being perpetuated and to undo the effects of past discrimination. The criteria is the relevancy of colour to a legitimate governmental purpose."[100]

It is to be viewed that in post anti-discrimination law period the doctrine of colour-blindness is used against the Negroes interest protection. The truth is revealed by Richard Delgado who argues that racism is integral feature of [the] landscape and White elites will "tolerate or encourage racial advances for blacks only when they also promote the White-interest."[101] K. Crenshaw opposing the colour-blind theory of liberal scholars points out that "to be race-conscious' is to be aware that race is linked to identifiable communities in American society that are different from the community of Anglos in America." He elaborates that to recognise that "belief in colour-blindness and equal process, makes no sense...in a society in which identifiable groups had actually been treated differently historically and in which the effect of this difference in treatment continued into the present."[102] Americans are more alert, argumentative and thought provoking. The White scholars criticise colour consciousness. Thus, the critic of Critical Race Theory like Bell, Delgado and Matsuda deny race consciousness. But Black scholars approve it as saviour of their right.[103] The race conscious approach to help Negroes has found support in some of judicial opinions in the United State of America. Justice P.B. Sawant cited a number of such opinions in his decision in ***Indra Sawhney v. Union of India***[104]. Thus, in ***Regents of the University of California v. Bakke***[105] Justice Marshall approved the giving of race consideration in effort to increase the number and percentage of Negro doctors and by doing so a national cause could be served.

Said, the learned Judge: "in the light of history of discrimination and its devastating impact on the lives of Negroes, bringing the Negroes into the mainstream of American live should be a state interest of the highest order." Justice Blackburn was also of the view that it would be impossible to arrange an affirmative action programme in a racially neutral way and have it successful. Justice Brennan expressed the view that the colour-blind well wishing is more an aspiration rather than a description of reality. He was emphatic on the point that remedial measures under Title VI of the Civil Rights Act, 1964, does not prohibit its remedial use of race where such action is constitutionally permissible. Justice Brennan's view was that under the 14th Amendment racial classification are not per se invalid. Similar opinion was expressed by Chief Justice Warren Burger while speaking for himself and White and Powell JJ., in ***H. Earl Fullilove v. Philip M. Klutzick***[106]. Burger C.J. was dealing with the constitutionality of the provision in the Public Works Employment Act, 1977 requiring that at least 10 per cent of the Federal funds granted for local public works projects should be utilised by the State to procure services or supplies from business owned by minority group members. The learned Judge upheld the view expressed in the earlier decisions that if the race was the consideration for earlier discrimination in remedial process, steps will almost invariably require to be based on the racial factors and any other approach would freeze the status quo which is the very target of all remedies to correct the imbalance introduced by the past racial discriminatory measures..."[107] (Emphasis supplied). But, status quoism was seen in the opinion of Justice Stewart's dissent. He cited 84 year earlier dissenting opinion of Justice Harlan in ***Plessy v. Ferguson***[108] of the colour-blindness. But majority upheld the statute according preference to Negroes, Spanish-speaking, orientals, Indians, Eskimos and Aleuts. However, in post-1970s, again status quoism began to dominate the Court. Thus, in ***Adarand Constructors v. Pena***[109] *Justice Thomas,* though accepting the worth of race consideration to remedy injustice done in past to the deprived classes that "it is true that remedial racial preferences may reflect a desire to foster equality in society "but did not approve such measures on notion of spreading poison and resentment and stamping minorities with badge of interiority. This view prevailed in **Parents involved in *Cmty. Schs. V. Seattle Sch. Dist. No. 1,***[110] wherein Chief Justice Roberts wrote, "[t]he way to stop discrimination on the basis of race is to stop discrimination on the basis of race."[111] Roberts C.J. again based his argumentative reason on wrong premise that race no longer matters. It shows that the decisions of the American Supreme Court during the last decade of the twentieth century and and the first decade of the twenty first century show complete retreat from Negro beneficial construction developed in post-Brown period. But it is devoid of social reality and visionary approach to give the racial problems prevalent during the current decade (2010s i.e. 2010-) The 2014 and 2015 racial incidents of unarmed Negroes killing by White police and spread of riot prove beyond doubt that race still matters in America. The dissenting opinion of ***Sotomayor J. in Schuette v. Coal***[112] is presents the correct position. Justice Sotomayor wrote, "Race matters, in part because of the long history of racial minorities being denied access to the political process – Race also matters because of persistent racial inequality in society – inequality that cannot be ignored and that has produced stark socio-economic disparities."[113]

The solution is suggested by Sotomayor is well convincing:

> "The way to stop discrimination on the basis of race is to speak openly and candidly on the subject of race, and to apply the Constitution with eyes open to unfortunate effects of centuries of racial discrimination."[114]

The position in India has been the same history of deprivation of depressed class has been alarming. Shambook was beheaded for excelling in knowledge on pretext that due to his worship a Brahmin's son had died as Veda had bitten taking the form of a Snake. It was totally irrational, prejudiced and iniquitous. Rationality could be: why not all the Brahmins including Bashistha and Kalmanish (whose son was said to have died of snake bite due to Shambook's Tapasya) did not give life to the dead boy by their excelling knowledge, Tapasya and virtuousness ? So was case of Eklabya. His Angutha was cut for Gurudakshina, eventhough Guru Dronacharya had refused to train Eklabya on caste and race consideration. Why did he not train his pupil Arjuna to excel ? What has been said of United States that 'segregation treats Blacks differently, and history shows that the seed of the different treatment lies in prejudice", so is the case with India. Depressed classes were segregated, excluded only and only on the basis caste based prejudices. They could not learn and earn but could only serve the Dwij classes. The degradation and very vulnerable conditions of depressed people known as Scheduled Castes and Scheduled Tribes and other backward classes was due to caste-conscious discrimination so what the Constitution did was the first step to ensure non-discrimination against such people. In legal terminology, it was equality in law. But, it was not enough to ensure equality in fact which was left with inequality. To this condition Jack M. Balkin comments "what law enforces is not equality, but equality in the eye of law."[115] So what our Constitution did by inserting Articles 15(1), (2), 16(2) and 29(2) was to enforce equality in the eye of law. To ensure equality of result some sort of race/ caste consciousness would be required. This is evident in the observation of Justice K. Ramaswamy in ***Ashok Kumar Gupta v. State of U.P.***[116] The Learned Judge said: "Equality prohibits state from making discrimination amongst citizens on any ground. However, inequality in fact, without differential treatment between the advantaged and disadvantaged subsists. In order to bridge the gap between inequality in result and equality in fact, protective discrimination provides equality opportunity. Those who are unequal they cannot be treated by identical standards...The State must, therefore, resort to protective discrimination for the purpose of making people who are factually unequal, equal in specific areas." Neither the framers, nor the different Commissions could ignore caste consideration for making equality effective i.e. equality in result too. Thus, like American Constitution our Constitution is both race-caste blind and race-conscious on analogy to remove thorn by thorn or diamond cuts diamond or poison cured by poison (विशस्य विशमौशधम्).

The Indian Constitution cannot be held to be caste-blind. This point was appreciated by Karnataka Backward Classes Commission headed by Havanur which reported that constitution suggests recognition of Castes for their equalisation."[117]

The most prominent researcher on Indian ways to resolve competing equalities, Marc Galanter in his article, "The Compensatory Discrimination: Theme in The Indian Commitment to Human rights" concludes: "The Constitution envisages a new order as to the place of caste in Indian life. There is clear commitment to eliminate inequality of status and invidious treatment and to have a society in which government takes minimal account of ascriptive ties. But beyond this the posture of the legal system towards caste is not as single-minded as the notion of a casteless society might imply. If the discourages some assertion of caste preference and caste solidarity in other respects the prerogative previously enjoyed by the caste group remain impaired. The law befriends castes by giving recognition and protection to the new social forms through which caste concerns can be expressed (caste associations, education societies, political parties, religious sects)."[118]

References

1. Article 15. Prohibition of discrimination on grounds of religion, race, caste, sex or place of birth–
   (1) The State shall not discriminate against any citizen on grounds only of religion, race, caste, sex, place of birth or any of them.

(2) No citizen shall, on grounds only of religion, race, castes, sex, place of birth or any of them, be subject to any disability, liability, restriction or condition with regard to-

(a) access to shops, public restaurants, hotels, and places of public entertainment; or

(b) the use of wells, tanks, bathing ghats, roads and places of public resort maintained wholly or partly out of State funds or dedicated to the use of the general public.

Article 16(1) ————

(2) No citizen shall, on grounds only of religion, race, caste, sex, descent, place of birth, resident or any of them, be ineligible for, or discriminated against in respect of, any employment or office under the State.

Article 29(1)————

(2) No citizen shall be denied admission into any educational institution maintained by the State or receiving aid out of State funds on grounds only of religion, race, caste, language or any of them.

Article 325. No person to be ineligible for inclusion in, or to claim to be included in a special, electoral roll on grounds of religion, race, caste or sex – There shall be one general electoral roll for every territorial constituency for election to either House of Parliament or to the House or either House of the Legislature of a State and no person shall be ineligible for inclusion in any such roll or claim to be included in any special electoral roll for any such constituency on grounds only of religion, race, caste, sex or any of them.

2. Oxford University Press (1966); Oxford India Paper backs 1999 and its 11th Impression 2007.
3. *Ibid.* p. 26.
4. Soli J. Sorabjee and Arvind P. Datar (ed.) "Nani Palkhivala – The Court room Cenius", Lexis Nexis – Butterworths Wadhwa, Nagpur, 2012 at p. 412.
5. *Ibid.* p. 413.
6. *Ibid.* p. 413.
7. *Ibid.*
8. (1973) 4 SCC 225.
9. G.S. Ghurye, Caste And Race in India, Popular Prakashan Bombay, 2006, p. 440. See Chapter 14, "A Casteless Society or a Plural Society", pp. 404 460.
10. C.A.D 30th Nov. 1948 (Mr. Mohamed Ismail Sahib (Madras: Muslim) C.A.D. Vol. VII, p. 692.
11. *Ibid.*
12. B. Shiva Rao, Framing of India's Constitution – A Study 2nd ed. Universal Law Publishing Co. New Delhi, 2004 (2012 Reprint) p. 193.
13. *Ibid.* p. 194
14. *Ibid.*
15. *Ibid.*
16. *Ibid.* p. 195.

17. *Ibid.* p. 196.
18. *Ibid.*
19. *Ibid.* This view as also subscribed by the Madras Legislative Council.
20. *Ibid.*
21. *Ibid.*
22. *Ibid.* p. 198 (But Sri Loknath Mishra preferred not to push the amendment, C.A.D. Vol. VII p. 682).
23. C.A.D. Vol. VII p. 679.
24. *Ibid.*
25. *Ibid.*
26. *Ibid.* p. 680.
27. *Ibid.* p. 681.
28. *Ibid.*
29. *Ibid.* p. 687.
30. *Ibid.* p. 688.
31. *Ibid.*
32. *Ibid.* p. 690.
33. *Ibid.* p. 690 (Shri T. Channiah).
34. *Ibid.* p. 691 (Shri Shantanu Kumar Dass).
35. *Ibid.* p. 691 (Shri Shantanu Kumar Dass).
36. *Ibid.* p. 682 (Mr. Aziz Ahmad Khan).
37. *Ibid.*
38. *Ibid.* p. 693.
39. *Ibid.*
40. *Ibid.* p. 686.
41. *Ibid.* p. 687.
42. *Ibid.* p. 691. (H.J. Khandekar)
43. *Ibid.* pp. 683-684.
44. *Ibid.* p. 681.
45. *Ibid.* pp. 687-688.
46. *Ibid.* p. 690 (T. Channiah).
47. *Ibid.* pp. 686-687 (Dr. Dharm Prakash).
48. *Ibid.* 688 (P. Kakkan).
49. *Ibid.* p. 689 (V.I. Muniswamy Pillay).
50. *Ibid.* p. 690 (Shantanu Kumar Dass).
51. *Ibid.* p. 691 (H. J. Khandekar).
52. *Ibid.* p. 697 (Dr. K.M. Munshi).
53. *Ibid.*
54. *Ibid.* p. 702.
55. *Ibid.*
56. *Ibid.*
57. *Ibid.* p. 701.

58. *Ibid.*
59. *Ibid.*
60. *Ibid.* pp. 701-702.
61. *Ibid.* p. 702.
62. The Scheduled castes have been the special trait Hindu society with untouchability. As a compromise with Sikh sentiments backward classes of Sikhs viz. Mazhabis, Kabirpanthis, Ramdasias, Balerias, Serars and Sikhligars who had got converted from Hinduism to Sikh religion based on equality) were included in the List of the Scheduled Castes.
63. To this end some times meetings were postpone and discussed threat bare later on. See, B. Shiva Rao, Framing of India's Constitution (Reprint 2012) pp. 741-780.
64. *Ibid.* pp. 752 and 757.
65. The Reports of Sardar Vallabhbhai Patel, Chairman, Advisory Committee on Minorities, Fundamental Rights, etc. on different dates, that is to say, No. CA/24/Com/47 dated 8th August, 1947, CA/60/Com/47 dated 25th Aug. 1947; CA/24/Com./47 dated 25th Aug., 1947; dated 11th May, 1949, etc. are clear example of changes in minorities claim.
66. *Ibid.*
67. Part XIV of the Draft Constitution consisting of Articles.
68. Article 275 Proviso, The Constitution of India.
69. Second Proviso (a) and (b) of Article 275. Article 244 provides for the formation of an autonomous State comprising of certain areas of Assam.
70. Article 275 (IA) (1) (ii).
71. (1992) Supp. 3 SCC 217 = 1992 SCC (L & S) Supp. 1.
72. *Ibid.* p. 89 (of L & S)
73. *Ibid.*
74. *Ibid.* p. 237-239.
75. *Ibid.* p. 239.
76. A.I.R. 1963, 3 S.C. 649.
77. *Ibid.*
78. (1972) 1 SCC 660- A.I.R. 1972, S.C. 1375.
79. A.I.R. 1968 S.C. 1012.
80. (1971) 1 SCC 38 = A.I.R. 1971 S.C. 2303.
81. Report of the First Backward Classes Commission, 1955.
82. *Ibid.*
83. State of Kerala v. N.M. Thomas, A.I.R. 1976 S.C. 490.
84. Udai Raj Rai, Fundamental Rights And Their Enforcement PHI Learning Pvt. Ltd., New Delhi, 2011, p. 595.
85. 1985 Supp. SCC 714 = A.I.R. 1985 S.C. 1495.
86. *Ibid.*
87. *Ibid.*
88. 60 U.S. (19 How.) 393 (1857).

89. *Ibid.* at p. 426.
90. Chief Justice Marshall in Marbury v. Madison 5 US (1 Cranch) 137.
91. 163 U.S. 537 (1896).
92. *Ibid.*
93. *Ibid.*
94. *Ibid.*
95. *Ibid.*
96. *Ibid.*
97. 347 U.S. 483 (1954).
98. Lester F. Ward, "Applied Sociology", Boston : 1906. p. 22.
99. 372 F. Ed. 836 (1967).
100. *Ibid.*
101. Critical Race Theory : The Cutting Edge (1995) see also D. Bell's Comment on Brown v. Board of Education (in) (1980) 93 Harvard L. Review 518 at 524-525.
102. K. Crenshaw, Race, Reform and Retrenchment : The Transformation and Legitimation in Anti- Discrimination Law (1988) 101 Harvard L. Rev. 1331.
103. For detail study of material on the point see, M.D.A. Freeman's (ed.) Lloyd Introduction to jurisprudence (Eighth edition, Sweet Maxwell, 2008) pp. 1496-1530).
104. 1992 Supp. SCC 217 = 1992 SCC (L and S) Supp. 1.
105. 438 U.S. 265 (1978).
106. 448 U.S. 448 (1980).
107. Quoted from the decision of Justice P.B. Sawant in Mandal case p. 237.
108. 163 U.S. 537 (1996).
109. 515 U.S. 2000 (1995).
110. 551 U.S. 701 (2007).
111. *Ibid.* p. 748.
112. 134 S. ct. 1623.
113. *Ibid.* 1676.
114. *Ibid.* For critical study see Daria Roithmayr, Reproducing Racism; How Everyday Choices Lock in White Advantage, New York University Press, 2014 and its review by Richard R. W. Brooks under caption. The Banality of Racial Inequality, 124 The Yale Law Journal 2015 pp. 2626-2662.
115. Jack M. Balkin, "Constitutional Redemption – Political Faith in an Unjust World," Harvard Univ. Press, 2011 p. 141.
116. (1997) 5 S.C.C. 201.
117. Karnataka Backward Classes Commission, Report, p. 36.
118. Marc Galanter : The Compensatory Discrimination : Theme in the Indian Commitment to Human Rights (in) Buxi (ed.) The Right to be Human, Lancer International, New Delhi, pp. 77-94 at p. 90; see also Galanter "Changing Legal Conceptions of Caste" (in) Structure and Change in Indian Society edited by Milton Singer and Bernard S. Cohn, Chicago : Aldine.

Chapter - 5

Preferential Treatment to SCs and STs and their Identification

5.1 Peculiar Problems of SCs and STs in Peculiarly Caste-ridden Indian Society

The earlier Dasyus, Das, Antyaj, untouchables and post 1935 Scheduled Castes and Scheduled Tribes form a peculiar part of the Indian society. They were, have been and are likely to remain part of the Hindu fold. But they have never been treated on equal footing by their Hindu co-religion followers. Whatever might have been the theory of the origin of Shudras one point is clear that such group was excluded, out cast, despised and therefore deprived of status, property and social mingling. One theory is that such groups are original inhabitants of the country – adivasi and they were relegated to the periphery by Aryans. Since they were deprived of means of livelihood they adopted slavery and became das of some Aryan or They adopted the vocation of Dasyus –looting etc. The second theory is that they were part of Aryan clan but due to despised means of livelihood were declared outcast. The third theory of Jotirao Phoole clarifies that Shudras/ untouchable were great warrior who challenged the dominance of brahminical order. Aryans/Brahmins thought them great enemy (Mahaari). They were defeated by Parshuram and were relegated to the condemned status of Mahar – a clan to which Dr Ambedkar also belonged. The fourth theory of Dr B.R. Ambedkar also subscribes the similar view which he expressed in his writing – Who were Shudras ? Dr Ambedkar explained reasons for untouchables living outside the village and their impurity with permanence and untouchability. Since this earlier warrior class was defeated and broke; "(i) they could not live within the 'settled village community' and had to live outside the border of the 'settled village community', and (ii) by living at the border of the village they could also meet the raids of the hostile tribes;[1] Dr Ambedkar differs from 'divine creation' theory that 'antya', 'Antyaja' and 'antyavasin' signified end of creation i.e. from feet. He said that 'antya' were at last is ladder of creation.[2] He interpreted 'antya' to mean the end of Hindu village system which has double significance – (a) that living in separate quarters was such a peculiar phenomenon that a new terminology had to be invented to give expression to it; (b) the word chosen express, the conditions of the people to whom they applied, namely, that they were alien. The further set of facts justifying the claim that the untouchables were broken men is evident from the lives of Mahars of Maharashtra. The following facts show relationship that exist between the Mahars and upper castes:[3]

- (i) the Mahars are found in every village;
- (ii) every village has a wall around it and the Mahars live outside the wall;
- (iii) they do the watch and ward on behalf of the village;
- (iv) Mahars claim many rights against villagers viz.
    - (a) the right to collect food from the villagers;
    - (b) the right to collect coin from each villagers at the harvest season;
    - (c) the right to appropriate dead animals belonging to the villagers.

Dr Ambedkar gives two theories regarding the origin of untouchability; first, contempt of caste Hindus for Buddhism which preached equality and second beef eating. Whatever causes of untouchability it indicates certain characteristics:

- (1) There is no racial difference between the Hindus and the untouchables;
- (2) The original distinction was in the form of settled tribes men and the broken men and it is the broken men who came to be treated as untouchables;
- (3) Just as untouchability has no racial basis it has also no occupational basis;
- (4) There are two roots from which untouchability must have sprung:
    - (a) Contempt and hatred for broken men of Buddhists by Brahmanas;
    - (b) Continuation of beef eating by the broken men after it was given up by the brahmanas.[4]

Result of Untouchability: Sarvpalli Radhakrishnan pointed out the effect of untouchability that, 'the Hindu social order degenerated into an instrument of exploitation, tyranny and oppression. It tended to perpetuate inequality and inhumanity and developed the spirit of separation, hatred and enmity, low and high.'[5]

Statutory Recognition of SCs and STs

The problem of the Scheduled Castes and the Scheduled Tribes is ***sui-generis***. The 'Scheduled Castes' is the latest of the long line of official euphemisms for 'untouchables'. In 1909, the bottom of the Hindu caste system and the lowest castes was for the first time conceptualised under the rubric of 'untouchability'. But 'Depressed Classes' remained the official term. During the Round Table Conference in 1931, Dr Ambedkar and R. Srinivasan expressed the view that the term 'depressed classes' was degrading and contemptuous. They preferred in its place 'Non Caste Hindu's, 'Protestant Hindus' or 'Non-Conformist Hindus' as an alternative. Gandhi used a new term 'Harijan' and finally the Government of India Act, 1935 used the term 'Scheduled Castes' to denote special electoral arrangements for untouchables and depressed classes. The Government of India Act, 1935 read, 'the Scheduled Castes' means such castes, races or

Table 5.1: Percentage of Untouchables in British India (Indian Statutory Commission, 1930)

Provinces	***No. of untouchables (millions)***	***Per cent of Hindu population***	***Per cent of total population***
Madras	6.5	18	15.5
Bombay	1.5	11	8.0
Bengal	11.5	57	24.5
Uttar Pradesh	12.0	31	26.5
Punjab	2.8	42	13.5
Bihar and Orissa	5.0	20	14.5
Central Provinces	3.3	33	24.5
Assam	1.0	24	13.0
Total	**43.6**	**28.5**	**19**

Source: Indian Statutory Commission, 1930: 40.

tribes or parts of or groups within castes, races or tribes, being castes, races, tribes parts or groups which appear to His Majesty in Council to correspond to the classes of persons formerly known as 'the depressed classes', as His Majesty in Council may specify. According to Indian Statutory Commission, 1930 the population of untouchables varied from eight per cent to 26.5 per cent in different Provinces of British India. The following table shows the scattered population of untouchables.

The untouchables were inflicted to many disabilities. J.H. Hutton, the famous author of 'Caste in India', has proposed a series of tests, as a Census Commission in1931, to identify disabilities:

1. Whether the caste or class in question be served by Brahmins or not.
2. Whether the caste or class in question can be served by the barbers, water-carriers, tailors, etc., who serve the caste Hindus.
3. Whether the caste in question pollutes a high-caste Hindu by contact or proximity.
4. Whether the caste in question is one from whose hands a caste Hindu can take water.
5. Whether the caste in question is debarred from using public conveniences, such as roads, ferries, wells or schools.
6. Whether the caste in question is debarred from the use of Hindu temples.
7. Whether in ordinary social intercourse a well-educated member of the caste or class in question will be treated as an equal by the high-caste men of the same educational qualifications.
8. Whether the caste in question is merely depressed on account of its own ignorance, illiteracy or poverty and but for that, would be subject to no social disability.
9. Whether it is depressed on account of the occupation followed, and whether, but for that occupation it would be subject to no social disability.

The tests may not be decisive of disabilities but they show a societal outlook to the issue. No single test was sufficient to identify the untouchables and led Ambedkar to say that the task was to identify those who suffer from the contempt and aversion of higher caste Hindus. The majority of Franchise (Lothian) Committee preferred stricter criteria of deciding depressed classes, ie., denial of entry into temples and causing pollution by touch. The list was published in 1936 in the form of the Government of

India (Scheduled Caste) Order. It contained over 40 million persons. The 1941 Census revealed 19 per cent population of Hindus and 42.6 per cent of total population as Scheduled Castes.

The sizable number of the depressed classes and their vocal assertion was felt by the time of framing the Constitution Scheduled Castes and Scheduled Tribes had acquired special attention. The objective of the

Table 5.2: Population of Scheduled Castes in 1941

Provinces	**S.C. *Population (millions)***	***Per cent of Hindu Population***	***Per cent of Total Population***
British India	39.92	20.90	13.49
Madras	8.068	18.85	16.49
Bombay	1.855	11.20	8.89
Bengal	7.378	29.44	12.23
U.P.	11.717	25.57	21.39
Punjab	1.248	16.53	4.38
Bihar	4.340	16.37	11.49
	5.58	16.74	12.37
Orissa	1.238	18.12	14.18
Central Provinces	3.051	23.57	41.34
Assam	0.676	16.04	6.62
N.W.F.P.	-	-	-
Sind	0.191	15.58	4.22
Pamer Mer Wara	-	-	-
Total	39.80	20.87	13.45
States and Agencies	8.892	13.86	9.78
Cochin	0.141	15.73	9.92
Hyderabad	2.928	21.99	17.92
Mysore	1.405	21.03	19.16
Rajputana		-	-
Travancore	0.395	11.15	6.50
Total (Throughout India)	**48.81**	**19.15**	**12.62**

Constituent Assembly was to achieve social revolution getting out of the medievalism based on birth, religion, custom and community. Article 366 (24) defines "Scheduled Castes" on the line of its definition under the Government of India Act, 1935. It reads: "Scheduled Castes" means such castes, races or tribes or part of or groups within such castes, races or tribes as are deemed under Article 341 to the Scheduled Castes for the purposes of this Constitution. Article 341 clause (1) provides, "The President may with respect to any state or Union Territory, and where it is a State, after consultation with the Governor thereof, by public notification, specify the castes, races or tribes or parts of or groups within the castes, races or tribes which shall for the purposes of this Constitution be deemed to be Scheduled Castes in relation to that State or Union Territory, as the case may be". Likewise Article 366(25) defines Scheduled Tribes to mean, "such tribes or tribal communities or parts of or groups within such tribes or tribal communities as are deemed under Article 342 to be Scheduled Tribes for the purposes of this Constitution". And, Identification of Problems in Protective Discrimination Policy.

Article 342(1) provides: "The President may with respect to any State or Union Territory, and where it is a State, after consultation with the Governor thereof, by public notification, specify the tribes or tribal communities or parts of or groups within tribes or tribal communities which shall for the purposes of this Constitution be deemed to be Scheduled Tribes in relation to that State or Union territory, as the case may be". However, Presidential promulgation of the Scheduled Castes and Scheduled Tribes Orders under Articles 341(1) and 342(1) are subject to revision by the Parliament under Articles 341(2) and 342(2) respectively.

The President promulgated a Scheduled Castes Order, 1950 which was mainly based on 1936 list. Some discrepancies, errors and oversights were corrected by the Scheduled Castes and Scheduled Tribes Order (Amendment) Act, 1956. The earlier order specified that "no person professing a religion different from Hinduism shall be deemed a member of Scheduled Caste". And, 1956 act amended it so as to read, "No person who professes a religion different from the Hindu or Sikh religion shall be deemed a member of a Scheduled Caste. Four Sikh Castes, namely, Mazhabis, Ramdasis, Kabirpanthis and Sikligars were included in the Scheduled Castes. It was so agreed in the Report of Chairman, Advisory Committee on Minorities, Fundamental Rights, etc. submitted to the President, Constituent Assembly of India on May 11, 1949 but was overlooked in Presidential Promulgation of the Constitution (Scheduled Castes) Order; 1950. The 1956 Parliamentary Act, also added about a million

Table 5.3: Population of Scheduled Castes and Scheduled Tribes, 1981 Census

	Scheduled Castes	*Scheduled Tribes*
1	*2*	*3*
INDIA[1,2]	10,47,54,623	5,16,28,638
States		
1. Andhra Pradesh	79,61,730	31,76,001
2. Assam[1]	-	-
3. Bihar	1,01,42,368	58,10,867
4. Gujarat	24,38,297	48,48,586
5. Haryana[5]	24,64,012	-
6. Himachal Pradesh	10,53,958	1,97,263
7. Jammu and Kashmir[2,5]	4,97,363	-
8. Karnataka[4]	55,95,353	18,25,203
9. Kerala	25,49,382	2,61,475
10. Madhya Pradesh	72,58,533	1,19,87,031
11. Maharashtra	44,79,763	57,72,038
12. Manipur	17,753	3,87,977
13. Meghalaya	5,492	10,76,345
14. Nagaland[3]	-	6,50,885
15. Orissa	38,65,543	59,15,067
16. Punjab[5]	45,11,703	-
17. Rajasthan	58,38,879	41,83,124
18. Sikkim	18,281	73,623
19. Tamil Nadu	88,81,295	5,20,226
20. Tripura	3,10,384	5,83,920
21. Uttar Pradesh	2,34,53,339	2,32,705
22. West Bengal	1,20,00,768	30,70,672
Union Territories		
1. Andaman and Nicobar Islands[3]	-	22,361
2. Arunachal Pradesh	2,919	4,41,167
3. Chandigarh[5]	63,621	-
4. Dadra and Nagar Haveli	2,041	81,714
5. Delhi[5]	11,21,643	-
6. Goa, Daman and Diu	23,432	10,721
7. Lakshadweep[3]	-	37,760
8. Mizoram	135	4,61,907
9. Pondichery[5]	96,636	-

of persons in Rajasthan and in U.P. in the list of the Scheduled Castes and thereby raised Scheduled Castes figure of over 52 millions (in 1951) to 53.3 million (in 1956). In 1971 census, the population of the Scheduled Castes raised to 80 millions, i.e., 14.6 per cent of the population and by 1981 census it crossed 100 million (10,47,54,623). The total Scheduled Tribes population raised to 5,16,28,638 and the Scheduled Castes and the Scheduled Tribes cumulatively formed 23.51 of the country's population. The following table indicates the State-wise and Union Territory-wise population of the S.Cs. and S.Ts.

1. Excludes Assam where census could not be held owing to disturbed conditions.
2. The population figures exclude population of areas under unlawful occupation of Pakistan and China.
3. No castes were scheduled by the President for Nagaland and Nicobar Islands and Lakshadweep.
4. Scheduled Tribe population figure of Karnataka would appear to include high returns relating to certain communities with nomenclature similar to those included in the list of Scheduled Tribes consequent on the removal of area restrictions.
5. No Scheduled Tribe has been scheduled by the President for Haryana, Jammu and Kashmir, Punjab and the Union Territories of Chandigarh, Delhi and Pondichery.

The census Reports reveal one remarkable trend of increase in the percentage of Scheduled Castes and Scheduled Tribes. In pre-Independence period Scheduled Castes formed 12.3 per cent of the country's population. It increased to 14.59 per cent in 1971 and further a little over 15 per cent of the country's population in 1981. Similarly, 5 per cent figure of the Scheduled Tribes in pre-Independence has gone over 7.5 per cent by the 1981 census.

5.2 Four Kinds of Reservational Benefits to SCs/STs

SCs and STs are indisputably backward, as has been seen in earlier chapter on vision of the framers, there was already unanimity on the point of the amelioration of the condition of these classes through reservation. The framers as well as the post Constitution Parliament have provided for four kinds of reservation:

1. Reservation of Seats for SCs and STs in the Legislative bodies i.e. Lok Sabha, Legislative Assemblies (Articles 330 and 332).

2. Reservation in Local bodies i.e. Gram Panchayats and Municipalities (Articles 343D and 343T).
3. Reservation in educational institutions (Article 15(4).
4. Reservation of Seats for SCs and STs in services (Article 16(4).

5.2.1 Reservation of Seats for SCs & STs in Legislative Bodies

Articles 330 and 332 provide for reservation of Seats for SCs and STs in the Lok Sabha and State Legislative Assemblies respectively Article 330 reads:

330. Reservation of seats for Scheduled Castes and Scheduled Tribes in the House of the People.- (1) Seats shall be reserved in the House of the People for-

(a) the Scheduled Castes;

(b) the Scheduled Tribes except the Scheduled Tribes in the autonomous districts of Assam; and

(c) the Scheduled Tribes in the autonomous districts of Assam.

(2) The number of seats reserved in any State [or Union territory] for the Scheduled Castes or the Scheduled Tribes under clause (1) shall bear, as nearly as may be, the same proportion to the total number of seats allotted to that State [or Union territory] in the House of the People as the population of the Scheduled Castes in the State [or Union territory] or of the Scheduled

(3) Notwithstanding anything contained in clause (2), the number of seats reversed in the House of the People for the Scheduled Tribes in the autonomous districts of Assam shall bear to the total number of seats allotted to that State a proportion not less than the population of the Scheduled Tribes in the said autonomous districts bears to the total population of the State]

[Explanation].- In this article and in Article 332, the expression "population" means the population as ascertained at the last preceding census of which the relevant figures have been published.

Provided that the reference in the Explanation to the last preceding census of which the relevant figures have been published shall, until the relevant figures for the first census taken after the year [2026] have been published, be construed as reference to the [2001] census.

Article 332 provides for SCs and STs seats in State Legislative Assemblies. It reads as follow.

[6]**332. Reservation of seats for Scheduled Castes and Scheduled Tribes in the Legislative Assemblies of the States.**- (1) Seats shall be reserved for the Scheduled Castes and the Scheduled Tribes, [except the Scheduled Tribes in the autonomous districts of Assam][7], in the Legislative Assembly of every State[8][***].

(2) Seats shall be reserved also for the autonomous districts in the Legislative Assembly of the State of Assam.

(3) The number of seats reserved for the Scheduled Castes or the Scheduled Tribes in the Legislative Assembly of any State under clause (1) shall bear, as nearly as may be, the same proportion to the total number of seats in the Assembly as the population of the Scheduled Castes in the State or of the Scheduled Tribes in the State or part of the State, as the case may be, in respect of which seats are so reserved, bears to the total population of the State.

[9][(3-A) Notwithstanding anything contained in clause (3), until the taking effect, under Article 170, of the re-adjustment, on the basis of the first census after the year [2026)[10], of the number of seats in the Legislative Assemblies of the States of Arunachal Pradesh, Meghalaya, Mizoram and Nagaland, the seats which shall be reserved for the Scheduled Tribes in the Legislative Assembly of any such state shall be, -

(a) if all the seats in the Legislative Assembly of such state in existence Amendment) Act, 1987 (hereinafter in this clause referred to as the existing Assembly) are held by members of the Scheduled Tribes, all the seats except one;

(2) in any other case, such number of seats as bears to the total number of seats, a proportion not less than the number (as on the said date) of members belonging to the Scheduled Tribes in the existing Assembly bears to the total number of seats in the existing Assembly.]

[11][(3-B) Notwithstanding anything contained in clause (3), until the readjustment, under Article 170, takes effect on the basis of the first census after the year [2026][12] of the number of seats in the Legislative Assembly of the State of Tripura, the seats which shall be reserved for the Scheduled Tribes in the Legislative Assembly shall be, such number of seats as bears to the total number of seats, a proportion not less than the number, as on the date of coming into force of the Constitution (Seventy-second Amendment) Act, 1992, of members belonging to the Scheduled Tribes in the Legislative Assembly in existence on the said date bears to the total number of seats in that Assembly.]

(4) The number of seats reserved for an autonomous district in the Legislative Assembly of the state of Assam shall bear to the total number of seats in that Assembly a proportion not less than the population of the district bears to the total population of the States.

(5) The constituencies for the seats reserved for any autonomous district of Assam shall not comprise any area outside that district. [***].[13]

(6) No person who is not a member of a Scheduled Tribe of any autonomous district of the State of Assam shall be eligible for election to the Legislative Assembly of the state from any constituency of that district [***][14].

[Provided that for elections to the Legislative Assembly of the State of Assam, the representation of the Scheduled Tribes and non-Scheduled Tribes in the constituencies included in the Bodoland Territorial Areas District, so notified, and existing prior to the constitution of the Bodoland Territorial Areas District, shall be maintained.][15]

Articles 330 and 332 of the Constitution provide for reservation of seats for the Scheduled Castes and the Scheduled Tribes in the House of the People and Legislative Assemblies of the States in proportion to their population. Initially such reservations were intended to continue for 10 years. But, said period, has been successively extended by the expiry of the stipulated ten years. Now by Constitution Ninety Fifth (95th) (Amendment) Act, 2009, the Article 334 has been amended with a view to extend the period of reservation of 2030 A.D. It has become phenomena to continue the reservations of SCs and S.Ts. and due to no change in mind set of people end political atmosphere in the country is such that there is no possibility of revert back in near future. The same extension is accorded to the two members of Anglo-Indian Communities to be nominated by the President under Article 331. The following table shows reservation of seats for S.Cs. and S.Ts. in the Lok Sabha and Vidhan Sabhas.

There is no reservation of seats for S.Cs. and S.Ts. in the Council of the States and the Legislative Councils of the States. And, to this extent the present reservation policy is improvement upon the Government of India Act, 1935 which ensured reservation of seats on communal lines in both Houses of the Legislatures.

Table 5.4: Percentage of the total population of SCs and STs in 2011

Sl. No.	State/ Central Territories	Total Population			Total Population in	
		Person	Man	Woman	Per-centage	Part of Per-centage
1	2	3	4	5	6	7
	INDIA	12,10,570	201,376	104281	16.6	8.6
1.	Jammu & Kashmir	12,541	925	1493	7.4	11.9
2.	Himanchal Pradesh	6,865	1,729	392	25.2	5.7
3.	Punjab	27,743	8,860	NST	31.9	NST
4.	Chandigarh	1,055	199	NST	18.9	NST
5.	Uttarakhand	10,086	1,893	292	18.8	2.9
6.	Haryana	25,351	5,114	NST	20.2	NST
7.	Delhi	16,788	2,812	NST	16.8	NST
8.	Rajasthan	68,548	12,222	9239	17.8	13.5
9.	Uttar Pradesh	1,99,812	41,358	1134	17.8	0.6
10.	Bihar	104,0999	16,567	1337	15.9	1.3
11.	Sikkim	611	28	206	4.6	33.8
12.	Arunachal Pradesh	1,384	NST	952	NST	68.8
13.	Nagaland	1,979	NST	1711	NST	86.5
14.	Manipur	2,570	97	903	3.8	35.1
15.	Mizoram	1,097	1	1056	0.1	94.4
16.	Tripura	3,674	655	1167	17.8	31.7
17.	Meghalaya	2,967	17	2566	0.6	86.1
18.	Assam	31,206	2251	3884	7.2	12.4
19.	West Bengal	91,276	21,463	5297	23.5	5.8
20.	Jharkhand	32,988	3,960	8645	12.1	26.2
21.	Odisha	41,974	7,188	9591	17.1	22.8
22.	Chhattishgarh	25,545	3,274	7823	12.8	30.6
23.	Madhya Pradesh	72,627	11,342	15317	15.6	21.1
24.	Gujarat	60,440	4,074	8917	6.7	14.8
25.	Daman & Diu	243	6	15	2.5	6.3
26.	Dadar & Nagar Haveli	344	6	179	1.8	52.0
27.	Maharashtra	1,12,374	13,276	10510	11.8	9.4
28.	Andhra Pradesh	64,581	13,878	5918	16.4	7.0
29.	Karnataka	61,095	10,475	4249	17.1	7.0
30.	Goa	1459	25	149	1.7	10.2
31.	Lakshadweep	64	NST	61	NST	94.8
32.	Kerala	33,406	3,040	485	9.1	1.5
33.	Tamil Nadu	72,147	14,436	795	20.0	1.1
34.	Pudducherry	1245	196	NST	15.7	NST
35.	Andman Nicobar	381	NST	29	NST	7.5

Note: For 2001 census in data of India and Manipur data of Mao Marxism, Pvomata and Purut data are also included.

Source: India 2015 p. 26.

Table 5.5: Reservation of Seats in Legislatures

States/ Union Territories	***Number of seats***	***Seats reserved for scheduled castes***	***Seats reserved for scheduled tribes***	***Number of seats***	***Seats reserved for scheduled castes***	***Seats reserved for scheduled tribes***
1	2	3	4	5	6	7
1. Andhra Pradesh	42	62	2	294	39	15
2. Assam	14	1	2	126	8	161
3. Bihar	54	8	5	324	48	28
4. Gujarat	26	2	4	182	13	26
5. Haryana	10	2	-	90	17	-
6. Himachal Pradesh	4	1	-	68	16	3
7. Jammu and Kashmir	6	-	-	762	6	-
8. Karnataka	28	4	-	224	33	2
9. Kerala	20	2	-	140	13	1
10. Madhya Pradesh	40	6	9	320	44	75
11. Maharashtra	48	3	4	288	18	22
12. Manipur	2	-	1	60	1	19
13. Meghalaya[3]	2	-	-	60	-	-
14. Nagaland[3]	1	-	-	60	-	-
15. Odisha	21	3	5	147	22	34
16. Punjab	13	3	-	117	29	-
17. Rajasthan	25	4	3	200	33	24

18. Sikkim	1	-	-	32	2	124
19. Tamil Nadu	39	7	-	234	42	3
20. Tripura	2	-	1	60	7	17
21. Uttar Pradesh	85	18	-	425	92	1
22. West Bengal	42	8	2	294	59	17
23. Andamans and Nicobar Islands	1	-	-	-	-	-
24. Arunachal Pradesh[3]	2	-	-	30	-	-
25. Chandigarh	1	-	-	-	-	-
26. Dadra and Nagar Haveli	1	-	1	-	-	-
27. Delhi[5]	7	1	-	56	9	-
28. Goa, Daman and Diu	2	-	-	30	1	-
29. Lakshadweep	1	-	1	-	-	-
30. Mizoram[3]	1	-	-	30	-	-
31. Puddicherry	1	-	-	30	5	-
Total	**542**	**79**	**40**	**3,997**	**557**	**3156**

1. Four seats are reserved for two autonomous districts- North Cachar Hills and Mikir Hills.
2. Excluding 24 seats in the territory held by Pakistan.
3. No reservation has been made.
4. Reserved for Sikkimese of Bhutia-Lapcha origin.
5. Metropolitan Council.
6. Includes 12 seats reserved for Sikkimese of Bhutia-Lapcha origin.

5.2.2 Reservation of seats for SCs and STs in Panchayats and Municipalities

The Constitution (73rd Amendment) Act, 1992 and the Constitution (74th Amendment) Act, 1992 provide for S.Cs. and S.Ts. reservation in Panchayats and Municipalities.

(a) Reservation for SCs and STs in Panchayats

Article 243-D. Reservation of Seats .-(1) Seats shall be reserved for-

(a) the Scheduled Castes; and

(b) the Scheduled Tribes.

In every Panchayat and the number of seats so reserved shall bear, as nearly as may be, the same proportion to the total number of seats to be filled by direct election in that Panchayat as the population of the Scheduled Castes in that Panchayat area or of the Scheduled Tribes in that Panchayat area bears to the total population of that area and such seats may be allotted by rotation to different constituencies in a Panchayat.

(2) Not less than one-third of the total number of seats reserved under clause (1) shall be reserved for women belonging to the Scheduled Castes or as the case may be, the Scheduled Tribes.

(3) ....

(4) The offices of the Chairpersons in the Panchayats at the village or any other level shall be reserved for the Scheduled Castes, the Scheduled Tribes and women in such manner as the Legislature of a State may, by law, provide:

Provided that the number of offices of Chairpersons reserved for the Scheduled Castes and the Scheduled Tribes in the Panchayats at each level in any State shall bear, as nearly as may be, the same proportion to the total number of such offices in the Panchayats at each level as the population of the Scheduled Castes in the State or of the Scheduled Tribes in the State bears to the total population of the State:

Provided also that the number of offices reserved under this clause shall be allotted by rotation to different Panchayats at each level.

(5) The reservation of seats under clauses (1) and (2) and the reservation of office of Chairpersons (other than the reservation for women) under clause (4) shall cease to have effect on the expiration of the period specified in Article 334.

(b) Reservation for SCs and STs in Municipalities

Article 243-T. Reservation of seats.- (1) Seats shall be reserved for the Scheduled Castes and the Scheduled Tribes in every Municipality and the number of seats so reserved shall bear, as nearly as may be, the same proportion to the total number of seats to be filled by direct election in that Municipality as the population of the Scheduled Castes in the Municipal area or of the Scheduled Tribes in the Municipal area bears to the total population of that area and such seats may be allotted by rotation to different constituencies in a Municipality.

(2) Not less than one-third of the total number of seats reserved under clause (1) shall be reserved for women belonging to the Scheduled Castes or as the case may be, the Scheduled Tribes.

(3) ....

(4) The officers of Chairperson in the Municipalities shall be reserved for the Scheduled Castes, the Scheduled Tribes and women in such manner as the Legislature of a State may, by law, provide.

(5) The reservation of seats under clauses (1) and (2) and the reservation of offices of Chairpersons (other than the reservation for women) under clause (4) shall cease to have effect on the expiration of the period specified in Article 334.

The reservation of seats for SCs and STs in Panchayats and Municipalities is different from reservation for such classes in educational institutions or services under Article 15(4) or 16(4).[16] It is akin to reservation for such classes in representative bodies like Parliament and State Legislature and limitation akin to Article 334 is put under Article 243 D(5) and Article 243T(5). Thus 10 year time as extended under Article 334 for Parliament and State Legislatures will automatically be applicable to Panchayats and Municipalities. In Local representative bodies representation of SCs and STs is ensured proportionate to their populations. The other distinguishing feature is that the representation of women is ensured through reservation.

The Supreme Court of India has taken very favourable attitude towards disadvantaged SCs and STs. Thus, they can contest elections for Chairmanship under reserve category even if they have not been chosen from reserved category and have been elected from the general Constituency, In ***Kasambhai F. Ghanchi v. Chandubhai D. Rajput***[17] the apex Court ruled that it is not necessary that SC or ST candidate for Chairmanship under reserved category be elected only from a reserved category. He can contest for reserved Chairmanship even if he has been chosen on the unreserved seat.

5.2.3 Reservation of Seats for S.Cs & S.Ts in Services and Educational Institutions

On the basis of the population of the SCs and STs the Union Government has provided for the following percentage of seats under the Union Services:

Table 5.6: Date wise reservation percentage fixed for the S.Cs and S.Ts.

Sl. No.	*Reservation percentage with description*	*Date of orders*
1.	@ 8.33 per cent direct recruitment made through open competition in favour of S.Cs	Oct. 1943
2.	@ 12.5 per cent recruitment made by open competition in favour of S.Cs.	21.9.47
3.	@ 16.66 per cent recruitment made otherwise than open competition in favour of S.Cs.	21.9.47
4.	@ 5 per cent in favour of S.Ts	13.9.50
5.	@ 15 per cent and 7.5 per cent in favour of S.Cs and S.Ts. respectively, in direct recruitment on All India basis through the UPSC or by means of open test held by any other authority	25.3.70
6.	@ 16.66 per cent and 7.5 per cent in favour of S.Cs and S.Ts. in case of direct recruitment on all India basis by open competition otherwise than mentioned in column 5	25.3.70

Article 46 of the Constitution provides that: "The State shall promote with special care the educational and economic interests of the weaker sections of the people, and, in particular, of the Scheduled Castes and the Scheduled Tribes, and shall protect them from social injustice and all forms of exploitation". Article 335 says that, "the claims of the members of the Scheduled Castes and the Scheduled Tribes shall be taken into consideration, consistently with the maintenance of efficiency of administration, in the making of appointments to services and posts in connection with the affairs of the Union or of a State" Article 15(4) speaks of special provisions for the advancement of the Scheduled Castes and the Scheduled Tribes and Article 16(4) speaks of reservations of appointments or posts in services under the State for any backward class of citizens which is not adequately represented in such services. Here backward class definitely included Scheduled Castes and Scheduled Tribes. To quote K.M. Munshi, "The word backward signifies that class of people" – does not matter whether you call them untouchables or touchables belonging to this community or that – a class of people who are so backward that special protection is required (for them) in the services.

Table 5.7: Reservation in State service*

(in per cent)

States	***S.Cs.***	***S.Ts.***	***O.B.Cs.***	***Total***
1. Andhra Pradesh	25		25	50
2. Assam	7	12	-	19
3. Bihar	14	10	26	50
	24			
4. Gujarat	5	10	10	25
5. Haryana	20	-	5	25
6. Himachal Pradesh	22.5	5	15	42
7. Jammu and Kashmir	8	-	42	50
8. Karnataka	15	3	50	68
9. Kerala	8	2	40	50
10. Madhya Pradesh	15	18	25	58
11. Maharashtra	13	7	14	34
12. Orissa	16	24	-	40
13. Punjab	14	-	1	15
14. Rajasthan	16	12	-	28
15. Tamil Nadu	2	16	50	68
16. Uttar Pradesh	18	2	15	35+15**=50
17. West Bengal	15	5	-	20

* Reservation in jobs for O.B.Cs.does not exist in Central Government, West Bengal, Orissa, Assam, Rajasthan, Union Territories and North East States.

** 2 per cent for physically handicapped, 5 per cent dependents of freedom fighters and 9 per cent for disabled army men, S.S.C., emergency commissioned officers and ex-servicemen.

The following figure shows percentage of reservation in State service for SCs & STs alongwith OBCs, ...in Central services Seats have been reserved in ratio of 15:75 per cent for SCs and STs. The Table is worth noting.

5.2.4 Group Membership Entitling Reservation Benefit to SCs and STs

Group membership may be acquired by birth, adoption, conversions and marriages. Group membership is relevant for contesting elections, admission in the educational institutions and seeking jobs under the State services, first the issue of Group membership benefit relation to Articles 341 and 342 are discussed here.

The cases relating to elections and services have come to the Courts. Mostly, in election cases they are result of intra SCs and STs disputes on distribution of booty. On the other hand, in service cases challenge has come, mostly from affected higher caste employees. In election matters cases involve whether a specific caste is or is not SC or ST. In service matters the challenge come on the basis of legality of the governmental move to provide reservation to SCs and STs. The common issue which confronts both the election and service matters is: Whether benefit of reservation is legally permissible in adoption, conversion or marriage case? The false certification issue has affected both types of cases.

The courts have preferred the propriety of institutional deference and have given due credence and finality to the Presidential order under Article 341(1) or Article 342(1) and Parliamentary exclusion or inclusion under Article 341(2) or Article 342(2). In cases of Caste or tribe determination the courts have taken restrictive interpretation of Presidential Orders.

5.2.4.1 Who are SCs and STs ?

The recipient of reservational benefit SCs and STs are identified groups of beneficiaries. There is more or less certainty as to determination of SCs and STs and not any uncertainty like the riddle of SEBCs.

Scheduled Caste is defined in the definition clause of the Constitution Article 366. Clause 24 of Article 366 reads, 'Scheduled Castes means such castes, races or tribes or other parts of or groups within such castes, races or tribes as are deemed under Article 341 to be Scheduled Castes for the purposes of the Constitution."

Article 341 reads,: "[1] The President may with respect to any State or Union Territory and where it is a State after consultation with the Governor thereof, by public notification, specify the castes, races or tribes or parts of or groups within castes, races or tribes which shall for the purposes of this Constitution be deemed to be Scheduled Castes in relation to that State [or Union territory, as the case may be].

(2) Parliament may by law include in or exclude from the list of Scheduled Castes specified in a notification issued under clause (1) any caste, race or tribe or part of or group within any caste, race or tribe, but save as aforesaid a notification issued under the said clause shall not be varied by any subsequent notification.

"Scheduled Castes" has been defined in Article 366 (25) to mean "such tribes or tribal communities or parts of or groups within such tribes or tribal communities as are deemed under Article 342 to be Scheduled Tribes for the purposes of this Constitution."

Article 342, reads:

342. Scheduled Tribes: The President may with respect to any State or Union Territory, and where it is a State, after consultation with the Governor thereof, by public notification specify the tribes or tribal communities or parts of or groups within tribes or tribal communities which shall for the purposes of the Constitution be deemed to be Scheduled Tribes in relation to that State [or Union territory, as the case may be].

(2) Parliament may; by law include in or exclude from the list of Scheduled Tribes specified in a notification issued under clause (1) any tribe or tribal community or part of or group within any tribe or tribal community, but save as aforesaid a notification issued under the said clause shall not be varied by any subsequent notification.

Thus, Constitution has detailed programme for the reservational benefits of the Scheduled Castes and Scheduled Tribes. Their case is different from other classes of the recipients of reservational benefits. First, they form the unimpeachable classes of backward people, as: (i) Scheduled Castes and Scheduled Tribes list is recommended by the State Government and finality is attached to the Union Government (President); (ii) though initiative is taken by the executive branch of the Government, finality in the matter is given to the Parliament; and (iii) Scheduled Castes and Scheduled Tribes are words of neutral import distinct from backward or depressed to designate the castes. The judiciary has attached great importance to the Presidential promulgation or S.C. and S.T. orders and have declared the construction of the Scheduled Castes in terms of the relevant orders. Thus, in K. ***Appa Rao v. Director P. and T.***,[18] the Orissa High Court refused the extension of Kanda Kapu Scheduled Tribe of Andhra Pradesh mentioned in Presidential order to include Kanda Kapu caste of Orissa. In ***Dharam Chand Ramesh Chand v. Babulal***,[19] member of Moghya Tribes residing in Guna district was declared not to be covered under

Scheduled Tribes as Guna resident of that caste were not recognised as S.T. It is so because the same caste may have different status at different places. The objective of Articles 341(1) and 342(1) is to provide additional benefit to the members of S.Cs. and S.Ts. having regard to the economic and educational backwardness from which they suffer. It is not the caste which attracts special treatment. It is the backwardness which attracts special care and educational and social backwardness of the castes, races or tribes, may not be uniform or of the same intensity in the whole of the State; it may vary in degree or in kind in different areas and that may justify the division of that State in to convenient and suitable areas for the purpose of issuing the public notification. Even the cases showing some departure and expressing the willingness to include some castes under the S.C. or S.T. through the same have not been mentioned in the Presidential order are moved by the special measurable conditions of such castes. Thus, in ***Bisavalingappa v. Munichlnappa***,[20] the Supreme Court had to decide whether Bhovi caste mentioned in Presidential order was same as Voddar caste. On inquiry it found that though Presidential order referred to Bhovi caste in Mysore as a Scheduled Castes whereas in fact there was no such caste in that State. The official record established that Voddar caste was known as Bhovi in Mysore and therefore in peculiar circumstances Voddar caste was allowed to be included in order as Bhovi caste. The Supreme Court has drawn a distinction between two categories of cases: (i) cases involving determination of issue if a caste or tribe was sub- caste or sub-tribe of a caste or community specified in the Presidential order as S.C. or S.T. and (ii) cases involving inquiry whether a caste or tribe, though not included in the Presidential order was same as the caste specified in the Order. In the case of former category, the Court's attitude was clearly negative and in the case of later too no inquiry was thought permissible unless unusual and peculiar circumstances justified some inquiry. Thus, in ***Bhaiya Lal v. Harikishan Singh***,[21] the Court did not inquire as to question whether Dohar caste was a sub-caste of Chamar caste designated as Scheduled Caste in order. Again in ***Parasram v. Shivachand***,[22] the Supreme Court refused to inquire whether Mochi and Chamar in some part of Punjab meant same caste. But some departure was made in ***Bhaiya Ram v. Anirudh***,[23] wherein the Supreme Court entertained evidence to show that 'Patars caste was the sub-caste of Munda'. The Court took liberal view and pointed out that it is a question of law whether particular person is covered under Presidential declaration under Article 342. On perusal of relevant facts the Court found that Patars are sub-caste of Mundas. The Court made clear that because some sub-tribes of Mundas are enumerated in the Presidential order and others are not will not lead inference that those are not enumerated are not Mundas. It included Patars in general category of Munda, even though **patar** was not specifically mentioned in order. Likewise in ***Shailbala Baxi v. Johanas Bissoi,***[24] the 'Bhotras' tribes was established to be same as 'Bhottadas' tribe mentioned in the Presidential order. In ***Kumari Tanuja M. Rajpal v. State of Bombay***,[25] Bawa tribe from Sindh which was in existence in Bombay was allowed to claim benefit of entry Gosavi as included in the list of Nomadic Tribe. The cases on the point indicate the liberal judicial approach to award preferential benefit to those classes which are too backward so as to attract protective discrimination, even State is not allowed to issue any clarification regarding the Presidential order, as that would amount to tinkering with. Different issues have arisen with respect to the group identity of SCs / STs.

5.2.4.2 Validity/recognition of one State's certificate of SC or ST in another State.

Presidential Order is made on the basis of the consultation with Governor of a specific state. Articles 341 and 342 provide for SC/ST declaration of Lists by the President, "for the purpose of this Constitution" and, "in relation to that state. Lists are separately drawn for each state." Therefore, the certificate of S.C. or S.T. of one state does not provide any benefit of reservation in another state.

Marrichandra Shekhar Rao v. Seth G.S. Medical College[26] refused to concede the benefit of S.T. to a candidate who had moved to a state wherein that caste was not recognised as Scheduled Caste. An employee of the Central Government had moved from Andhra Pradesh to Maharashtra. He was enjoying Scheduled Tribe benefit. He lived there for a decade. His son after passing12th class applied for admission in medical college as Scheduled Tribe. The Court did allow the benefit of Caste as that caste was not mentioned in the Presidential order issued for Maharashtra. The rationale behind judicial approach was that a member of ST does not suffer the same degree of handicap and disadvantage in the State where his tribes is not mentioned as ST as he suffers in a state where it is so specified. However, the Court realised its effect on mobility in services and suggested legislative measures to remove it. In ***Action Committee on Issue of Caste Certificate to SCs/STs v. Union of India***,[27] the Court upheld the Constitutionality a Government communication dated 22.3.1977 dissenting benefit of SC/ST in migrated States. Again in Subhash Chandra v. Delhi Subordinate Services Selection Board.[28] The Supreme Court ruled that SC/ST would not automatically come in purview of backward classes in recipient State or Union Territory. It can be done only through Parliamentary and only circular would not entitle them.

However, the Supreme Court three judge bench consisting of V.N. Khare C.J. and S.B. Sinha and Dr A.R. Lakshman, JJ, took a practical view in ***Sudhakar Vithal Kumbhare v. State of Maharashtra***[29]. The appellant belonged a ST community known as Halba/Harbi. It was recognised as S.T. both in Maharashtra and Madhya Pradesh. Due to state reorganisation that tribe was shifted from one State another. The question arose. Whether the appellant being a member of such a tribe and originally resident in M.P. was entitled to the benefit of reservation in Maharashtra ? In other words whether a member of the S.T. belonging to one region could continue to get the same benefit despite bifurcation of the region in terms of the States Reorganisation Act ? Allowing the benefit to the appellant, the unanimous order made observation that-

> "The Scheduled Castes and Scheduled Tribes have suffered disadvantages and been denied facilities for development and growth in several States. They require protective preferences, facilities and benefits ***inter alia*** in the form of reservation, so as to enable them to compete on equal terms with the more advantaged and developed section of the community."[30]

5.2.4.3 SC/ST Benefit to Migrated Person to another State for central Services

The Supreme court has allowed benefits and privileges of SCs/ Sts in Central services throughout the country. Thus, in ***Union of India v. Schantiranjan Sarakar***, [31] the apex court ruled that, "a member of a Scheduled Caste, thus notified in any of the states within the territories of India, having regard to the provisions contained in Article 341 of the Constitution, was entitled to get the benefit of the said status for the purpose of entering into the central civil services."

5.2.4.4 Benefit of SC/ST status not available to Union Territory Migrated Person

In Article 341 and 342 the SCs and STs lists are declared for each separately and for the purpose of this constitution "and in relation to that state." But Union Territory stands on somewhat different footing due to the Central Administration of the Union Territory. Does it make any difference ?

It is well established that SC/ST benefit based on caste certificate issued for one state is not available to such persons if they are migrated to the another State. It is also established that benefits ensuing from SC/ST certificate of any state would be available everywhere for the purposes of

Central services. But, what is position if a SC/ST member migrates to any Union Territory ? A Union Territory is administrated by the Central Government. And, on this analogy in ***S. Pushpa v. Sivachanmughavelu***[32] a three judge bench consisting of R.C. Lahoti, C.J. and K.G. Balakrishnan and G.P. Mathur JJ., speaking through G.P. Mathur, J., was confronted with the issue: whether selection and appointment made of migrant SC candidate of other states against quota reserved for SC candidates on the post of Selection Grade teachers in the Union Territory of Pondicherry was legal and valid ? CAT (Madras bench) had declared it illegal and invalid. The apex court set aside the CAT order. Delvering the Judgement Justice Mathur conceded that the identification of SC/ST has to be done strictly in accordance with the Presidential order and a migrant Scheduled Caste of another state cannot be taken into consideration otherwise it may affect the number of seats which have to be reserved in the "House of the People or Legislative Assembly". But he observed:

> "Though, a migrant SC/ST person of another State may not be deemed to be to within the meaning of Articles 341 and 342 after migration to another State but it does not mean that he ceases to be an SC/ST altogether and becomes a member of forward caste."[33]

On the above logic agreeing to the position that SC/ST list is meant for the State for which it is drawn, the learned judged observed:

> "However, there would be no infraction of clause (4) of Article 16 if a Union Territory by virtue of its peculiar position being governed by the President as laid down in Article 239 extends the benefit of reservation even to such migrant Scheduled castes or Scheduled Tribes who are not mentioned in the Schedule to the Presidential order issued for such Union Territory. The UT of Pondicherry having adopted the policy of the Central Government where under all Scheduled Castes or Scheduled Tribes, irrespective of their state are eligible fo posts which are reserved for SC/ST candidates, no legal infirmity can be ascribed to such a policy and the same cannot be held to be contrary to any provision of law."[34]

But in Subhash Chandra v. Delhi Subordinate Services Selection Board[35], a division bench of two judges consisting of S.B. Sinha and Cyriac Joseph JJ., speaking through S. B. Sinha J. departed from S. *Pushpa* case on grounds that: (i) it had not taken into consideration the constitution bench decision in State of ***Maharashtra v. Milind***[36] which was binding on three judge bench in S. *Pushpa* Case; (ii) it felt bound by the constitution bench decision in ***E.V. Chinnaih v. State of A.P.***[37], (iii) though U.T. is administered by the Union Government, the socio-economic aspect cannot be mixed with the administrative aspect; (iv) the services for UT and the Central Services are different, and (v) scheme of Article 341 and 342 has to prevail and backwardness is based on socio-economic policy of State and UT as a unit.

Some departure is shown in three judge bench decision of the Supreme Court in Puduchery S.C. ***People Welfare Association v. U.T. Pondicherry***.[38] Speaking for the Court for himself and on behalf of Madan B. Lokur and Kurian Joseph JJ., Chief Justice R.M. Lodha allowed the benefit of Scheduled Caste to the Scheduled Caste migrated from other State/UT to the UT of Pondicherry. The learned Chief Justice pointed out that person migrated from other State/Union Territory could also enjoy benefit of reservation for SC/ST along with original Scheduled Caste residents of Puducheery. The put literal interpretation to the Presidential order, 1964 which used the expression 'resident'. The Court declared the Government order reading 'resident' as men of origin of Puducherry and barring migrants from reservation as invalid. The court ruled that Presidential order, 1964 issued under Article 341(1) and 342(1) cannot be amended, modified, altered or varied by any executive order.

The decision allowing migrants too entitled to the reservation along with original SC residents was based on technical interpretation of 'resident'. Resident may be original, may be migrated. But it left open the wider question relating to effect of migration of persons of reserved categories to other States/Uts.

5.2.5 Benefit of SC/ST Category on Change due to Conversion, Reconversion Adoption and Marriages

In early cases the Supreme Court had taken very liberal view to allow the benefit SC/ST even on conversion. In ***Chatturbhuj Vithaldas Jasani v. Moreshwar Parasram***[39] the Supreme Court did not disqualify a Mahar who had joined Mahanubhava Panth. The Court issued three tests to adjudge whether the member remained in the old clan, (1) the reaction of the old body ; (2) the intentions of the individual himself; and (3) the rules of the new order. The Court took cognizance of the facts that he was admitted to Mahar Caste functions and had been allowed to marry twice the Mahar girls. He himself identified himself as Mahar. The Court concluded that "conversion to this sect imports little beyond an intellectual acceptance of certain ideological tenets and does not alter the converts' caste status."[40] Thus, the main emphasis was given on the intention of the convert expressed through his consistent conduct and dealings. As Marc Galanter points out the prime test of intention needed to be confirmed through acceptance by the old group.[41] Much flexibility was shown by Mysore High Court in ***Shyam Sundar v. Shankar Deo Udgir***[42] where a Samgar Caste member had accepted Arya Samaj membership, married a Sonar girl according to Arya Samaj rites and in 1951 census had reported as "Arya". The High Court strenuously said that his old caste status could not be divested unless there was expulsion by the old caste and intentional abandonment or renunciation by the convert. Anyway, the two decisions, discussed earlier are the cases not changing the train in Ambedkarite version but changing the compartment of the same train – the Hindu cult. The liberalism shown in ***Jasani*** and ***Udgir*** found extended concessionary interpretation in ***Kartie Oraon v. David Munzi***[43] in a member of an Oraon family had been Christian since his grand father's time. The Court found certain similarities between Christian Oraon and Non-Christian Oraon life intermarry and descendents treated as full member of tribe. Patna High Court applying ***jasani*** ruling ruled that, "conversion did not extinguish membership in the tribe". The judicial liberalism shifted on another side i.e. benefit of new tribe in ***Wilson Rende v. C.S. Booth***[44] the son of English father and Khasi mother was given benefit of Khasi tribe for election purposes. The High Court made clear that even though he was an Anglo-Indian within the definition of Anglo-Indian given Article 366(2) of the Constitution this did not prevent him from being a member of Khasi tribe or some other community. The High Court observed that his being a Khasi depended not on purity of blood but on his conduct and community acceptance.

V.V. Giri v. D. Suri[45] a quite innovative trend was discernible both in the attitude of the High Court and the Supreme Court of India. The issue was, whether a community described in all documents from 1885 to 1928 as Moka Dora, a Schedule Tribe community could avail benefit of reservation in Parliamentary election which after 1928 had followed Sankritisation and adopted Kshatriya custom, marriage style, marriage connection with Kshatriyas, employed Brahmin priest and wore sacred thread (Yagyopavit). Tribunal emphasised on jasani test of intention of the member and declared that due to lack of intention on part of the person concerned to remain Moka Dora, he was not entitled to claim benefit of S.T. Taking radical turn the A.P. High Court ignored the question whether he remained Moka Dora and shifted to the question whether he had become Kshatriya. The High Court ruled that caste is a matter of both rather than choice and on that principle higher caste could not be gained.[46] Court found that there was no evidence to prove that Kshatriya recognised him as Kshatriya and recognition by one or two families would not be sufficient.[47] The Supreme Court took third line i.e. Jasani third test – reaction of new group. The Apex Court noted the, "recognised features of the hierarchical social structure prevailing amongst the Hindus"[48] and the "inflexible and exclusive nature of the caste system. Status was recognised to come only by birth and it is too difficult for a person born in depressed class to attain higher caste status by volition, education, culture and status."[49] Hierarchic and inflexible nature of Hindu society does not allow upward caste movement. J. L. Kapur J. dissented and rejected the primacy of birth and pointed out that caste varies as a consequence of ***Guna, Karma*** and ***Subhavana***. He pointed out that the candidate had lost his original caste status and by "his conduct raised himself to the position of a Kshatriya and he was no longer a member of the Scheduled Tribe."[50]

The Supreme Court, however, took different stand in cases of conversion to Buddhism. Thus, in ***Pujbarao v. Meshram***[51], the incident of mass conversion, eye witnesses and Buddhist ritual was found enough to embrace Buddhism and therefore, loss of Scheduled Caste status. The Supreme Court did not agree with contention that he was treating Buddha as 11th incarnation of Lord and observed that he was not of that sophisticated class that have discarded altogether the picture and the blessing and "had [he] considered himself to be a Hindu, he would have followed the usual practice."[52] But after a decade the court adopted latitudarian and flexible approach with sympathetic view of Buddhism in ***Ganpat v. Presiding Officer.***[53] In this case the Court did not agree with argument that Buddhist assimilation in functions, garlanding Dr Ambedkar, Pali mantras show that he had become Buddhist. He was treated to be Hindu since was born as Hindu. The Court observed and appreciated tolerant Hindu religious practices.

5.2.5.1 Conversion

There are two sets of opinions among the Courts. One view is that conversion operates as an expulsion from the caste. Two reasons are preferred- **first**, the convert ceases to have any caste because caste is predominantly a feature of Hindu society and **second**, a person who ceases to be Hindu ordinarily would not be regarded as Hindu by others. This view was expressed by the Madras High Court in ***Michael v. Venkateswaran.***[54] However, Rajamannar C.J. was agreeable to accept exception to this general rule and held that in spite of conversion the caste distinction might continue. The second set of opinion is guided by this exception conceded by Rajamanar C.J. in *Michael's* Case. In ***Kathapalli Narsayy V. Jammana Jogi,***[55] The A. P. High Court had expressed the view that, "notwithstanding conversion, the converts, whether an individual or family or group of converts, may like to be governed by the law by which they were governed before they became convert and the community to which they originally belonged may also continue to accept within their fold not withstanding conversion". This line of augment finding support from Rajamanar C.J. was fully appreciated in ***C. M. Arumugham v. S. Rajgopal (II)***[56] and relied upon with approval in ***State of Kerala.* v. *Chandramohanan***[57]. In *Chandramohanan* the Supreme Court placed more emphasis on social reality while dealing with the issue whether conversion to Christianity by itself will result in loss of the status of ST. The issue has to be decided taking into consideration the fact of each case. It cannot be governed by circular as circular is not law within the meaning of Article 13. It has to be proved that a person who has embraced another religion is still suffering from social disability and following the customs and traditions of the original community. The Supreme Court ruled: "Upon conversion, a person may be governed by a different law than the law governing the community to which he originally belonged, but that would not mean that notwithstanding such conversion, he may not continue to be a member of the tribe". This approach was approved by the Constitution Bench in ***E. V. Chinniah* v. *State of A.P.***[58]

However, the courts have been cautious of the misuse of conversion process. Thus, in ***Kurupati Miria Das* v. *Dr Ambedkar Seva Smajam***[59], the apex court ruled that if after getting elected as a Scheduled Caste person, the elected person renounces his caste and embraces another religion, then a writ of Quo Warranto will lie not challenging his election but his subsequently continuing in his capacity as a person belonging to the particular caste on the basis of which he had contested election. Likewise a person is not eligible to contest as a Scheduled Caste candidate an election if before the nomination paper is filed, he had embraced/converted to another religion, e.g. Christianity.[60]

5.2.5.2 Revival of Scheduled Caste on Reconversion to Hinduism

In ***Kailash Sonkar* v. *Maya Devi***[61] a three Judge bench of the Supreme Court speaking through S Fazal Ali J.(on behalf of himself and R.B. Mishra and M.P.Thakar JJ.) expressed the view that where a Hindu embraces non-caste recognising system as Christianity, Buddhism or Islam there is loss of caste on such conversion.

But, the real issue is what is position after reconversion? That is to say, a Scheduled Caste Hindu converted to Christianity and again he or his issue get reconverted to Hinduism. In ***C. M. Arumugham* v. *S. Rajagopal***[62] Justice P. N. Bhagwati had noted the factual position that in some cases converted persons also retain the earlier caste. Said Bhagwati J., "This is not indeed infrequent phenomenon in south India where, in some of the castes, even after conversion to Christianity, a person is regarded as continuing to belong to the caste. There are castes, particularly in South India, where this consequence does not follow on conversion, since such castes comprise both Hindus and Christians". On the issue of regaining of caste on reconversion the above observation is weighty and as Marc Galanter commenting on ***Arumugham* v. *Rajgopal***[63] said the decision rested on the principle of tolerance of Adi Dravida community to accept Christian do not cease to belong Adi Dravid caste[64].

On the question whether caste will revive if the members of community accept the reconverts, the Judges are silent and Justice Bhagwati held that *prima facie* on conversion to Christianity the respondent would not cease to belong to the Adi Dravida caste, yet he refrained from expressing final opinion on the point.[65] In ***Anbalangan* v. *R. Devarajan***[66], a three Judge bench comprising of S. Murtaza Fazal Ali, O.Chinnappa Reddy and E. S. Venkataramaiah JJ. speaking through Chinnappa Reddy J. reiterated the same view and further explained with remark, "if it (caste) disappears, it disappears to reappear on reconversion." Chinnappa Reddy J. said. "Unless the practice of caste makes it necessary no expiatory rites need to be performed, ordinarily he regains his caste unless the community does not accept him. The practice of caste, however, irrational it may be appear to our moral and social sense, is so deep-rooted in the Indian people that its mark does not seem to disappear on conversion to different religion. If it disappears, it disappears only to reappear on reconversion."[67]

"In fact, this process goes on continuously in India and generation by generation lost sheep appear to return to the caste fold and are once again assimilated in that fold. This appears to be particularly so in the case of members of the Scheduled Caste, who embrace other religions in their quest for liberation, but return to their old religion on finding that their disabilities, have clung to them with great tenacity (emphasis added)."[68]

Indian cases have favoured revival of old caste on reconversion. In earlier times expiatory ceremony on reconversion was needed.[69] Later on even expiatory ceremony compulsion was loosened.[70] The Court observed in case of a convert from Balaji Caste to Christianity and reconversion to Balaji Caste there was evidence of necessary expiatory ceremony and therefore, it ruled, "Where there was no evidence of expiatory ceremonies, it was hardly right for the Court to erect barrier which the autonomy of the caste did not require."[71] In this context, a three-Judge bench consisting of Chandrachud, Bhagwati and Sarkaria JJ., took a pragmatic and liberal view in *Arunamugham Case*[72], discussed earlier, and O. Channa Reddy J. look more liberal and pragmatic view in *S. Ambalagan*[73] case, quoted extensively earlier. Justice Mustafa Fazal Ali took a more pragmatic approach going a step further giving due credence to the choice of the reconvertee. Thus, in ***Kailash Sonkar* v. *Maya Devi***[74] in which one Maya Devi was born of a converted Christian father and mother and married Jai Prakash Shalwar of Katia Scheduled Tribe. Issue was: could a girl born of converted Christian get reconverted on her choice to Hinduism? On becoming major she opted to get reconverted to Hinduism. A letter showing her voluntary embracing of Hindu religion was presented to the Court. The relevant part of the letter read thus:

> "I am prepared to own Hindu religion with all sincerity and to follow all its customs and rites.

Today, on 6.11.76, I am fully major. Hence the above decision is my own where in no external interference exists".

> Immediately thereafter, she married to Jay Prakash on 6.11.76 in Arya Samaj, Gorakhpur according to Vedic rites.

She had produced certificate to that effect from secretary, Arya Samaj Gorakhpur along with marriage certificate dated 14.11.1976. She had received Abhinandan Patra from Katia Caste community to the effect that " We mention her in this Abhinandan Patra as belonging to Katia Caste as we were proud as she was the first M.L.A. in our caste". Murtaza Fazil Ali, J. arrived at conclusion that " the case fulfils the conditions required for being reconverted to Hinduism from Christianity in order to revive the original caste".[75] The fact that on reconversion she was elected as a member of the Legislative Assembly from a constituency reserved from the Scheduled Caste was treated to be a positive proof of her old community having accepted her back to old fold. The Courts have not been rigid as to express assent of the community approving reconversion. Thus, in ***Nara* v. *Nadis Basi*,**[76] the Orissa High Court expressed the view that it would be sufficient if it is shown that community men did not protest. The acceptance of reconverted person had been asserted by Justice Bhagwati speaking for the unanimous constitution bench of the apex court consisting of A. N. Ray C.J. and Bhagwati J. himself and A.C. Gupta, S. Murtaza Fazal Ali and Jaswant Singh JJ. in ***Guntur Medical College* v. *Moha Rao*.**[77]

The parents of the respondent Modiga SC had converted to Christianity. On 20th Sept. 1973 he renounced Christianity and re-embraced Hinduism after going through Shuddhi Ceremony and thus he was received back into Madiga Caste of Hindu fold. He got admission provisionally in Guntur

Medical College as S.C. Relying on Govt. of A.P. note, "No candidate other than Hindu including a Sikh can claim to belong to Scheduled Castes. No Candidates can claim to belong to the Scheduled Caste except by birth," the principal of the college cancelled his admission. In the High Court the government counsel himself had conceded that government stand was not repugnant to clause (3) of the constitution (Scheduled Castes) order, 1950. The Scheduled Caste has specific meaning vide Article 366(24) read with Article 341. The government had undertaken to admit him irrespective of the fate of case. But state had disputed his acceptance as Madiga by that community is absence of sufficient evidence to prove that. The Supreme Court accepted no automatic category absorption in S.C. and cited with approval observation of Krishnaswami Ayyangar J. in ***Durgaprasada Rao v. Sudarsenswami***[78] that "In matters affecting the well being or composition of a caste, the caste itself is the Supreme Judge". Bhagwati J. observed: "On conversion to Hinduism a person born of Christian converts would not become a member of the caste to which his parents belonged prior to their conversion to Christianity, automatically or as a matter of course, but he would be such member, if the other members of the caste accept him as a member and admit him within the fold".[79]

The constitution bench expressed the view that the respondent could take benefit of S.C. reservation only if he could show that he was accepted by Madiga S.C. But, the Court did not go to inquire that because of government assurance to not disturb his admission, whatever, be the result of the appeal. Thus, this case did not touch the important issue of misuse of reconversion as the respondent Mohan Rao adopted reconversion method to get reservation benefit after having failed to get admission in Gandhi Medical College in 1973 as a backward class candidate because Christians converts are treated as such. And after failing that he resorted the way of reconversion as Madiga on Sept. 20, 1973. The facts show that the respondent had been educated as Christian and only for the purpose of admission in medical college he resorted to that recourse. Even if the community had accepted him as Madiga, could not the test of stresses and strains of backwardness been raised in that case? This case does not throw any light on this aspect, as it was not raised at all.[80] The challenge came from the third party, Principal and not from some S.C. candidate himself. Had it been raised by some S.C. claimant the issue of suffering the stresses and strains would have been raised and the court would have been compelled to decide that.

In the above case one important constitutional issue was left open which appears to have been undertaken, though not elaborately dealt by Chief Justice K. G. Bala Krishnan in ***Deshraj* v. *Bodhraj***[81]. Respondent was elected from S.C. reserved constituency. Witnesses belonging to his village stated that they knew respondent and his family well and that the respondent belonged to Tarkhan Caste (which was not S.C.) Cross examine could not discredit them.

Documentary evidences – records of the Government School, the birth register maintained by the police station concerned, Village Pariwar Register, maintained by Gram Sabha, all showed that he was son of M. belonging to Tarkhan Caste. He could show his caste as a S.C. only after 1990. He produced caste certificate as Lohar (S.C.) dated 16.12.1991 issued by an Executive Magistrate. He had got altered earlier entry in Village Pariwar Register, maintained by Gram Sabha in 1990 i.e. about 34 years after his birth. The High Court failed to look into facts. But, the Supreme Court of India speaking through K.G. Bala Krishnan C.J. declared his election void. This was a case SC vis-à-vis SC. It was decided on the basis of facts only and not on disadvantage or otherwise.

This aspect was appreciated by three-Judge Bench in ***Soosai v. Union of India.***[82] The bench consisted of P.N. Bhagwati, C.J. and R.S. Pathak and Amarnath Sen, JJ. Bhagwati, CJ had been member of Mohan Rao's case. Soosai case was decided by R.S. Pathak, J. Soosai belonged to Adi Dravid, A Scheduled Caste. He was converted to Christianity. He was cobbler by profession and worked on the roadside at one of the crossroads in Madras. Under the government scheme as per Presidential Order that is Constitution (Scheduled Castes) Order, 1950, the cobbler belonging to Hinduism and Sikh Religion were allotted bunks free of cost by Regional Deputy Director, Khadi and Village Industries Board. The petitioner was not allotted bunks. He challenged the validity of Presidential Order on the ground that only Hindu and Sikh members of the Castes enumerated in the Scheduled Caste to that order are deemed to be scheduled castes for the purposes of the Constitution of India. Pathak, J. made clear that since depressed classes of Hindu and Sikh communities suffered from economic and social disabilities and cultural and educational backwardness so gross in character and degree that the members of those castes in Hindu and Sikh communities called for constitutional protection, they have been incorporated in section 3 of the said Order. Pathak, J. did not find mere submission that after conversion to Christianity the petitioner remained Adi Dravid, a Scheduled Caste, sufficient. In order to establish discrimination, he had to establish that he suffered from a comparable depth of social and economic disabilities and cultural and educational backwardness and similar levels of degradation within the Christian community necessitating intervention by the State under the provisions of the Constitution.

But, some confusion has further been created by the Supreme Court decision in K.P. Manu v. Chairman, Scrutiny Committee for Verification of Community Certificates.[83] This was a case of reconversion. The appellant's great grandfather was a member of Hindu Pulaya community, a scheduled caste. His grandfather got converted into Christianity. The petitioner's father remained Christian. At the age of 24, the petitioner converted himself to Hindu religion. On the basis of conversion to Hinduism he got a caste certificate under the Kerala (SC's and ST's) Regulations Act, 1996. The scrutiny committee cancelled said Caste Certificate on the ground that he was born of Christian parents and there was no evidence to establish that after conversion, the parents followed the traditions and customs of the community.

However, the apex court reverted back to S. Rajgopal decision and re-asserted that as a general rule on conversion from Hinduism to Christianity a person would cease to be a member of the Caste and that is not an absolute rule, it would depend upon the structure of the Caste and its rules and regulations whether a person would cease to belong to his caste on his embracing Hinduism. The Supreme Court talked the principle of eclipse and said in the case of conversion, the original caste merely gets eclipsed which resurfaces when a person reconverts to the original religion.

The Supreme Court too liberal view of the object and purpose of the Constitution (Scheduled Castes) Order 1950 and opined that when a person is reconverted to Hinduism, the social and economic disabilities again revive and become attached from which he suffered prior to his conversion. The court evolved/asserted the test of genuine willingness to go back to the old fold without any protest from the members of the erstwhile community. Will such decision not upset the social arrangement ? Look at the situation –

Great grandfather – Adi Dravid, SC

Grandfather – Christian

Parents – Christian

Appellant – Christian up to 24 years of age

Appellant – Scheduled Caste after the age of 24

If after generations gap, reconversion is allowed for getting the benefit, what would happen to the social cohesion in view of post-2014 election

Ghar Vapsi Concept? Will it not encourage misuse of caste certificate and tensions in society ?

5.2.5.3 Benefit of SC/ST on Marriage: March from Acceptance Theory to Disadvantage Suffered

The issue of allowing the benefit of SC/ST to a woman who has married with SC/ST is complex matter. It has spiritual, social and legal complications. Many social reformers and exponents of caste consciousness demolition theory and promoters of harmony among upper caste and SC/ST have preferred inter caste marriage between the upper caste people and SCs/STs. Both Dr Ambedkar and Mahatma Gandhi suggested inter-caste marriage to root out the evil of untouchability. Many governmental proposals favoured such move and policy was adopted to honour and help them financially. On the other hand, there is chance of motivated marriage to seek benefit of service or contesting elections.

The former view is supported both by spiritual consideration of the change of a women on marriage by acquiring gotra and name of her husband and social policy to encourage inter-caste marriage to attack at social evil of casteism. Report of Scheduled Castes and Scheduled Tribes 1973-74 narrates many State programmes of gifts and grants to couples entering to inter-caste marriages. As per Overseas Hindustan Times, 8 June, 1978 on the visit of Prime Minister Morarji Desai, a public reception at Ahmedabad was organised wherein 18 couples entering Harijan-Caste Hindu marriages were honoured and were awarded Rs 5,000 along with assurance to provide various benefits to the offsprings of such marriages.[84] On recommendation of JPC set up in 1967 to include wives of SCs/STs in that category a bill was introduced in Parliament to the effect, "Notwithstanding anything in any law, in any custom or usage to the contrary, a woman who marries a person belonging to a Caste specified in any part of the Schedule shall be deemed to belong to the Scheduled Caste to which her husband belongs". It was thought to be a good incentive for upper caste girls to marry SCs/STs. But, later it was abandoned in 1976 when the bill again came to be discussed.[85] "The justification adduced was that such legislation would be redundant as on inter-marrying a wife would automatically become member of such groups because a women in India took on her husband's social identities."[86]

In early stages of the functioning of the Constitution, the apex court adopted acceptance theory as a determinative factor of the status a non-tribal woman on marriage with a tribal person. The Supreme Court of India evolved this concept in ***N.E. Horo V. Jahanara Jaypal Singh.***[87] In this case a Tamil Christian woman was married with a prominent scheduled caste politician Jaypal Singh. After his death a Parliamentary seat 51, Khunts reserved for S.T. fell vacant. His wife filed her nomination to contest election, but her nomination form was rejected on the ground that she was not a Munda Scheduled Tribe but a Christian and the status of a Munda ST could be acquired by birth and not by marriage. The Supreme Court division bench examined the Munda Tribe custom prevalent in Chhotanagpur and material evidences. Speaking for himself and M. H. Beg J., Justice A. N. Grover found the following matters established:

1. The Munda are endogamous and inter-marriage with non-Mundas is normally prohibited;
2. That a Munda male along with his family on marrying a non-Munda girl is after ex-communicated or out casted;
3. That the rule of endogamy is not so rigid that a Munda cannot marry a non-Munda after performing special ceremonies;
4. That such marriages have been or being sanctioned by the Parha Panchayat.
5. That were a Munda male and his family outcasted for marrying a non-Munda, they are admitted to the tribe after certain special ceremonies being performed.

The Court concluded that "Once the marriage of a Munda male with a non-Munda female is approved or sanctioned by the Parha Panchayat they become members of the community."[88] The Supreme Court approved the decision of the High Court to give wide import to the expression "tribal communities". Said the Court;

"The use of the term "Tribal communities" in addition to the term "Tribes" in Article 342 shows that a wide import and meaning should be given to these words and even if the respondent is not a member of the Munda Tribe by virtue of birth she having been married to a Munda after obtaining the approval of the elders of the tribes would belong to the tribal community to which her husband belongs on analogy of the wife taking the husband domicile."[89]

Thus, the Supreme Court emphatically said that even without invoking the domicile doctrine the membership of the wife could be upheld on account of the marriage being approved and sanctioned by Parha Panchayat of Munda Tribe.[90]

Some attempts have been made to justify the married women status on the plea of 'spiritual consideration'. But, they have not succeeded.

Thus, in ***Urmila Ginda* v. *Union of India***[91] an upper caste girl married to a Scheduled Caste claimed the benefit of reservation based on the Hindu theory of marriage that she had become Sapinda and caste fellow of her husband. It was argued that on marriage a girl does not remain a member of her parent's family but becomes member of her husband's family by snapping all ties from parental home. Delhi High Court was not convinced with such spiritual considerations and adopted the test of suffering of disadvanges. The High Court ruled that she was not one of them who had suffered disadvantage and being a high caste Hindu girl she was not subject to any backwardness –social or educational. In similar vein the Bombay High Court ruled in ***Vaishali* v. *Union of India***[92] that a lady belonging to the upper caste by marrying to the Schedule Caste is not entitled to reservational benefit under Article 16(4) of the Constitution. The Division Bench decision of the Supreme Court is ***Valsamma Paul* v. *Cochin University***[93] is very informative judicial pronouncement with Judicial awareness of the living stream of national life. In the instant case a Syrian Catholic, Forward Class girl married a Latin Catholic (Backward Class). She had applied for the one post reserved for Latin Catholic, backward fisherman. It was argued that she was married under the cannon law and therefore, could claim the benefit of reservation on principle that a lady on marriage becomes the member of the family of her husband. Delivering the Judgment of the Supreme Court for himself and B. L. Jansria J., Justice K. Ramaswamy pronounced the practical way to took at the matter. Said, the learned Judge:

> "When a member is transplanted into the Dalits, Tribes and OBC, he/she must of necessity also have had under gone the same handicaps, and must have been subjected to the same disabilities, disadvantages, indignities or sufferings so as to entitle the candidate to avail the facility of reservation."

The learned Judge made clear –

"A candidate who had the advantageous start in life but is transplanted into the Backward Caste by adoption or Marriage or conversion, does not become eligible for the benefit of reservation either under Article 15(4) or 16(4), as the case may be."[94]

In ***State of Tripura v. Namita Majumdar (Barman)***[95] a female born of forward caste married a Scheduled Caste man of Namsudra community. Before her appointment as Stenographer junior grade a complaint was made and she was not given the benefit of the Scheduled caste. Valsamma Paul rule was applied. So was case in ***Meera Kanwaria v. Sunita***[96] a Rajput girl married to Jatav Scheduled Caste, contested and won municipal election but was deprived of benefit as a Scheduled Caste candidate.

5.2.5.4 Benefit of SC/ST to the Offsprings of Marriages with SC/ST: Suffering of Disadvantage Test

Ordinarily a Child gets title, caste and other traits from father. But, ***Wilson Reade v. C.S. Booth***[97] presents exception. The issue was whether a child born of English Father and Khasi S.T. could contest election for a reserved seat. He was accepted as tribe man by tribes people where matrilineal rule applied and anyone born of a Khasi mother was regarded as the tribe member. He had followed "the tribal custom and the way of life". Tribes men accepted as their leader in politics. Assam High Court ignore the principle of the purity of blood and accepted the conduct of the person concerned and acceptance by the community.

But, ***Punit Rai* v. *Dinesh Chaudhary***[98] presents a different set of opinion. In this case issue arose whether the respondent was eligible to contest election as S.C. candidate. He was the issue born of father Bhagwan Singh a Kurmi and Dev Kumari Pasi mother. The majority decision delivered by Brijesh Kumar J. for himself and V.N. Khare C.J. held the view that the respondent could not prove that he was treated as a member of 'Pasi' community. In his concurring Judgment S.B. Sinha J. was more categorical. Sinha J. ruled that caste of the father was determinative factor in the absence of any law. Sinha J. observed: "The caste system in India is ingrained in the Indian mind. A person, in the absence of any statutory law, would inherit his caste from his father and not his mother even in a case of inter-caste marriage. How the caste or tribe of the person is to be determined depends upon several factors including the customary laws. A person under customary Hindu law would be inheriting his caste from his father."[99]

Though there was a Bihar government circular dated 3.3.1978 to the effect that, for the determination of a child born from a non-Scheduled Caste father and Scheduled Caste mother........the child born from such parents will be counted in the category of Scheduled Caste, but the court refused to accept the circular as law within the meaning of Article 13 of the constitution.

In ***Anjan Kumar* v. *Union of India***[100] a division bench H.K. Sema and Dr A.R. Lakshmanan JJ. Re-inforced the test of suffering the disadvantages. The appellant was born of non-tribal Forward Class Kayastha father and a Scheduled Tribe mother. Delivering the Judgment of the Court, H.K. Sema J. ruled that in view of the catena of decisions of the Supreme Court the question raised before the court were no more *res integra* and observed that, "the condition precedent for granting tribe certificate being that one must suffer disabilities wherefrom one belongs. The offshoots of the wedlock of a tribal woman married to a non-tribal husband-Forward Class (Kayastha in the present case) cannot claim Scheduled Tribe status. The reason being such offshoot was brought up in the atmosphere of Forward Class and he is not subjected to any disability."[101]

The courts have maintained a distinction between two types inter-caste marriages- a forward class woman marrying to a tribal man and a tribal or SC girl marrying with a forward class person. In the former case courts have given some latitude. Though a woman of forward caste after marriage with a tribal cannot automatically attain the status of tribal but on acceptance by the tribal community by resolution of the community on observance of rituals and traditions of the tribe and resolution being registered in Village Register kept for that purpose, she may attain the tribal status on analogy of the wife taking the husband's domicile.[102] In such cases, the children from such marriage will be tribal. On the other hand, if a non-tribal man marries a tribal woman, their children will not be tribal.[103] Even the acceptance of marriage between the non-tribal woman and a tribal man will not grant him tribal status and furthermore, even the government circular to that effect would not benefit her, as it would not amount to law within meaning of Article 13. The reason given is that such marriages performed against the wishes of their parents is objected to by parents and village community and may involve even excommunication.

The off-springs of a Hindu Scheduled Caste mother and a Christian father have not been allowed to enjoy SC status.[104] The courts allow the benefit of reservation to the children out of inter-caste marriages only if they have been subjected to the same disabilities attached to SCs and STs. The onus to prove that he/she is subjected to the same handicap and disadvantages and disabilities of a member of SC/ST lies on the claimants of the benefit.[105]

However, the Courts have not failed to appreciate the facts and realities of life. They have searched ratio of earlier decisions and explained the variation on account of facts. Thus, in ***Rameshbhai Dabhai Naika* v. *State of Gujrat***[106] a division bench of the Supreme Court consisting of Aftab Alam and Rajana P. Desai JJ. explained and clarified earliest decisions in *Valsamma Paul,* [107] *Punit Rai*[108] and *Anjan Kumar*[109] cases. In the instant case the fact was that the mother of the appellant was undeniably a Nayak, one of the Scheduled Tribes and the appellant himself and his other siblings were also married to Nayaks. His father was non-tribal (Kshatriya) and on that simple basis the High Court did not pay any heed to his upbringing as a member of the Nayak community and his acceptance in that community. Since the High Court declined to record any finding on whether the appellant was in fact, brought up as a tribal and consequently shared all the indignities and handicaps and deprivations normally suffered by the tribal communities and, therefore, the appellant lost his tribal certificate and the fair price shop that was allotted to him on that basis. Speaking for the Apex Court Aftab Alam J. clarified that the High Court had read the three earlier cited cases, as laying down the rule that regardless of other considerations the offsprings of an inter-caste marriage or marriage between a tribal and a non-tribal would take his/her caste from the father. Indeed such observations in those cases were not ratio-decidendi.

The learned Judge narrated, elaborated and explained the situation in those cases that the concerned children were brought up in environment of forward caste community and had not suffered any social disabilities or backwardness. Justice, Aftab Alam observed that–

> "The legal position that seems to emerge is that in an inter-caste marriage or a marriage between a tribal and non-tribal the determination of the caste of the offspring is essentially a question of fact to be decided on the basis of the facts adduced in each case. The determination of the caste of a person born of an inter-caste marriage or a marriage between a tribal and non-tribal cannot be determined in complete disregard of attending facts of the case."[110]

The learned Judge further made clear that the presumption about the caste of child determination on the basis of father's caste may be, even more strong, if husband is forward caste and wife is tribal. But, such presumption is by no means conclusive and irrebuttable. Pointing out the legal position that such presumption may be rebutted by the child by producing the evidence that he/she was brought up by the mother who belonged to the SC/ST fold. He/She could prove that, "by virtue of being the son of a forward caste father he did not have any advantageous start in life but on the contrary suffered deprivations, indignities, humilities and handicaps like any other member of the community to which her mother belonged.[111] He was treated so by the communities to which her mother belonged as well as the people outside that community."[112]

Thus, the main consideration for determination of the caste of child born out of wed-rock between tribal and not-tribal espouse would be the bringing up of the child. This is decisively determinative factor. In ***Sobha Hymavathi Devi* v. *Setti Gangadharswami***[113] a three-Judge bench of the

Supreme Court consisting of R. C. Lahoti C.J. and G. P. Mathur and P. K. Balasubramanyan, JJ. did not allow the benefit of reservation to Sobha Hymavathi Devi to contest election as a ST candidate on the ground that she was not only born of a Sistu Karnam forward caste father and evidentiary proof was to recognise as such, she was always being educated at Visakhapatnam and she was never living as a tribal in Bhimaveram Village to which her mother's family belonged and there was no occasion for that community to treat her as a member of that community nor was proved that she followed the way of life of that community. The facts that she was daughter of a mother belonging to Bhagatha S.T. community and married Appala Raju of that community did not help her as document showed her caste as Sistu Karnam, an upper caste and she was always educated at Vishakhapatnam.

Table 5.8: Suffering of disadvantages a determinative factor

Case	***Marriage/adoption /conversion***	***Suffering of disadvantage***	***Decision***
Valsamma Paul	Marriage : backward caste girl married ST.	Advantage of starting life as Backward Class	No benefit granted
Punit Rai	Offspring of marriage: father Kurmi mother S.C.	Suffering disadvantages not proved	No benefit granted
Sobha Hymavathi Devi	Father Forward caste mother ST Herself married ST	Upbringing as Forward caste, education always at Visakhapatnam	No benefit granted
Anjan Kumar	Offshoot of tribal woman non-tribal father Forward caste-Kayastha	Not suffering disadvantage	No benefit granted
Rajeshbhai Dabhai Naika	Father Kshatriya Mother ST(Nayak)	Brought as tribal suffered disadvantages	Benefit Granted

Ratio: Transplantation in SC/ST by way of adoption, marriage and conversion does not automatically makes claimant entitled of reservation. Only those can claim entitlement of reservation who have really suffered disadvantages, indignities and social disabilities from which SC/ST suffer.

5.2.5.5 Rationality of the Test of Suffering Disadvantages by the Claimant

In allowing the benefit of the SC/ST status and benefit the courts have applied the test of suffering handicaps in cases of adoption, marriage and conversion with equal vigour. Reason and rationality is to avoid fraudulent advantages and ensure benefit to genuinely needy claimants. Thus, in ***D. Neelima v. Dean, PG. Studies, A.P. Agricultural University***[114]. A. P. High Court on line of creamy layer formula enunciated by the apex court in ***Indra Sawhney* v. *Union of India***[115], ruled that, "by the device of marriage just before the time of applying for admission into post-graduate course, if they were permitted to invoke the benefit and protection available to the class of persons who really suffer from environmental disadvantages and incidental stresses and strains, it amounts to letting of the purpose of reservation to whittledown, besides permitting entry of citizens better, if not equally, placed as those constituting creamy layer."[116] In ***Valsamma Paul* v. *Cochin University***[117], K. Ramaswamy J. pointed out the object of reservation is to remove handicaps, disadvantages, sufferings and restrictions to which the members of the Dalits or Tribes or OBC were subjected and bring them in the mainstream of the nation life by providing them opportunities and facilities and said that a candidate who had advantageous start as a Forward Caste and is transplanted in backward caste by adoption, or marriage or conversion can not enjoy the benefit of reservation. To allow them to acquire status of Scheduled Castes etc. by voluntary mobility into these categories "would play fraud on the constitution and would frustrate the benign constitutional policy under Articles 15(4) and 16(4) of the Constitution".[118]

5.2.5.6 Finality of the Lists issued for SCs/STs by the President

The language of Article 341(1) or Article 342(1) is clear enough to convey the message that the lists announced by the President intend to be final. The purpose of giving exhaustiveness and finality to the SCs/STs lists is to avoid any uncertainty as to the caste as being SC or ST. The Presidential order is determinative.[119]

Presidential order is exhaustive. Since the list is prepared keeping into the backwardness of a caste or castes, races, tribes or parts of or groups within castes, races or tribes no issue can be raised as to the inclusion of these parts or groups which have been left out and not mentioned in the Presidential order. In *Gurmukh Singh* V. *Union of India*[120] the High Court of Punjab ruled that Presidential order cannot be challenged on the ground that it grants benefit of SCs only Hindu Bawarias to the exclusion of

Sikh Bawarias so as to deny them privileges enjoyed by a S.C. Thus, Article 15(1) is to be read with Article 341(1) and to allow Presidential power to divide castes into groups for the purpose of granting benefits meant for SCs. The list is prepared after examination of the social and economic backwardness of group and the President may come to conclusion that not the whole caste, race or tribe but the only parts or groups within them should be specified. Likewise the specification may be only for a part of the state and not the entire state.[121] Whatever is done by the President-specification of SC/ST for the whole caste, race or tribe or only the part or group of them or the whole state or only a specified local area, that is final for the State actions. State can make provision for the purposes of educational admissions under Article 15(4) or reservation in state services under 16(4). But, it can make no alteration in beneficiaries. If the whole caste is specified as SC/ST, the state cannot sub-classify. It would be violative of equality, as well as, principle of reasonableness.[122] Likewise, if the Presidential order intends to give benefit of S.C. on account of 'residence' it cannot be restricted on ground of birth.[123]

The finality and exhaustiveness of the Presidential order under Article 341(1) or Article 342(1) is such that

1. Nobody is competent to argue that a caste not mentioned in the list is equal in status to caste mentioned in list or it is part of that and therefore be deemed to have been in that for the purposes of benefits.[124] Even mention of that not included caste in Gazetteers or glossaries would not serve any purpose.
2. No change/addition can be made by way of circular.[125]
3. The State Government cannot de-notify certain castes as SC/ST if it is not mentioned in the Presidential order. Thus, in ***Vijay Prakash* v. *State of U.P.***, The Allahabad High Court refused to treat 'Bhar' and Rajbhar as ST on the basis of Government Notification, because they had not been included in the Presidential order issued for U.P. and government has no power to do so.
4. Even the State legislative cannot bring any change in the Presidential list.[126]
5. Even Judiciary is incompetent to make any change in the status of any caste/tribe. It cannot declare a tribe equivalent to ST.[127] The Court is devoid of power to declare any caste or tribe as synonymous to a SC/ST.[128] The Judiciary has mere interpretative role and while doing so the Court can have limited role to allow substitution of the old name of a caste in Presidential order.

Thus, In ***Basavalingappa* v. *Munichinnapla***[129] it was found that 'Bhovi' was mentioned in Presidential order before 1956, the name was changed by a conference of the Vodder Caste in Mysore. The evidence was given that Voddar meant Bhovi in Mysore before 1956. The Court admitted it. So was done in the case of admitting popular name Patar included in Tribe specified in the President's order Munda (Bihar).[130] But, these are cases positively meant for the whole group. Otherwise, the Supreme Court refused in ***Palaghat zilla Thandan Samudhya Samiti* v. *State of Kerala***[131] to restrict the application of "Thandan" SC. Presidential order had used 'Thandan' as S.C. for the whole state. The state's plea was that benefit of order was confined Thandan residing in particular part of the State and any other community called "Thandan" should be excluded from that order and the High Court had accepted that interpretation, the Supreme Court did not approve such interpretation. The Supreme Court declared Judicial hands off in giving restrictive interpretation to the Presidential order.

6. Now the Court prefers the complex issues of Caste falling under the Presidential order or not to be decided by statutory bodies like the National Commission for SC/ST or the State Commission. Thus, in ***A.S. Nagendra* v. *State of Karnataka***[132] the issue whether the caste known as Maaleru is the same as 'Maleru' which was specified in the Presidential order, the state commission for SCs/STs was to decide it. But, on its non-serious attitude, the apex court directed the National Commission for SCs/STs to determine the issue.

5.2.5.7 Determination of the Membership of SCs/STs

There have been many cases of false certificates of SCs/STs. The issue arises: who has to decide whether a person is a member of SCs or STs ?

The certificate issues by a revenue officer or other administrative authority may be a *prima facie* evidence. But, it may not be conclusive proof.[133] The dispute has to be finally decided by the competent authority. Who is competent authority ? The judiciary has favoured determination by scrutiny committee constituted for that purpose. In ***Kumari Madhuri Patel* v. *Additional Commissioner Tribal Development***[134], the Supreme Court laid down the procedure for the issuance of certificate. It was further explained in ***Madhuri Patel* v. *Addl. Commissioner for Tribal Development***[135]. The apex court ordered the determination of disputed SC/ST caste by a scrutiny committee consisting of five members with a quorum of three members. It was to act as a quasi-Judicial body and consider relevant materials before taking any decision to cancel the certificate. Consequently in ***Baswal* v. *State of Maharashtra***[136], the Supreme Court declared the issuance of certificate in defiance of *Madhuri Patel* decision's direction and issued by a two-member committee as invalid. The Scrutiny Committee has to follow the rule of natural Justice to give opportunity of being heard the person whose certificate is under challenge. Caste Certificate issuing order of the scrutiny committee is reviewable. Thus, consideration of irrelevant material and non-consideration of material facts/materials may prompt the Court to quash the order of the scrutiny committee.[137] The object behind the constitution of the scrutiny committee is to serve the social and constitutional purpose that the benefit of the caste certificate is taken by a genuine claimant and no undue advantage is obtained on the basis of ingenuine certificates.[138]

5.2.5.8 Alteration in Presidential Order

As has been discussed earlier the Presidential order is issued under Article 341(1) or 342(1). It is final. The only competent body to make any alteration in the Presidential order is the Parliament. Article 341(2) specifically and mandatorily provides-

> "(2) Parliament may by law include in or exclude from the list of Scheduled Castes specified in a notification issued under clause (1) any caste, race or tribe or part of or group within any caste, race or tribe, but save as aforesaid a notification issued under the said clause shall not be varied by any subsequent notification". As power to declare the SC/ST lists under clause (1) of Article 341 and clause: (1) of Article 342 lies exclusively in the President, the power to make any alteration by way of inclusion or exclusion of any caste, race or tribe exclusively lies in the Parliament.

The Supreme Court has maintained a distinction between its power to review and interpret SEBC in such a way as to skim off creamy layer from it in famous *Mandal Case*[139] and reiterated in subsequent cases. When asked to so on facts with respect to SCs/STs in ***E. V. Chinnaiah* v. *State of A.P.***[140], and the determination of SC's/STs, the court bluntly refused to so and ruled that whether creamy layer among Scheduled Castes be excluded from reservation, can be decided only by the Parliament by enacting law to that effect under Article 341(2). Scheduled Caste declared by the President is an unbreakable class and the court is not competent to break or divide it. The doctrine of Parliament's exclusivity to alter the Presidential order was reaffirmed by S.B. Sinha J. in ***Shree Surat Valsad***

Jilla K.M.G. Parishad* v. *Union of India[141]. Speaking for the Division Bench of himself and M. Katju J., Sinha J. asserted that "List prepared by President under Article 341(1) forms one class of homogeneous group. Only on list is to be prepared by the President and if any amendment there to is to be made, the same is to be done by Parliament".

The rationality behind giving the exclusive power of inclusion or exclusion in Presidential order to the Parliament appears to be the nature of decision to that effect. It is a policy matter. It need to be debated in Parliament and only on evaluation pros and cons of the matter the parliament may make alteration by enacting law.The representative of the people know better the need of the people and therefore, Parliament has been given the upper hand to the exclusion all-state executive, state legislature and Judiciary itself.

However, in view of the chances of misuse of caste certificate the Supreme Court became cautious and did not allow benefit of Laskar[142] tribe to fall under Deshi Tripura Tribe because none of them was included in the Presidential order. Declaring the finality of Presidential order the court put emphasis on reading Presidential order as such and observed that nobody can add to or remove from the list of the SCs or STs as notified by the President under Article 341(2) or 342(2). A Constitution bench of the Supreme Court in ***State of Maharashtra v. Milind***[143] made it clear that-

1. It is not at all permissible to hold any inquiry or let in any evidence to decide or declare that any tribe or tribal community or part of or group; within any tribe or tribal community is included in the general name even though it is not specifically mentioned in the entry in the Scheduled Tribe Order if they are not specifically mentioned in it.
2. The Scheduled Tribe Order must be read as it is. It is not even permissible to say that a tribe, sub-tribe, part of or group of any tribe or tribal community is synonymous to the one mentioned in Scheduled Tribe Order if they are not so specifically mentioned in it.[144]

On the above basis the Supreme Court refused to include "Halba Koshti" in the entry mentioned in Order as 'Halba, Halbi'. The apex court categorically said that any change – by way of exclusion or inclusion in the Presidential order can be done only by the Parliament under Article 341(2) or 342(2). In ***E.V. Chinniah v. State of A.P.***[145] the Supreme Court clarified that Scheduled Caste is no caste in traditional sense. Ray C.J. pointed out in state of ***Kerala v. N.M. Thomas*** that Scheduled Castes and Scheduled

Tribes are not a caste within the ordinary meaning of the caste. Iyer J. expressed the view that "Scheduled Castes are not castes in the Hindu fold but an amalgam of castes, races, groups, tribes or parts thereof found on investigation to be lowliest." In ***Akhil Bharatiya Soshit Karamachari Sangh (Rly). v. Union of India***, Iyer J. again pointed out the "Scheduled Castes need not be castes in the conventional sense and, therefore, may not be a caste within the meaning of Articles 15(1) and 16(2) of the Constitution". Be it treated as a caste or not one thing is clear that Presidential order under Article 341(1) notifying Scheduled Castes is not based on any caste characteristic but their abysmal backwardness. Thus, the reservational benefit in favour of the Scheduled Castes and the Scheduled Tribes was a constitutional necessity.

5.2.5.9 Can there be Sub-division Among SCs/STs

This class unit and well nit entity cannot be sub-divided by anybody after the Presidential order. There has been enough discussion earlier on the point. In post Indra Sawhney period and evolving of creamy layer principle an issue has been raised from time to time as to creamy layerisation of certain group or layer amongst SCs and STs. The issue confronted is: Can SC or ST once declared by the President be divided in macro category of creamy layer and non-creamy layer. The issue is not very recent. As early as, 1970s in N.M. Thomas Krishna Iyer J. talked of benefit of reservations snatching away by heady berth occupant among Harijan. In Akhil Bharatiya Soshit Karamchari Sangh, exposing the problem, he left the matter to be handled by the Government and at opportune time in the future. In first part of para 94 in that case, he defended and in the latter, exposed the problem. Said, Iyer J.:

> "....Nor does the specious plea that because a few Harijans are better off, therefore, the bulk of the bottom deserves no Jack-up provisions, merit scrutiny. A swallow does not make a summer. May be, the state may, when social conditions warrant, justifiably restrict Harijan benefit to the Harijans among the Harijans and forbid the higher Harijans from robbing the lowlier brethren."

Again in para 98, Iyer J. observed:

> "The argument that there are rich and influential Hrijans, who rob all the privileges leaving the serf-level sufferer as suppressed as ever. The administration may well innovate and classify to weed out the creamy of SCs/STs. But, the court cannot force the State in that behalf."

The opinions of Krishna Iyer J. leave three obvious conclusions

(a) It for the government to tackle the issue;

(b) It may be tackled in future, when the opportune time arise, and

(c) Judiciary will not force in that behalf.

But, the judicial trend shows that even State cannot do that, because State Government or Union executive cannot make any alteration in the presidential well knit classification as SC or ST and no sub-classification is allowed. The issue directly arose in ***E. V. Chinnaiah v. State of A.P.***[146] The State of Andhra Pradesh had enacted The Andhra Pradesh Scheduled Castes (Rationalisation of Reservations) Act, 2000. It divided 15 per cent reservation meant for the Scheduled Castes by further sub-dividing the SCs. into four categories; Group –A, Group-B, Group – C, and Group –D. Considering the issue raised before Apex Court, whether the State had the right to sub-divide the SCs and STs as declared in the Presidential Order into further sub-categories, it held that –

> "19 This part of the Constituent Assembly coupled with the fact that Article 341 makes it clear that the State Legislature or its executive has no power of disturbing" (term used by Dr Ambedkar) the Presidential List of Scheduled Castes for the State. It is also clear from Articles in Part XVI of the Constitution that the power of the State to deal with the Scheduled Caste list is totally absent except to bear in mind the required maintenance of efficiency of administration in making of appointment which is found in Article 335. Therefore, any executive action or legislative enactment which interferes, disturbs, re-arranges, regroups or re-classifies the various castes found in the Presidential List will be violative of scheme of the Constitution and will be violative of article 341of the Constitution."[147]

Taking inspiration from N.M. Thomas case the Supreme Court arrived at conclusion that the castes once included in the Presidential List, form a class by themselves. If they are one class under the constitution, any division of these classes of persons based on any consideration would amount to tinkering with the Presidential List.[148] The court bluntly said that the State have no right to further classify SCs or STs into different categories.[149] In his concurring judgment S.B. Sinha J.[150] pointing out the special place of SCs/STs and President as sole repository of specifying.......said that any legislation which would bring them out of the purview thereof or tinker with the order issued by the President of India would be unconstitutional.

In ***Ashok Kumar Thakur v. Union of India***,[151] K.G. Balakrishnan C.J. ruled that for the purpose of reservation, the principles of creamy layer are not applicable for Scheduled Castes and Scheduled Tribes. In ***Avinash Singh Bagri v. Registrar, IIT, Delhi***[152] a thre judge bench consisting of K.G. Balakrishnanan C.J. and P. Sathasivam and Dr B.S. Chauhan JJ., reaffirmed the non-applicability and creamy layer rule to SC and ST categories students for study in IIT. Speaking for the unanimous Court P. Sathasivam J. pointed out that SCs and STs are a separate class by themselves and creamy layer principle is not applicable to them.[153]

A three judge Special Bench of the Tripura High Court, consisting of Deepak Gupta C.J., U.B. Saha and S.C. Das JJ. ***Jayata Chackraborty v. State of Tripura***[154], speaking through C.J. Gupta was confronted with the issues that even if the creamy layer test is not to be applied, those categories, classes and castes amongst the SCs and STs who have corned amongst all the benefits at the cost of the more depressed classes of the SCs and STs should be excluded by the State from getting the benefit of reservation. The facts narrated are revealing. Representation of STs in upper echelons of service are as follow:

ST community of "Dabbarma"	more than 90 per cent
'Debbarmas' and "Jamatias"	almost all 100 per cent
About 12 to 13 STs	virtually no representation
Total STs 17	

The full bench of Tripura High Court in view of precedent deference of E.V. Chinnaiah decision[155] did not allow any division among SCs and STs and E.V. Chinnaiah decision[156] is based on well knit class identification of SCs/STs under Articles 34/and 342 and finality of Residential order passed there under. But the Judicial outlook appears to be the missed opportunity of setting practical and just trend so as to reach the benefit of reservation to really deprived courts have ignored the wild of change in direction of making Justice reality to the serf-level sufferers and suppressed among SCs/STs. The fact narrated in Jayanti Chakraborty case[157] are eye opener. How long technicality of law will be allowed to continue the deprivation of worst among SCs/STs and privileges of reservation be swallowed by rich and influential upper strata of SCs/STs is crying for solution. If the parliament fails to enact appropriate law due to political reasons that the class which is swallowing reservational benefit is more vocal and politically suitable to political parties, should not judiciary take lead in this matter as it has taken in many spheres? A very informative comment came in The Hindu 25th September 2015 p. 12 under heading

"Dalit Sub-Castes Seek Reservation Review".[158] A morcha of still deprived SCs/STs is coming up with such demand. A retired bureaucrat belonging to the Valmiki Caste and President of Rashtriya Dalit Bachao Andolan, O.P. Shukla (as the sir name stands) feels that some state governments' efforts to provide quota for Ati Dalits have been frustrated by Judiciary.[159] There are over 1200 Scheduled Castes in India. A teacher of Social Exclusion at J.N.U., Y. Chinna Rao pleads that "Rather than excluding castes, it should be found out which groups have not benefited at all from scheduled caste quota and these should be given the priority within the quota, after which there should be an open competition among all Scheduled Castes"[160]

- It is felt that the un-benefited deprived SCs are Second Among Equals. The following figures are quite informative.

<table>
<tr><th colspan="6">Second Among Equals</th></tr>
<tr><td colspan="6">Some Dalit groups claim they are not benefiting as much from reservation as the 'advanced' Dalits</td></tr>
<tr><td colspan="2">The 'Deprived' Dalits
• Valimiks (sanitation workers) in North India
• Mangs in Maharashtra
• Madigas in Andhra Pradesh</td><td colspan="2">Their Demand
A sub-quota within the Scheduled Caste category</td><td colspan="2">The 'Advanced' Dalits
• Leather workers caste in North India
• Mahars in Maharashtra
• Malas in Andhra Pradesh</td></tr>
<tr><td colspan="4">Usha Mehra Commission in Andhra Pradesh (2008)</td><td colspan="2">Sociologist S.S. Jodhika'[s Study in Punjab</td></tr>
<tr><td colspan="4">Findings</td><td colspan="2">Findings</td></tr>
<tr><td>• 'Advanced' Mala caste in IAS and IPS</td><td>76 per cent to 86 per cent</td><td>• Represen-tation of Madiga community</td><td>13 per cent to 23 per cent</td><td>105 Number of IAS officers from Scheduled Castes</td><td>3 IAS Officers from Balmiki-Mazhabi (same as Valmikis) Community</td></tr>
</table>

Source: The Hindu, 25.09.2015, p. 12.

In 2001, U.P. Scheduled Castes and Scheduled Tribes Commission prepared a survey of population and representation of percentage of different castes of Scheduled Castes in services which revealed the following figures:

Table 5.9: Population and Representation per cent of different castes of SCs in Services

(Figures in percentage)[161]

Sr. No.	*Caste*	*Percentage of Population*	*Police*	*Revenue*	*Consoli-dation*	*Basic Education*	*Secondary Education*	*Total*
1.	Chamar	56.06	61.50	56.55	73.77	26.76	–	58.55
2.	Pasi	1502	9.94	12.3	7.00	8.11	–	8.94
3.	Dhobi	6.24	9.17	8.50	7.00	8.77	–	8.94
4.	Kori	6.06	2.50	7.20	3.34	7.93	–	3.82
5.	Balmiki	3.26	3.67	1.18	0.82	–	–	3.44
6.	Shilpkar	2.26	1.01	0.53	0.82	–	–	0.88
7.	Khatika	2.16	2.68	2.21	1.36	–	–	2.70
8.	Dhanuk	1.45	1.92	1.95	1.29	–	–	2.41
9.	Gaur	0.90	1.02	0.20	–	–	–	0.82
10.	Kol	0.86	0.53	0.22	–	–	–	0.41
11.	Dusadh	0.62	1.12	0.89	–	–	–	0.97
12.	Mushar	0.55	0.11	0.11	–	–	–	0.16
13.	Beldar	0.41	0.58	0.20	–	–	–	0.46
14.	Basor	–	0.17	0.15	–	–	–	0.15
15.	Nat		0.63	0.40	–	–	–	0.83
16.	Dharkar		0.23	–	–	–	–	0.23
17.	Bahelia		0.29	–	–	–	–	0.25
18.	Kharwar		0.28					0.22
19.	Dome		0.21					0.28
20.	Rawat		0.12					0.78
21.	Kanjar		0.32					0.27
22.	Bengali		0.04					0.07
23.	Hela		0.17					0.33
24.	Saharia		0.04					0.01
25.	Dhangar		0.05					0.05
26.	Beria		0.40					0.33
27.	Domar		–					0.03
28.	Bansphor		0.10					0.18
29.	Chweeron		–					–
30.	Baiswar		0.02					0.02
31.	Baiga		0.01					0.02
32.	Ban		0.01					0.01
33.	Majhwar		0.03					0.03
34.	Bhuihar		0.17					0.12
35.	Agariya		0.01					0.30
36.	Karwal		0.01					0.12
37.	Barbar		0.04					0.12
38.	Turaiha		0.03					-

(Contd...)

39.	Bhuiya		0.01					0.01
40.	Guwal		0.01					0.05
41.	Badhik		0.02					0.02
42.	Kapadia		*0103*					0.04
43.	Majhabi		0.01					0.01
44.	Bhantu		0.08					0.06
45.	Kalabaj		0.01					0.01
46.	Balhar		-					-
47.	Bawaria		0.02					-
48.	Dhasia		0.11					0.050
49.	Badi		0.01					0.01
50.	Pankha		-					0.06
51.	Habura		0.01					0.02
52.	Dabkar		0.03					0.02
53.	Hari		0.002					0.002
54	Beriay		0.01					0.02
55.	Kokha		0.01					0.02
56.	Bajgi		0.002					0.002
57.	Bajania		0.002					0.002
58.	Balia		0.02					0.04
59.	Patari		0.01					0.02
60.	Parahia		0.01					0.01
61.	Kharot		0.08					0.06
62.	Khariata		-					-
63.	Sansiay		0.08					0.07
64.	Dharmai		0.01					0.01
65.	Sanoria		0.01					0.01
66.	Lalbegi		0.002					0.02

The learned Judge did not allow any division in view of EV Chinnaiah decision.

References

1. Dr. Ambedkar, Writings and Speeches, Education Department, Government of Maharashtra (1990 Vol. I., pp. 266-267.
2. "last in ladder of creation" indicates being last both spatially and temporarily. It exposes cumulative effect on the Dalits due to heinious inequality of caste order. See Prakash Louis, Political Sociology of Dalit Assertion. Gyan Publishing House, New Delhi, 2003 p. 82 f.n. 15.
3. *Ibid.* pp. 44-45.
4. *Ibid.* p. 46.
5. The Hindu view of Life. 1949. p. 93.
6. Arts. 331 and 332 shall not apply to the State of Jammu and Kashmir.
7. Subs. For "except the Scheduled Tribes in the tribal areas of Assam, *in Nagaland and in Meghalaya" by the Constitution (51st Amendment) Act, 1984, S. 3(1) (w.e.f. 16.6.1986).S. 3(2) of this Act provides :

(2) The amendment made to Article 332 of the Constitution by sub-section (1) shall not affect any representation in the Legislative Assembly of the State of Nagaland or the Legislative Assembly of the State of Meghalaya until the dissolution of the Legislative Assembly of the State of Nagaland or the Legislative Assembly of the State of Meghalaya existing at the commencement of this Act. [*The words "and in Nagaland" inserted by the Constitution (23rd Amendment) Act, 1969, S.3. Further for "and in Nagaland" the words "in Nagaland and in Meghalaya" were substituted by the Constitution (31st Amendment) Act, 1973, S.4].

8. The words and letters "specified in Part A or Part B of the First Schedule" omitted by the Constitution (7th Amendment) Act, 1956, S. 29 and Sch.
9. Ins. By the Constitution (57th Amendment) Act, 1987, S.2(1) (w.e.f. 21-9-1987). S.2(2) of this Act provides :

   The amendment made to Article 332 of the Constitution of sub-section (1) shall not affect any representation in the Legislative Assembly of the State of Arunachal Pradesh or the Legislative Assembly of the state of Meghalaya or the Legislative Assembly of the State of Mizoram or the Legislative Assembly of the state of Nagaland until the dissolution of the Legislative Assembly of the State of Arunachal Pradesh or the Legislative Assembly of the state of Meghalaya or the Legislative Assembly of the State of Mizoram or the Legislative Assembly of the State of Nagaland existing at the commencement of this Act.
10. Subs. For "2000" by the Constitution (84th Amendment) Act, 2001, S.7.
11. Ins. By the Constitution (72nd Amendment) Act, 1992, S. 2(1) (w.e.f. 5-12-1992). S. 2(2) of the Amending Act, provides:

   (2) The amendment made to Article 332 of the Constitution by sub-section (1) shall not affect any representation in the Legislative Assembly of the State of Tripura until the dissolution of the Legislative Assembly existing at the commencement of this Act.
12. Subs. For "2000" by the Constitution (84th Amendment) Act, 2001, S. 7.
13. The words "except in the case of the constituency comprising the cantonment and municipality of Shillong" omitted by the North-Eastern Areas (Re-organisation) Act, 1971 (81 of 1971), S. 71 (w.e.f. 21-1-1972).
14. The words "except from the constituency comprising the cantonment and municipality of Shillong" omitted by the North-Eastern Areas (Re-organisation) Act, 1971 (81 of 1971), S. 71 (w.e.f. 21-1-1972).
15. Ins. By the Constitution (90th Amendment) Act, 2003, S.2.
16. Union of India v. Rakesh Kumar (2010) 4 SCC 50 = A.I.R. 2010 S.C. 3244.
17. (1998) 1 SCC 285 = A.I.R. 1998 S.C. 815.
18. A.I.R. 1969 Ori. 220.
19. A.I.R. 1977 M.P. 186.
20. A.I.R. 1965 S.C. 1269.
21. A.I.R. 1965 S.C. 1557.
22. A.I.R. 1969 S.C. 597.
23. A.I.R. 1971 S.C. 2533.
24. A.I.R. 1975 S.C. 216.

25. A.I.R. 1989 Bom. 101.
26. (1990) 3 SCC 130.
27. (1994) 5 SCC 244.
28. (2009) 15 SCC 458.

    Prior to the Supreme Court decision in Mari Chandra Shekhar Rao there was difference of opinion among the different High Courts. In Manju Singh v. Deon, B.J. Medical College, A.I.R. 1986 Guj. 175 and Ghanshyam Kiggan Borikar v. L.D. Engineering College, A.I.R. 1987 Guj. 83, the Gujrat High Court had given benefit to SC/ST migrants to the new State. The Supreme Court overruled them. On the other hand, the Bombay High Court in M.S. Malathi v. Commissioner Nagpur Division, A.I.R. 1989 Ban. 138, the Punjab and Haryana High Court in V.B. Singh v. State of Punjab ILR (1976) 1 P.H. 769; in Tapan Kumar Roy v. A.P. University, A.I.R. 1989 A.P. 132, the A.P. High Court and the Orissa High Court in K. Appa Rao v. Director of Posts and Telegraphs A.I.R. 1969 Ori. 220 had disallowed the benefit of the SC or ST in migrant states. The Supreme Court approved their stand and ruled that on migration a member of SC or ST could not carry his special benefits and privileges with him to the migrated State.
29. (2004) 9 SCC 481.
30. Ibid. p. 484 (para 5).
31. (2002) 3 SCC 90 (S.B. Sinha J).
32. (2005) 3 SCC 1 (d/on 11 Feb., 2005).
33. *Ibid*, p. 14 (para 20).
34. *Ibid*, p. 15 (para 21).
35. (2009) 15 SCC 458.
36. (2001) 1 SCC 4 (dt. Nov. 28, 2000 by the CB consisting of G.B. Patnaik, S. Rajendra Babu, D.P. Mahopatra, Doraiswamy Raju and Shivraj v. Patil, JJ.)
37. (2005) 1 SCC 394 (dt. Nov. 5, 2004 by the Constitution bench consisting of N. Santosh Hegde, S.N. Variava, B.P. Singh, H.K. Sema and S.B. Sinha JJ.).
38. (2014) 9 SCC 236.
39. (1954) SCR 817.
40. *Ibid* p. 890.
41. Marc Galanter, Competing Equalities, (1984) p. 291.
42. A.I.R. 1960 Mys. 27.
43. A.I.R. 1964 Pat. 201
44. A.I.R. 1958 Ass. 128.
45. A.I.R. 1959 S.C. 1318.
46. A.I.R. 1958 A.P. 735.
47. *Ibid.*
48. A.I.R. 1959 S.C. 1318 at p. 1327.
49. *Ibid.*
50. *Ibid.* p. 1331.
51. A.I.R. 1965 S.C. 1179.

52. *Ibid.* p. 1182.
53. A.I.R. 1973 S.C. 420.
54. A.I.R. 1952 Mail, 474, see also *Raj Gopal* v. *Arumugham*(I) A.I.R.1969 S.C.101 where in the Supreme Court ruled that upon youth, conversion to Christianity, the person loose his membership of Adi David Hindu caste.
55. 30 FLR 199 (A.P.)
56. A.I.R.1976 S.C.939 = (1976) ISCC 863. The Supreme Court did not accept Rajgopal I.
57. A.I.R.2004 S.C. 1672: (2004) 3SCC 429.
58. (2005) ISCC 394.
59. (2009) 7 SCC 387: A.I.R.2009 S.C. 2475.
60. Punjab Rao V. Meshram A.I.R.1965 S.C. 1179; see also Ramalingam Goka V. Abraham Boddu, A.I.R. 1970 S.C.741(1969) ISCC 24: *Soosai v. Union of India* A.I.R. 1986 S.C. 733; *Swvigardar v. Zonal Manager* A.I.R. 1996 S.C. 1182.
61. A.I.R. 1984 S.C. 600.
62. A.I.R.1976 S.C. 939
63. *Ibid.*
64. Competing equalities, how of Backward Classes in India (1984), p. 331.
65. Observations Fazal Ali in *Kailash Snakar v. Maya Devi* A.I.R. 1984 S.C.600 at b. 605 (para 18).
66. A.I.R. 1984 S.C. 411. This case was decided on 5.12.1983 where as Kailash Sonkar case was decided on 16.12.1983.
67. *Ibid.*
68. *Ibid.*
69. *Gurupadsami Nadar v. Lrulappa Kanar* A.I.R. 1934 Mad. 634 (Varadachaiar J.)
70. *Goona Durga Prasad Rao v. Sudarsanswami* A.I.R.1940 Mad, 513. (Mockett and Krishnaswami Ayyangar JJ.)
71. A.I.R. 1976 S.C. 939.
72. A.I.R. 1976 S.C. 939.
73. A.I.R. 1984 S.C. 411.
74. A.I.R. 1984 S.C. 600.
75. *Ibid.* p. 611 (para 50).
76. A.I.R. 1986 or 255 (273).
77. A.I.R. 1976 S.C.1904.
78. A.I.R. 1940 Mad. 513.
79. A.I.R.1976 S.C.1904 (1908).
80. Sec, H.M. Seervai, Constitutional Law of India Vol.1(fourth ed.) Universal Law Publishing Co. Pvt. Ltd. 1991, (2006 Reprint) p. 595.
81. (2008) 2 scc 196 (D/Nov.30,2007, bench: K.G. Bala Krishnan C.J. and R.V. Raveendraj J.).
82. AIR 1986 SC 733.
83. 2015(3) SCALE 1.

84. Marc Galanter, Competing Equalities (1984)k.341(f.n.255)
85. *Ibid* (f.n.256).
86. Shri G. Kuchelar, LSDC (4th series), Vol. 45, No. 9 Col. 270 (Nov. 1970).
87. A.I.R. 1972 S.C.1840 (d/on 2.1.1972).
88. *Ibis* p.1849 (para 22).
89. *Ibid* p.1850 (para 23).
90. *Ibid.*
91. A.I.R.1975 Del. 115.
92. (1978) 80 Bom. L.R.182.
93. (1996) 3SCC 545. (D/4.1.1996).
94. *Ibid.*
95. (1998) 9 SCC 217.
96. (2006) 1 SCC 344.
97. A.I.R. 1958 Ass. 128.
98. (2003) 8SCC 204.
99. *Ibid.* pp. 219 and 222.
100. (2006) 3SCC257: A.I.R. 2006 S.C. 1177.
101. *Ibid.* 265.
102. *N.E.Horo* v. *Jahanara Janardan Singh* A.I.R. 1972 S.C. 1840; *Kailash Sonkar* v. *Maya Devi* A.I.R. 1984 S.C.600.
103. *Anjan Kumar* v. *Union of India* (2006) 3SCC257.
104. *Sapna Jacob* v. *State of Kerala* A.I.R. 1993 Ker.75.
105. *Indira* v. *State of Kerala.* A.I.R. 2006 Ker.I; *State of Tripura* v. *Namita Majumdar* (Barman) (1998) 9SCC 217; *Urmila Binda* v. *Union of India,* A.I.R.1975 Del.115.
106. (2012) 2 SCC (Cr.)190.
107. (1996) 3 SCC 545.
108. (2003) 8 SCC 204.
109. (2006) 3SCC 257.
110 Ramesh Bhai Dabhi Naika (2012) 2SCC(Cr.)190z pp. 210-111.
111. *Ibid.* p. 211.
112. *Ibid.*
113. (2005) 2SCC 244.
114. AIR 1993 AP 229.
115. A.I.R. 1993 SC 477; 1992 Supp (3) SCC 217.
116. D. Neelima, A.I.R. 1993 A.P. 229.
117. (1996) 3SCC 545.
118. *Ibid,* b. 566 (para 34).
119. Bhaiyal Lal V. Harikishan Singh A.I.R. 1965 S.C. 1557.
120. A.I.R. 1952 Punj.143.

121. *Bhaiyalal* v. *Harikishan* A.I.R.1965 S.C. 1557.
122. E.V. *Chinnaiah* v. *State of Andhra Pradesh* (2005) ISCC 394.
123. Punducherry Scheduled Caste People *Welfare Association* v. *Union Territory* of Pondichery (2014) 9SCC236.
124. *Bsavalingappa* v. *Munichinnappa* A.I.R. 1965 S.C. 1269.
125. A.I.R.1989 Bim.(5A-A.I.R. 2005 All 18).
126. Shree Surat Valsad Jilla *K.M.G Prishad* v. *Union of India* (2007) 5 sec 360.
127. *Nityanand Sharma* v. *State of Bihar* (1996) 3 SCC 576.
128. *Pankaj Kumar Shaha* v. *S.D.O.* (1996) 8 SCC 264.
129. A.I.R.1965 S.C.1229, see also, Chinnappa V. Venkatramani (1996) 3 SCC 585.
130. *Bhavia* v. *Anirudh* A.I.R.1971 S.C.2533.
131. (1994) 5 SCC 359.
132. (2005) 10 SCC 301.
133. Rama Krishna V. Asstt. Collector (1987) 3 ATC70.
134. (1994) 6 SCC 241.
135. (1997) 5 SCC 437.
136. (2007) 12 SCC 800.
137. *Sayana* v. *State of Maharashtra* (2009) 10 SCC 268.
138. *State of Maharashtra* v. *Ravi Prakash Babala Singh Parmar,* (2007) ISCC 80.
139. (1992) Supp. (3) SCC 217; AIR 1993 SC 477.
140. (2005) 1 SCC 394.
141. (2007) 5 SCC 360: A.I.R. 2007 S.C 2056.
142. *Srish Kumar Choudury* v. *State of Tripura,* 1990 Supp. SCC 220 = A.I.R. 1990 SC 991.
143. (2001) 1 SCC 4.
144. *Ibid.* pp. 30-31.
145. (2005) 1 SCC 394 : A.I.R. 2005 S.C. 162.
146. (2005) 1 SCC 394.
147. *Ibid.* (para 19).
148. *Ibid.* (para 16).
149. *Ibid.* (para 37).
150. *Ibid.* (paras 52, 111, 39)
151. (2008) 6 SCC 1 at p. 513.
152. (2009) 8 SCC 220.
153. *Ibid.* at p. 230.
154. A.I.R. 2015 Tri. 43 (F.B.) dt. 9.4.2015.
155. (2005) 1SCC 344.
156. *Ibid.*
157. A.I.R. 2015, Tripura 43.
158. Vikas Pathak Dalit Sub-Castes Seek Reservation Review, The Hindu, 116. The Hindu 259, 2012, p. 12.

159. *Ibid.* The Punjab Government Efforts in 1970s, Haryana in 1990 and Rajnath Singh as C.M. in U.P. and Andhra Pradesh effects in 2000 are cited as examples.
160. The Hindu 25.9.2012, p. 12.
161. *Sources:* Unpublished Report August 2001, U.P. Scheduled Castes and Scheduled Tribes Commission, pp. 54-58.

Chapter - 6

Issues Arising Out of Preferential Treatment to SCs/STs

Preferential Treatment to SCs and STs at Promotional Stage

6.1 Should Reservation be confined to the initial appointments or it should include promotions too?

One of the most debated issues in service jurisprudence has been whether reservational benefits should be limited to the initial appointments or it should also be allowed in promotions. The issue of reservation at promotional stage has created heart-burning and dissatisfaction between reservationists and anti-reservationists. In pre-1990s cases the issue mostly related to SCs/STs as reservation in Central Services was only for them and not for OBCs. And therefore, discussion on them in principle may have relevance to OBCs also. The reservationists insisted that reservation should be at every stage, i.e. from initial appointment to top promotions. On the other hand, the argument of anti reservationists has been that reservation should be limited to initial appointments. Upto November 16, 1992, i.e. the day on which Mandal case was decided the judiciary had supported the view of reservationists. The story started with judicial approval of governmental move to provide reservation to SCs/STs at the level of promotion too. Thus, in ***General Manager, Southern Railway v. Rangachari***,[1] the Supreme Court had to decide the claim of the respondent who had been successful before Madras High Court in assailing the circular of Railway Board providing for reservation of Selection posts in Class III of the railway service in favour of the members of the Scheduled Castes and the Scheduled Tribes and in particular the reservation of selection posts among the court Inspectors in Class III, one of which held by the respondent. The impugned circular read:

"There are different grades of Class III posts. Some of those posts are 'non-Selection' posts, promotion to which is made on "Seniority-cum-suitability" basis while in the case of others which are 'Selection' posts promotion is made by a positive act of selection. There will be no quota for Scheduled Castes and Scheduled Tribes candidates in respect of promotion to 'non-selection' posts".

"For promotion to 'Selection' posts however, there will be the prescribed quota for reservation. The field of consideration in the case of Scheduled Castes and Scheduled Tribes candidate should be for times the number of posts reserved without any condition of qualifying period of service in their case, subject to the condition that consideration should not normally extend to such staff beyond two grades immediately below the grade for which selection is held."[2]

The circular was given retrospective effect since January 4, 1957.

Another circular was issued on June 12, 1959 giving guidance and direction as to the mode of the implementation of earlier circular.

"2(ii). The Special Roster in force for SCs and STs in direct recruitment categories are to be followed to work out the number of posts to be reserved for SCs and STs. in promotions made in Selection Grades and for promotion from Class IV to Class III.

2(iii). As the Board's orders have retrospective effect from 4th January, 1957, it is necessary that the promotions made in each selection grade on your Division/Office from 4th January, 1957, are reviewed and the number of posts due to SCs. and STs. worked out applying the Roster referred to in item (ii) above."

First, had the circular not been given retrospective effect the dispute was not likely to arise, as it arose in the case.

The main issue for consideration was: whether reservation was intended to be assured only at the stage of initial appointment or even to all stages of post-appointment attracting employment ? There was somewhat agreement on the point that under Articles 16(1) and (2) promotion was included[3] but there was difference as to its inclusion under Article 16(4). And even Attorney General did not contest the inclusion of promotion under clause (1) and clause (2) of Article 16[4] and therefore there was no contest on the point. Still, the majority expressed the view on the point by giving liberal interpretation of the provisions to include not only initial matters prior to the act of employment but also others like matters of salary and periodical increments, terms as to leave, as to gratuity, as to pension and as to the age of superannuation. This was concluded on the basis that Articles 16(1) and (2) really give effect to equality before law guaranteed by Article 14 and to the prohibition of discrimination guaranteed by Article 15(1). The three provisions were held to form part of the same constitutional code of guarantees and supplement each other. The majority pointed out that for treating preferentially to the backward classes the condition precedent is the conclusion of the State that they have not adequate representation the services of the state. Thus, it can be exercised only to make inadequate representation of backward classes in the services adequate.[5] The court accepted reservation in two senses: reservation of appointments by fixing a certain percentage in that behalf as well as reservation of certain initial posts. Taking liberal view of[6] "appointments" and "posts", the majority ruled:

> "The power of reservation which is conferred on the state under Article 16(4) can be exercised by the state in a proper case not only by providing for reservation of appointments but also by providing for reservation of selection posts."[7]

This was conclusion of the three learned Judges on the bench – Gajendragadkar, C.J. and A.K. Sarkar and K.C. Das Gupta, JJ. The two learned Justices on the bench differed diametrically. Wanchoo, J. pointing out how reservation is to be effectuated, said:

> "Article 16(4) tells us that it may be made either by reserving appointments to the services or reserving posts in the services. Appointments in my opinion clearly mean the initial appointments to a service, for a person is appointed only once in a service and thereafter there is no further appointment. Therefore, when the Article speaks of reservation of appointments it means reservation of percentage of initial appointments to the service."[8]

He further clarified:

> "Posts refer to the total number of posts in the service and when reservation is by reference to posts it means reservation of a certain percentage of posts out of the total number of posts in the service."[9]

Wanchoo, J. pointed out that the two methods of reservation in Article 16 have two purposes – the method of reservation of appointments is a long-range policy of achieving the adequate representation and the method of reservation of the posts has the goal of achieving adequate representation for shorter period.[10]

Ayyangar, J. did not subscribe the view of other Judges including Wanchoo, J. that 'posts' means posts in service itself and pointed out that every appointment in a service must be to "a post" in a service, because there cannot be appointment in the air but can only be to a 'post' in a service."[11] In context of Article 16(4) the learned Judge was of the view that "it meant not posts in a service but ex-cadre posts".[12] Perhaps this was reason for him to write a separate judgment in this case. On two vital issues he expressed his entire agreement with Wanchoo, J. referring to scheme of Article 16(4) and Article 335 he concluded that constitutional scheme:

> "Contemplates and permits reservation only in respect of appointments to services at the initial stage and not at each stage even after the appointment has taken place."[13]

Ayyangar, J. also agreed with Wanchoo, J. on the point that posts refer to total number of 'posts' in a service. He elaborately supported this conclusion and exposed ingenuity of holding otherwise. He elaborated:

> "In some of the top grades there are single posts in the service. If at any point of time the incumbent is not a member of the backward class, it would certainly be a case of inadequate representation as regards that post which would meant that such posts which are single may be reserved for all times to be held by members of the backward classes, because if at any moment such a person ceases to hold the post there would be inadequate representation in regard to the post."[14]

The learned Judge drew attention to this aspect because:

> "It pointedly demonstrates that the correct view is that when inadequacy of representation" is referred to in Article 16(4) as justifying a reservation, the only rational and reasonable construction of the words are that it refers to a quantitative deficiency in the representation of the backward classes in the service taken as a whole and not to an adequate representation at each grade of service or in respect of each post in the service."[15]

Of course, what *Rangachari Case* did was that it paved way for reservation at promotional stage about which there had been difference of opinions among the High Courts. In ***Sukhanandan v. State of Bihar***[16] and ***P.K. More v. Union of India***[17], the Patna and the Bombay High Courts had ruled that the expression "matters relating to employment" used in Article 16(1) was wide enough to include within its scope not only initial appointments to any service but all other conditions related to employment. On the other hand, in ***Mohinder v. State of U.P.***[18] the Allahabad High Court had held that the expression 'matters relating to employment' was confined to initial appointment.

In ***R. N. Pramanick v. Union of India***[19] the Calcutta High Court interpreted Rangachari ruling in the context of its emphasis on the requirement of administrative efficiency in Article 335. It held that Article 16(4) must be read with Article 335, so that no reservation or special provision in favour of the members of SCs. can be carried to the extent of impairing 'the efficiency of administration'. The Court pointed out that the respondent did not violate the Constitution in providing that merit was to be the only consideration for promotion to the higher grade even though there was reservation for Scheduled Castes for recruitment to the lower post. Similarly, in ***Sudhakar v. State of Orissa***[20] the Orissa High Court ruled that in view of paramount importance of efficiency in administration despite reservation for SC., a SC. candidate found unfit for appointment cannot be appointed in the public service. This spirit may very well govern promotional case. Rangachari was approved and followed by the Supreme Court in ***State of Punjab v. Hiralal***[21]. The Court specifically ruled out the acceptance of the argument that the word 'posts' in Article 16(4) meant post filled by initial appointment and held 'posts' referred to selection posts. Though the policy of preferential promotion was not directly involved in ***State of Kerala v. N.M. Thomas***,[22] still it found some recognition by the Supreme court. The majority of Judges proceeded on consideration that in providing two additional chances of clearing qualifying tests did not involve reservation. However, one Judge readily thought it to had been involved. There are only two judgments referring to promotion. Conceding that promotion was not involved,[23] Ray, C.J. quoted Gajendragadkar, J.'s observation in Rangachari: "the power to make reservation, which is conferred on the State, under Article 16(4) can be exercised by the State in a proper case not only by providing for reservation of appointments but also by providing for reservation of selection posts". He also noted the necessity of reservation policy to be applied consistently with the requirement of administrative efficiency.[24] The other Judges except Beg, J. on the bench referred to Rangachari on the other points.[25] Beg, J. holding that promotion was involved, elaborately discussed the issue:

> "When citizens are already employed in a particular grade, as Government servants, considerations relating to the sources from which

they are drawn loose much of their importance. As public servants of that grade they could, quite reasonably and logically, be said to belong to one class, at least for purposes of promotion in public service for which there ought to be a real "equality of opportunity", if we are to avoid heart burning or a sense of injustice or frustration in this class. Neither as members of this single class nor for purposes of the equality of opportunity which is to be afforded to this class does the fact that some of them are also members of an economically and socially backward class continue to be material, or, strictly speaking even relevant. Their entry into the same relevant class as others must be deemed to indicate that they no longer suffer from the handicaps of a backward class. For purposes of Government service the source form which they are drawn should cease to matter. As Government servants they would, strictly speaking, form only one class for purposes of promotion."[26]

In ***Akhil Bharatiya Soshit Karamchari Sangh v. Union of India***,[27] the issue involved related also to reservations against non-selection posts. The exhaustive scheme of preferential treatment in favour of SCs and STs was launched by Railway Board in compliance of the directives of the Ministry of Home Affairs. In addition to raising percentage of reservation of directly recruited SCs and STs from 15 per cent to 22.5 per cent and in service training for them, an ambitious scheme of promotional reservation was announced:

1. Annexure 'F' provided for reservation for members of S.C. and S.T. only in 'selection posts' to be filled by promotion.
2. Annexure 'H' provided that in promotion by selection from Class-III to Class II, the eligible S.C. and S.T. candidates must be given one grading higher than the grading otherwise assignable to them on the basis of their record of service, i.e., if any S.C. and S.T. employee has been categorised by the Selection/Departmental Promotion Committee, on the basis of his record of service as 'good', he should be recategorised by the Committee as 'very good', and this recategorisation will then form the basis of allotment of marks in respect of 'Record of Service'. However, 25 per cent limit was fixed and posts involving safety were excluded from concessionary benefit.
3. Annexure 'K' the 15 per cent for S.Cs and 7½ per cent for S.Ts. quota were to be provided in promotion to the categories and posts in Classes I, II, III and IV filled on the basis of seniority-cum-

> suitability provided the element of direct recruitment to those grades, if any, did not exceed 50 per cent.

Since, it involved promotional reservation to both selection and non-selection posts, there was plea for the review of Rangachari. Obviously, the plea was based on very weak ground, as selection posts require more merits than the non-selection posts. Krishna Iyer, J. rightly pointed out that if promotional reservation could be held valid in Rangachari in relation to selection posts, there was no reason why such preferential treatment could not be held valid in relation to non-selection posts. The Court noted that:

> "Competitive skill is more relevant in higher posts, especially those where selection is made by competitive examinations. Lesser classes of posts, where promotion is secured mechanically by virtue of seniority, except where the candidate is unfit, do not require a high degree of skill as in the case of selection posts."[28]

> The learned Judge further noted:

> "It is obvious that as between selection and non-selection posts the role of merit is functionally more relevant in the former than in the latter". And if in Rangachari reservation has been held valid in the case of selection posts, such reservation in non-selection posts is a ***fortiorari*** case. If in selecting top officers you may reserve posts for S.Cs/S.Ts with lesser merit, how can you rationally argue that for the posts of peons or lower division clerks reservation will spell calamity ? The part that efficiency plays is far more in the case of higher posts than in the appointments to the lower posts."[29]

In Soshit Karamchari Sangh, the Court felt that competitive skill was more relevant in higher posts and promotional reservation was to put some setback to the legitimate expectations of majority of workers, still it preferred promotional reservation for S.Cs and S.Ts on the ground that, "the real power could be shared by the weakest section only if the doors of the higher decks were opened to them."[30] It was pointed out that:

> "Obviously Article 16(4) was not designed to get more Harijans into Government as scavengers and sweepers but as "Offices" and "bosses", so that administrative power may become the common property of the high or low, homogenised and integrated into one community.[31]

Had there been plea for review of *Rangachari Case* on the ground of the evaluation of promotional reservation in favour of S.C. and S.T. in light of Article 335 the argument would have been more weighty than on the ground of non-selection posts. But the result would have remained the same. The argument on the ground of inefficiency was declared as a 'riffle phoeny' because, "at the higher levels the Harijan/Girijan appointees are a microscopic percentage and even in the case of Classes III and II posts they are negligible."[32] Iyer, J. pointed out that: "Indeed, it will be gross exaggeration to visualise a collapse of the administration because 5 to 10 per cent of the total number of officials in the various classes happen to be substandard,"[33] and noted that "care has been taken to give in-service training and coaching to correct the deficiency."[34] In ***S.S. Sharma v. Union of India***[35] the Supreme Court has again reaffirmed the judicial verdict that Article 16(4) extends to reservation in the selection post. And, in ***Scheodhar Singh v. State of Bihar***[36], the Patna High Court allowed reservation for the Scheduled Castes to the cases of promotions both to the selection and non-selection posts even though the roster adopted resulted in a junior in lower cadre becoming senior in the higher cadre.

In ***Comptroller and Auditor General v. K.S. Jagannathan***[37] the Supreme Court ruled that-

> "It is now well settled by decisions of this court that the reservation in favour of backward classes of citizens, including the members of the Scheduled Castes and the Scheduled Tribes, as contemplated by Article 16(4) can be made not merely in respect of initial recruitment but also in respect of posts to which promotion are to be made."

Soon after the Union Government's decision to implement Mandal Report, the author made plea of a serious consideration on the review of Rangachari decision. Many grounds pleaded by author on principle have been accepted by Supreme Court (though there is no mention of his book on this point) in Mandal case, it would be most desirable to reproduce the points raised and discussed by the author in 1991 in his book, "Reservation Policy And Practice in India – A Means To An End" at pp. 181-84.

"***First***, the issue of reservation at promotional stage arose in Rangachari Case due to the retrospective operation of the scheme.

Second, on issue, whether the instructions issued in Board's letter contemplated reversion of already promoted to selection posts after January 4, 1957, to accommodate SCs and STs according to percentage basis, the respondent was assured before the High Court by the appellants during the proceedings that he need not have any apprehension of reversion as result of the implementation of the impugned circular and shortfall was to be made good against the existing as well as future vacancies.[38] Thus, there was no list at all and technically, decision is more or less ***obiterdicta***.

Third, in Rangachari, the majority confined itself to technical interpretation of the provisions of Article 16 and words like appointment and posts. It did not take the issue of balancing the two competing interests involved therein as it did in the subsequent year in Balaji. It is clear from the observation of majority in Rangachari which is demonstrative of the fact that Court was mainly concerned with issue of determining whether circulars were inside Article 16(4) or outside and it ruled that it was inside Article 16(4).[39] And that's all. Otherwise Gajendragadkar, J. speaking for majority had in mind that efficiency of administration is of paramount importance and it would be unwise and impermissible to make any reservation at the cost of efficiency of administration.[40] But he did not pursue the point. He noted 'reservation of appointments or posts may theoretically and conceivable mean some impairment of efficiency; but the risk involved in sacrificing efficiency of administration must always be borne in the mind when any State sets about making a provision for reservation of appointments or posts.[41] The dissenting Judge, Wanchoo, J. however, expressed his concern for the ill-effect which could ensue from reservations at promotional stage and exposed the double fold danger of such a policy. ***Firstly***, it was bound to impair and result in determination in the efficiency of administration[42], and ***Secondly***, it would make fundamental rights under Article 16(1) guaranteed to all the citizens [to which Article 16(4) is only an exception practically illusory.[43]

Fourth, the majority summarily disposed of the issue of the assessment of governmental policy vis-à-vis the requirement of efficient administration under Article 335. This attitude of the majority might have been due to the institutional deference which it had expressed in relation to the issue of retrospectively of governmental policy. The majority had conceded that giving retrospective effect to reservations might well cause heart-burning or dissatisfaction among the general class of employees and in that sense it would be an act of wisdom not to give effect to reservation affectively. But it expressed the view that, "with the propriety or wisdom of the policy underlying the circulars we are not directly concerned."[44]

Fifth, the ruling allowing reservation at promotional stage was by a very slender majority. In *Rangachari*, the decision was pronounced by 3: 2 majority. In *Thomas*, the only judge who addressed himself with the problem of promotion involved in the case was Beg, J. and his observations do not subscribe the view that there should be reservation at promotional stage. Again, in *Soshit Karamchari Sangh,* the majority decision is formed of two judges – Iyer and Chinnappa Reddy, JJ. And Pathak, J. contra. And there is much force in observation of Beg, J. in Thomas Case that in order to avoid heart-burning or sense of injustice or frustration there is need of a real equality of opportunity. There is serious need of the review of the issue afresh.

Sixth, there is vast difference between the initial appointment and promotional posts. First, in the case of initial appointment expectations are less clear. Reservation does not hit a vested interest. It only affects some future prospects. Reservation at promotional stage directly hits at vested interest, [45] frustrates reasonable expectations of those occupying certain posts for long. In hope of promotional avenues many people serve the institutions and not change trade. Further, the adjustment of mere opportunities for future benefits for the purpose of promoting employment equality may not have that adverse effect on individuals mind as the reallocation of vested rights.[46]

Seventh, reservation at promotional level is doubly dangerous to the efficiency of administration – the not so qualified person occupies a chair and finds himself incompetent to deal with matters and a more qualified person forced to work under reservational promotes gets frustration accelerated and stops taking interest in work. It is not based on impressionism but on the reality of offices works. In Gorakhpur, North Eastern Railway is the biggest employer. In some offices caste members having M.A., LL.B. degrees work as clerks or cashiers. On the other hand, an Intermediate or B.A. passed S.C. member appointed quite later jumps over their heads as O.S. or head cashier. The whole office roams on the road and on tea stall. If any body asks them about their duty, they vehemently retard: "What benefit do we have, if we perform our duties sincerely?" This generates a sense of reaction and resentment among government servants, epitomised in the mocking reference to the S.Cs. officers as a "son-in-law of the government" or a "Government Brahmin."[47]

Eighth, it gives birth to moral insensitivity. Seniority ensures many benefits and its denial may adversely affect the people. According to Carl Cohen:

> "Seniority entitlement are tied to individuals and competitive status. Seniority is, therefore, of great moral as well as practical importance and directly affects individual more importantly than it does the collective bargaining."[48]

Ninth, there should be limit of compassionate considerations and as Mr M.R. Yardi Study Group has pointed out, merit should be given top priority in the higher posts which require initiative, judgement and abilities and promotions should be made by selection of the best candidates.[49] Justice Iyer is right when he says that negligible percentage of S.C. and S.T. may not halt to efficient administration. But there is another aspect of the problem. They are scattered at different places. If a very junior member of the services is promoted not on account of merit but on account of his belonging to some depressed class, the whole office gets demoralised.

Lastly, there is sea of change in position of an unemployed depressed person striving for livelihood and survival and employed depressed person enjoying status with others. In the former compassion and sympathy may play sincere role. But in the latter they will have no place. Among equals law needs to be equal and be equally administered. A serious need of hour is to think over the matter whether a person who had been allowed the advantage of reservation once should be allowed to invoke the same again and again for furthering his future prospects and advancement. Compassion and right cannot go long way simultaneously. Promotional posts need be spared for right and deservedness. In one of extra-judicial pronouncements, one of the justices threw inspiring ideas on the issue: "...Backward people might continue to get weightage until they cross the first hurdle and thereafter they should have to compete with others. Even such weightage should not be perpetuated."[50]

The informative and reformative winds coming from American Supreme Court has reshaped our thinking on 'procedure established by law' in ***Maneka Gandhi v. Union of India***[51] and later prison reform and other cases. The same is needed in the area of protective discrimination heading towards reverse discrimination.[52] In America, judicial policy appears to be against quotas imposing promotion preferences.

Perhaps it is based on court's recognition of the potentiality of detestability under promotional preferential more than preferential treatment at the stage of entry. ***In Bridgeport Guardians Inc. v. Bridgeport Civil Service Commission***,[53] the court allowed preferential treatment at the stage of initial entry but disallowed preferential treatment at the promotional stage.

No doubt, preferential treatment is an inroad in the combined scheme of Articles 16(4) and 335. It is bound to cause imbalance in higher ranks as perpetuation of imbalance at the level of entry. In words of Khanna, J..

> "The ideals of supremacy of merit, the efficiency of services and the absence of discrimination in sphere of public employment would be

the obvious casualties if we once countenance inroads to be made into that valued principle beyond those warranted by clause (4) of Article 16."[54]

But these grounds go to the background in view of dominant caste preferences in promotions and inequality inpractice (it will be discussed in detail later).

6.1.1 Nine-Judge Bench took up the Issue for Final Verdict

The issue of reservation at promotional stage was raised before the Supreme Court in peculiar way. Kania, C.J. and Venkatachaliah and Jeevan Reddy, JJ. Conceded in Mandal Case that this question did not arise, as much as the impugned Memorandums did not provide for reservation in the matter of promotion.[55] So was the acceptance of Thommen J. in his concurring view on the point[56] and Sawant, J. in his concurring opinion that the question did not directly arise and therefore did not fall for consideration at all.[57] The leading majority (minus Ahmadi, J.) also accepted the well established principle of the constitutional law that constitutional questions should not be decided in vacuum and that they must be decided only if and when they arise properly on the pleadings of a given case and where it is found necessary to decide them for a proper decision of the case."[58] Sawant, J. went to the extent of issuing warning that any opinion expressed by the court on the said point would be obiter.[59] He also discussed the general principle: "it is well settled by the decisions of this Court that constitutional questions are decided only if they arise for determination on the facts and are absolutely necessary to be decided. The Court does not decide questions which do not arise. The tradition is both wise and advisable.[60] This is why A.M. Ahmadi, J. did not express any opinion on the point. Barring Ahmadi, J. all the other eight hon'ble judges expressed their views for one reason or the other. Sawant, J. was most reluctant. He said that "it is not necessary to answer the question since it does not arise in the present case." However, if it has to be answered, the answer is as follows. "The reservations in the promotions in the services are unconstitutional as they are inconsistent with the maintenance of efficiency of administration."[61] Thommen, J. thought it too vital an aspect of the concept of reservation under Article 16(4) to be overlooked and required to be dealt particularly in deference to the submissions at bar.[62] The leading majority remembered that reference to the larger Bench was made with a view to 'finally settle the legal position relating to reservations' and with a view to settle the law in an authoritative way majority was persuaded to express the opinion on the issue.[63]

6.1.2 Rangachari Departed but Major Premise Not Demolished

In the above background and reluctance the Supreme Court touched the issue and gave verdict against reservation at the stage of promotion. Kania C.J., Venkatachaliah and Jeevan Reddy judges drew the conclusion that reservation of appointments or posts under Article 16(4) is confined to initial appointment only and cannot extend to providing reservation in the matter of promotion.

The Court did not demolish the major premise of Rangachari Case.[64] It did not agree with the view in that case that Article 16(4) contemplates or permits reservation in promotions as well. But as to major premise it observed:

> "It is true that the expression "appointment" takes in appointment by direct recruitment, appointment by promotion and appointment by transfer. It may also be that Article 16(4) contemplates not merely quantitative but also qualitative support to backward class of citizens."[65]

Conceding it majority departed by putting emphasis on the answer of question not on reading of Article 16(4) alone but on a combined reading of Article 16(4) and Article 335. The majority in Mandal case was not agreeable to take any risk to efficiency of administration. The reasons preferred by Kania, C.J. and Venkatachaliah and Jeevan Reddy, JJ. Were as follow:

(1) While it is certainly just to say that a handicap should be given to backward class of citizens at the stage of initial appointment, it would be a serious and unacceptable inroad into rule of equality of opportunity to say that such a handicap should be provided at every stage of promotion throughout their career. That would mean creation of a permanent separate category apart from the mainstream a vertical division of the administrative apparatus.[66]

(2) It will encourage lack of initiative among reservationist and heart-burning among anti-reservationists. To quote the learned judges, "the members of the reserved categories need not have to compete with others but only among themselves. There will be no will to work, compete and excel among them. Whether they work or not, they tend to think, their promotion is assured. This in turn is bound to generate a feeling of despondence and 'heart-burning' among open competition members."[67] Consequently, efficiency of administration would be affected. In their view pulling the members of backward classes on a fast-tract would necessarily result in leap-fogging.[68]

(3) Efficiency of administration and larger interest of nation both require that crutches to backwards cannot be provided throughout one's career.

The learned judges were conscious of the charge of confining backward classes of citizens to the lowest cadres and clarified that they did not intend to do so. Because, "it is well-known that direct recruitments take place at several higher levels of administration and not merely at the level of Class IV and Class III. Direct recruitment is provided even at the level of All India Services. Direct recruitment is provided at the level of District Judge, to give an example nearer home."[69]

(4) Since there was no debate on the point in the Constituent Assembly and none referred to promotions; it does not appear to have been within their contemplation. Pandian, J. fully concurred with the conclusion of the majority that reservation is not permitted in matter of promotion among initial appointee. He cited with approval a three judge bench decision of the Supreme Court in ***Mohan Kumar Sinhania v. Union of India***[70] of which he had also been party of holding that reservation is referable only to initial appointment. Thommen, J. recorded the following reasons for depriving reservation at the stage of promotion.

(i) To be overlooked at the time of promotion in favour of a person who is junior in service and having no claim to superior merits is to cause frustration and passionate prejudice, hostility and ill-will not only in the mind of the overlooked candidate but also in the minds of the generality of employees. Any such discrimination is unfair and it causes dissatisfaction, indiscipline and inefficiency.[71]

(ii) Requirement of efficiency stated in Article 335 is an overriding mandate of the Constitution.[72]

(iii) With a view to ensure adequacy of representation of backward classes in services it is open to government to create sufficient number of posts for direct appointment.

(iv) Once appointed in service equality must be observed, any further discrimination is negation of equality, fairness and justice.[73]

Kuldip Singh, J. in his concurring decision disallowed reservation at the stage of promotion on ground of the nature of Article 16(4) which permits protective discrimination in favour of a class. He made it clear

"It is, therefore, mandatory that the opportunity to compete for the reserved posts has to be given to a class and not to the individuals. When Direct recruitment to a service is made the "backward class" as a whole is given an opportunity to be considered for the reserve posts. Every member of the said class has a right to compete. But that is not true of the process of promotion. Only the individuals are benefited."[74] Second, argument of Kuldip Singh, J. was based on difference between appointment and condition of service including promotion which is expected to be governed by Articles 16(1) and (2). Third reason given by the learned judge was based on equality after appointment. To quote him, "when two persons one belonging to the backward class and another to the general category enter the same service through their respective channels then they are brought at par in the cadre of the service. Both must be treated equally in the matters of employment after they have been recruited to the service.[75] Lastly, representation of backwards should be ensured by direct recruitment. Sawant, J. concurred on the ground of maintenance of efficiency of administration, lack of initiative among backwards and heart-burning and frustration among others.[76]

R. M. Sahai, J. concurred on two grounds: (i) after entry in service all become equal, and (ii) constitutional sanction requires class to be benefited whereas promotion involves individual to be benefited.

6.1.3 Short of Promotion Other Concessions Permissible

Kania, C.J., Venkatachaliah, Jeevan Reddy, Pandian, Thommen, Sawant and Sahai, JJ. All disallowed reservation at the stage of promotion. But, Kania, C.J. and Venkatachaliah, Jeevan Reddy, Thommen and Sawant, JJ. expressed the view that short of reservation other concessions may be conceded to backward classes at the level of promotion also. Kania, C.J. and Venkatachaliah and Jeevan Reddy, JJ. said:

> "It would not be impermissible for the state to extend concessions and relaxations to members of reserved categories in the matter of promotion without compromising efficiency of the administration. The relaxation concerned in Thomas and the concessions namely, carrying forward of vacancies and provisions for inservice coaching/training in Karamchari Sangh are instances of such concessions and relaxations."[77]

The Court however, cautioned: "it would not be permissible to prescribe lower qualifying marks or a lesser level of evaluation for the members of reserved categories since that would compromise efficiency of administration.[78]

Pandian, J. agreed to concession like relaxation of age etc.[79] Thommen, J. conceded short of reservation any affirmative action in favour of disadvantaged classes. Said, the learned judge, it is within the discretion of the State to extend to all disadvantaged groups including any backward class of candidates, preferences or concessions such as longer period of minimum time to pass qualifying tests etc.[80]

Sawant, J. conceded that backward classes may be provided with relaxations, exemptions, concessions and facilities etc. to enable them to compete for the promotional posts with others where the promotions are based on selection or merit-cum-seniority basis.[81]

6.1.4 A Critical Appraisal

The leading majority conceded ruling of *Rangachari* decision for more than 30 years but thought to depart from it on principle. However, it was not very much against reservational justice enabling switch over and issued a number of directions viz., (i) that the decision on the question shall operate prospectively, and shall not affect promotions already made, whether on temporary, officiating or regular/permanent basis, (ii) reservations already provided in promotions in Central services or State services or services under Corporations etc. shall continue for another 5 years, (iii) If any authority thinks that for ensuring adequate representation to 'backward classes of citizens' in any service, class or category, it is necessary to provide for direct recruitment therein, it shall be open to it to do so,

Table 6.1

Sl. No.	*Basis*	*Judges*	*No.*
1.	Violation of Equality	Kania, C.J., Venkatachaliah, Jeevan Reddy, Pandian, Sahai, Thommen and Kuldip Singh, JJ.	7
2.	Individualist nature in promotional benefit not warranted under Article 16(4)	Sahai and Kuldip Singh, JJ.	2
3.	Threat to efficiency of Administration	Sawant J., Thommen J., Kania, C.J., Venkatachaliah and Jeevan Reddy, JJ.	5
4.	Lack of initiative among BCs and heart-burning among others	Sawant, J. Thommen, J., Kania, C.J., Venkatachaliah, and Jeevan Reddy, JJ.	5
5.	Alternate of direct recruitment	Thommen and Kuldip Singh JJ.	2
6.	Promotion relates to condition of service and therefore not related to 16(4)	Kuldip Singh, J.	1
7.	Not in contemplation of the Constituent Assembly Members	Kania, C.J., Venkatachaliah and Jeevan Reddy, JJ.	3

(iv) government may grant relaxations short of reservation. Pandian, J. fully endorsed these views in his concurring judgement.[82]

On principle reservation at promotional level may not be permissible and that is reason why out of nine justices in *Mandal case* as many as eight judges contributed the above view. A summary of groundwise disapproval of reservation at promotion level may be presented as below:

But, keeping in view the Indian conditions some doubts may become obvious:

1. *Rangachari Case*'s basic premise that appointment includes different facets of employment including promotion and transfers etc. i.e. "in regard to employment, like other terms and conditions associated with and incidental to it, the promotion to a selection post is also included in the matters relating to employment and even in regard to such a promotion to a selection post all that Article 16(1) guarantees is equality of opportunity to all citizens who enter service"[83] has not been fully demolished but clarified by giving more and more emphasis on Article 335.

2. In *Rangachari* Case too Article 335 was given due credence. The learned judge, Gajendragadkar, J. who delivered the majority decision was conscious of the issue that advancement of the socially and educationally backward classes required not only, that they should have adequate representation in the lowest rung of services but that they should aspire to secure adequate representation in selection posts in the services as well.[84] In the context the expression 'adequately represented' imports considerations of size as well as values, numbers as well as the nature of appointments held and so it involves not merely the numerical test but also the qualitative one.[85] Rangachari decision itself conceded that "reservation of appointment or posts may theoretically and conceivable mean some impairment of efficiency; but the risk involved in sacrificing efficiency of administration must always be borne in mind when any state sets about making a provision for reservation of appointments or posts."[86]

In *Mandal* case the leading majority judgement found no justification to multiply the risk which would be the consequence of holding that reservation can be provided even in the matter of promotion. The clarification issued by the Court and its reiteration that "while it may be permissible to prescribed a reasonably lesser qualifying marks or evaluation for the OBCs, SCs and STs – consistent with the efficiency of administration and the nature of duties attaching to the office concerned –in the matter of direct recruitment, such a course would not be permissible in the matter of promotions" does not appear to be very much convincing. The court appears to be agreeable to ensure adequate representation in higher posts by creation of direct posts. It also recognises that direct recruitment inviting reservation includes highest services like I.A.S. If lowering of some qualification may be consistent with the mandate of Article 335 in initial appointment even to highest services how it will not be able to conform Article 335 if it is applied to the stage of promotion in rank lower than the highest service "If it may be consistent with Article 335 in the case of direct recruitment it may also be consistent in the case of promotion.

3. The analogy that Article 16(4) speaks of 'class' whereas promotion involves individual's benefit looses much of its force when we view the issue of individualisation of backwards for the purpose exclusion as creamy layer. If individual backwards may be deprived of benefit of reservation on account of certain economic upliftment why they may not be permitted to take benefit of reservation in promotions.

4. Promotion depends in part on favourable evaluation by superior officers who rate each subordinate in a 'Confidential Report' as outstanding, very good and good, etc.[87] It has widely been believed by Scheduled Castes employees that superior officers deliberately obstruct their promotion by giving them unfavourable rating.[88] The Report of Commissioner for S.Cs and S.Ts concurred that such reports are "generally biased."[89] The same may be true of O.B.Cs. As a matter of fact due to these reasons the government adopted different promotion schemes.[90] The class bias of upper caste officers may force even the ablest B.Cs. employees to suffer the loss of promotion. Perhaps this hard reality of service life was in the mind of Sawant, J. when talking of short of reservation concessions to backward classes he observed:

> "A provision can also be made to man the Selection Committees with suitable persons including those from the backward classes and to devise methods of assessment of merits on impartial basis. The Selection Committee should also ensure that the claims of the backward class employees are not superseded."[91]

The following sketch of the performance of reservations of government posts[92] may provide some light on the real issues –

(i) "Reservations succeed, where exhortation and goodwill do not, in getting members of the beneficiary groups into government service;

(ii) Generally reservations fall short of announced goals;

(iii) This is more so the higher the posts, except at the very peak;

(iv) Reservations are far fewer in number than the announced level conveys;

(v) Reservations tend to be clustered in certain services, departments and grades;

(vi) The process of achieving substantial representation is slower than indicated by the announced level and scope of reservation; and

(vii) Reservations are resented and resisted, resentment and resistance is more articulate and focused at the middle levels and at the promotion stage than the initial recruitment stage."[93]

5. Much will depend on preference of value in connection with Article 16(4). If it is to provide jobs to O.B.Cs., the judgment of S.C. is O.K. If value preference is ensuring adequate representation and sharing power of administration reservation at promotional stage is to be allowed because adequacy of representation of O.B.Cs. is to be ensured at all levels of services not the initial ones.

6. Status quoist approach of heart-burning, demoralisation are not well established and even if established they have to be discouraged because of upper caste mania and violent opposition against any fruitful measure of ensuring representation of backward classes.

7. Since the issue of reservation in promotion was not directly raised in Mandal case the observations of the Court may be treated as Obiter, instead of *ratio decidendi* of the case.

6.1.5 Legislative Attempt to Secure Reservation for SCs/STs at Promotion Level

The observation of the Supreme Court as to reservation in promotions was made in context of Article 16(4) read with Article 335 and therefore was intended to apply to all backward classes Including S.Cs/S.Ts. The Parliament was quick enough to enact the Constitution (Seventy-seventh, Amendment) Act, 1995 (assented on 17.6.1995). The object and Reason of the Amendment made clear, "since the representation of the Scheduled Castes and the Scheduled Tribes in services in the States have not reached the required level, it is necessary to continue the existing dispensation of providing reservation in promotion in the case of the Scheduled Castes and the Scheduled Tribes". In view of the Government commitment to protect the interest of the Scheduled Castes and the Scheduled Tribes, the continuing existing policy of reservation in promotion was to be ensured consequently Clause (4A) after Clause (4) of Article 16 which reads, *inter alia:*

"(4A) Nothing in this article shall prevent the State from making any provision for reservation in matters of promotion to any class or classes of posts in the services under the State in favour of the Scheduled Castes and the Scheduled Tribes which in the opinion of the State, are not adequately represented in the services in the State."

In view of the Judicial emphasis on 50 per cent limit of reservation, the Parliament passed the Constitution (81st Amendment) Act, 2000 to make unfilled posts category a distinct category unaffected by 50 per cent limit. It reads.

> [(4-B) Nothing in this article shall prevent the State from considering any unfilled vacancies of a year which are reserved for being filled up in that year in accordance with any provision for reservation made under clause (4) or clause (4-A) as a separate class of vacancies to be filled up in any succeeding year or years and such class of vacancies shall not be considered together with the vacancies of the year in which they are being filled up for determining the ceiling of fifty per cent reservation on total number of vacancies of that year.]

6.1.6 Judicial Interpretation

In ***Ashok Kumar Gupta v. State of U.P.***[94], a three judge bench of the Supreme Court consisting of K. Ramaswamy, S. Saghir Ahmad and G.B. Patnaik JJ. Unanimously upheld the reservation in promotion granted to SCs and STs in view of Article 16(4A). Speaking for the Court, Justice K. Ramaswamy made clear that Clause (4A) of Article 16 is a declaration of legislative policy.[95] Legislative policy is beyond the pale of assailment on the anvil of violation of the fundamental right. After *Mandal Case* Parliament has given effect to the legislative policy of reservation in promotion as a constitutional scheme. He observed that "Article 16(4-A) read with Articles 16(1) and (4) guarantees a right to promotion to Dalits and Tribes as fundamental right where they do not have adequate representation consistently with the efficiency in administration." He also pointed out that after overruling *Rangachari* case, prospectively, *Mandal Case* had provided 5 years continuance of reservation in promotion. In meantime Article 16(5-A) came into force from 17.6.1995. Therefore, the right to promotion continued as constitutionally guaranteed fundamental right.[96]

6.1.7 Judicial Jolt to Promotee SC/ST with Seniority- Catch up Rule[97]

In ***Union of India v. Virpal Singh Chauhan***[98] a division bench of S. C. Agrawal and B.P. Jeevan Reddy, JJ. ruled that while the reserved candidates are entitled to accelerated promotions, they would not be entitled to consequential seniority. The Court approved the government effort to deprive reserved category employees seniority consequent on promotion. It ruled, "it is open to the state, if it is so advised, to say that while the rule of reservation shall be applied and the roster followed in the matter of promotions or within a particular service, class or category, the candidate promoted earlier by virtue of reserved/ roster shall not be entitled to seniority over his senior in the feeder category and that as and when a general candidate who was senior to him in the feeder category is promoted, such general candidate will regain his seniority over the reserved candidate with withstanding that he is promoted subsequent to the reserved candidate."[99]

A three judge bench consisting of J. S. Verma, N.P. Singh and K. Venkataswami JJ. Reiterated the same view in Ajit Singh ***Januja v. State of Punjab***.[100] Speaking through N. P. Singh, the Apex Court ruled that by accelerated promotion reserved candidates did not supersede their seniors in the general category who were promoted subsequently.[101] The judicial pronouncements in *Virpal Chauhan* case and *Ajit Singh* case prompted to give effect by issuing the O.M. dated 30th January, 1997. It adversely affected the interests of the government servants belonging to SCs/ STs category in the matter of seniority on promotion to the next grade ***Ajit Singh II and Others v. State of Punjab***[102] consisting of Dr A.S. Anand C.J., and K. Venkataswami, G. B. Patnaik, S.P. Kurdukar and M. Jagannadha Rao JJ. reiterated *Virpal Singh* case and *Ajit Singh Case* rulings. Speaking through Jagannadha Rao J. the Supreme Court adhered "catch up" rule enunciated in earlier mentioned case and explained *Mandal* case II ruling as to balancing between different interests so as not to create reverse discrimination. It did not agree with statutory rule of seniority on the basis of "continuous officiation" on promotion. This ruling in *Ajit Singh* II Case gave a new interpretation to 5 years continuance of promotion since 16.11.1992 i.e. date of decision in Mandal case. Jagannadha Rao J. ruled that it is not permissible to accept the contention that Indra Sawhney permitted reservation in promotions for a further 5 years and that during that period Article 16 (4-A) was incorporated in Part III of the Constitution, and therefore, the concept of seniority attached to the roster promotion, as per certain ratings then in force, must be deemed to continue and deemed to be permissible in view of Article 16(4-A). The reason proffered was that Indra Sawhney did not have to go into issues relating to seniority and on the other hand it referred to the balancing Article 16(4) against the rights of the individual under Article 16(1). The logic of the Court was that Articles 16(4A) and 16(4) do not confer any fundamental right nor they create obligation on State enforceable in court of law. Ajit Singh II was decided on 16 September, 1999. The same bench on December 8, 1999 reiterated its earlier stand in ***Ajit Singh III v. State of Punjab***[103] and made clear that view reiterated in Ajit Singh II Case is unexceptional. Again the argument of enabling nature of Article 16(4) was pressed into.

Obviously, the line of argument in *Virpal Singh* case and *Ajit Singh* cases alongwith O.M. Dated 30th January, 1997 were bound to be commented upon and reacted by way of representation from S.Cs./ STs representatives including some of M.Ps. The Government decided to protect the interests of SCs/STs government servants. But mere withdrawal of O.M. was thought not to be enough and therefore, by the Constitution (85th Amendment) Act, 2001 Article 16(4A) was amended to ensure promotion of SCs/STs with consequential seniority. Section 2 of the Amendment Act, 2001 read, "In Article 16 of the Constitution in Clause (4A), for the words "in matters of promotion to any class", the words "in matters of promotion, with consequential seniority, to any class" shall be substituted.

Inspite of the above declared policy, a three judge bench consisting of V.N. Khare C.J. and S.B. Sinha and Dr A.R. Lakshmanan, JJ. ruled in ***Bimalesh Tanwar v. State of Haryana***[104] that an affirmative action in terms of Article 16(4) of the Constitution is meant for providing a representation to a class of citizenry who are socially or economically backward. Article 16 is applicable in the case of an appointment. It does not speak of fixation of seniority. Seniority is, thus, not to be fixed in terms of the roster. *Bimalesh Tanwar* case was decided on March 2003 and 85th Amendment had come in force since 17.6.1995. However, it was not considered in light of 85th Amendment Act, 201. The matter was directly raised in ***M. Nagraj v. Union of India***[105] wherein a Constitution bench upheld the constitutionality of Article 16(4A) as amended by 85th Amendment Act, 2001 and made clear that it was meant to abrogate the *Virpal Singh Chauhan* and *Ajit Singh* Cases.

Though Nagraj accepted that the 85th Amendment Act, 2001 had abrogated Chauhan and Ajit Singh Cases[106] it proceeded on preoccupied notion that there is no right of reservation, nor corresponding duty / obligation on part of State to give effect to reservation. It allowed qualified application of reservation. Thus, if the government with to exercise its discretion and make provision for reservation–

(i) the state has to collect quantifiable data showing backwardness of the class;

(ii) inadequacy of representation of that class in public employment in addition to compliance with Article 335.

(iii) Even if the State has compelling reasons, as state above, the State will have to see that its reservation procession does not lead to (a) excessiveness as to breach the ceiling limit of 50 per cent or (b) obliterate the layer; or (c) extend the reservation indefinitely.

This observation encourages qualified use of reservation in favour of SCs/STs. Though, in later cases like ***Ashok Kumar Thakur v. Union of India***[107] and others it has been held, rather reiterated that creamy layer rule does not apply to SCs/STs and 50 per cent limit is subject to Clause (4B) of Article 16, yet the Courts have given due credence to *Nagraj* ruling[108] and have invalidated reservation for SCs and STs in a number of cases. Thus, in ***Suraj Bhan Meena v. State of Rajasthan***[109], a division bench of the Supreme Court consisting of Altmas Kabir and A.K. Patnaik JJ. disallowed promotion of two government servant *Surajbhan Meena* (ST) and *Sriram Choradia* (S.C.) with consequential seniority on the plea that before doing that no exercise was undertaken in terms of Article 16(4-A) to acquire quantifiable data regarding the inadequacy of representation of the Scheduled Caste and Scheduled Tribe communities in public services. Again the argument proceeded on non-mandatoriness of Article 16(4.A) and (4.B). Speaking through Altmas Kabir J. the apex Court conditionalised the application these provisions. Putting interpretation on Nagraj ruling the learned judge observed:

> "In effect, what has been decided in *M. Nagraj* Case is part recognition of the views expressed in *Virpal Chauhan* Case but at the same time upholding the validity of the Seventy-seventh, Eighty-First, Eighty-second and Eighty-Fifth Amendments on the ground that the concept of 'catch-up' rule and "consequential seniority" are judicially evolved concepts and could not be elevated to the status of a constitutional principle so as to place them beyond the amending power of Parliament. Accordingly, while upholding the validity of the said amendments, the constitution bench added that, in any event, the requirement of Articles 16(4-A) and (4-B) would have to be maintained and that in order to provide for reservation, if at all, tests indicated in Articles 16(4-A) and (4-B) would have to be satisfied, which could only be achieved after an inquiry as to identity."[110]

The Court concluded that "the position of M. Nagraj Case is that reservation of posts in promotion is dependent on the inadequacy of representation of members of the Scheduled Castes and Scheduled Tribes and Backward Classes and subject to the condition of ascertaining as to whether such reservation was at all required."[111] Again, in

U.P. Power Corporation Ltd. v. Rajaesh Kumar,[112] a two judge bench consisting of Dr Dalveer Bhandari and Dipak Mishra, JJ. Speaking through Dipak Mishra, J. the court emphasised the non-mandatory nature of Articles 16(4-A) and (4-B) with certain qualifiers by taking recourse to the process of interpretation."[113] According to the learned Judge M. Nagraj Case[114] requirement of quantifiable data justifying reservation in terms of parameter of efficiency, backwardness and inadequacy of representation is a categorical imperative each time such reservation is sought to be imposed. To him "concepts of catch-up rule and consequential seniority are judicially evolved concepts to control the extent in reservation and the creation of this concept is relatable to service jurisprudence."[115] The *Nagraj Case* precondition of reservation was reiterated by Altmas Kabir J. in ***Salauddin Ahmed v. Samta Andolan***.[116] The Court ruled that since Article 16(4-A) was enabling and State was not bound to make reservation in promotion for SCs and STs; the same could be done only after compliance with mandatory precondition.

Not only precondition laid down in *Nagraj Case* has been emphasised before promotion scheme is applied, was pressed by division bench of the Supreme Court in Anil Chandra v. Radha Krishna Gaur but it was made clear that 'adequate representation does not mean proportional representation.'[117]

6.1.7.1 Judicial Jolt in Favour of SCs/STs Promotion Due to Enabling Nature of the Scheme

On 11.3.2016, a division bench of Dipak Mishra and Prafulla C. Pant JJ reiterated the enabling nature of Articles 16 (4-A) and 16 (4-B) of the Constitution, the Court declared judicial hands of in the matter of issuing order against the government to provide reservation to SCs and STs in promotion. It was ruled that the government has discretionary powers to frame laws for reservation in promotion and it cannot be forced to bring any regulation on the issue. The court ruled that, "The State is not bound to make reservations for SCs and STs in matter of promotions. Therefore, there is no duty. In such a situation, to issue mandamous to collect data would tantamount to asking the authorities whether here is ample data to frame the rule or regulation. This will be a way entering into the domain of legislation."[118] The Supreme Court rejected PIL to direct U.P. Government to grant reservation to SCs and STs in services. Such issue was treated as policy matter. The Court ruled;

"The Courts do not formulate any policy, remains away from making anything that would amount to legislation, rules, regulations or policy relating to reservation. The Courts can lest the validity of the same when they are challenged. The Court cannot direct for making legislation or for that matter any kind of subordinate legislation."[119]

6.2 Jolt to SCs/STs in Appointments to the State Services Due to Interpretation of Article 335

The claims of the members of the SCs and STs was to be taken into consideration consistently with the maintenance of efficiency of administration, in making the appointments to services in the posts in connection with the affairs of the Union and of a State. Reading Article 16 (4) and Article 335 some of the decisions of the Supreme Court created some problems. SCs and STs had been enjoying, in spite of Article 335/ in consonance with Article 335, the facility of relaxation of qualifying marks and standards of evaluation in matters of reservation in promotion on the basis of Government order dated 22.1.1997. The Supreme Court judgement in *S Vinod Kumar* v. *Union of India*[120] held that such relaxation in matters of reservation in promotions were not permissible under Article 16(4) in view of the command contending Article 335 of the Constitution. The Supreme Court also held that the law on subject of relaxation of qualifying marks and standards of evaluation in matters of reservation in promotion is led down by the nine judge Constitution Bench Judgement in the case of *Indra Sawhney* v. *Union of India* (Mandal Case)[121] vide para 831 of the judgement also held that such relaxation has been not permissible under Article 16(4) in view of the command contending in Article 335 of the Constitution. It is humbly submitted that Mandal case strictly related and was confined to SEBCs not SCs/STs still with a view to implement the S Vinod Kumar's judgement the Government withdrew the relaxation with effect from 22.7.1997. The withdrawal of relaxation had adverse effect on the interest of SCs and STs. It prompted representation to the Government from different quarters including members of Parliament. In view of such representation the Government of India decided to review the earlier withdrawal order and to restore the relaxations. As a consequence the Constitution (82nd Amendment) Act, 2000 was enacted. It added Proviso to Article 335 which reads "Provided that nothing in this Article shall prevent in making any provision in favour of the members of Scheduled Castes and Scheduled Tribes for relaxation in qualifying marks in any examination are lowering the standard of evaluation for reservation in matters of promotion to any class or classes of services or posts in connection with the affairs of the Union or of a State."

The Supreme Court upheld the constitutionality of this amendment in M Nagraj v. Union of India[122] and declared that the Vinod Kumar's case was legislatively superseded by the 82nd Amendment Act. But it also provided that the question as to how and in what manner the State as also the Public Service Commission would comply with the Constitutional requirement of Article 335 should not ordinarily be allowed to raised. It was made clear that lowering of marks for the candidates belonging to the reserved categories is not a constitutional mandate. At threshold and the proviso is applicable only for purpose of promotion. The Supreme Court also pointed out that even after the insertion of the proviso, the limitation of overall efficiency in Article 335 is not obliterated. It is for the State concerned to decide in a particular case whether over all efficiency of the system is affected by relaxation under proviso to Article 335. It also may clear that if the relaxation is so excessive that it ceases to be a qualifying mark then certainly the State is free not to allow relaxation. Before exercising power under proviso to Article 335 the state has to ensured. The compelling interest of backwardness, (2). Inadequacy of representation in the service and permitting such exercise only after identified by weighty and comparable data.

The decisions of the Supreme Court in post-2000 amendment period in one way or the other have not been very much encouraging and in the interest of the Scheduled Castes and Scheduled Tribes. In *Ashutosh Gupta v. State of Rajasthan*[123] the Supreme Court reiterated that-

> "Article 335 stipulates that the claim of the members of the Scheduled Castes and Scheduled Tribes shall be taken into consideration, consistent with the maintenance of efficiency of administration in the making of appointments to services and posts in connection with the affairs of the Union or of the State. It is thus apparent that even in the matter of reservation in favour of Scheduled Castes and Scheduled Tribes, the Founding fathers of the Constitution did make a provision relating to maintenance of efficiency of administration. In this view of the matter, if any statutory provision provides for recruitment of a candidate without bearing in mind the maintenance of efficiency of administration, such a provision cannot be sustained being against the Constitutional mandate."[124]

There also appears the change in emphasis of the Supreme Court between the pre-2000 amendment and post-amendment in *State of Kerala* v. *NM Thomas*[125], the seven judge bench had held that efficiency of administration may not require a high degree of qualification but minimum which is necessary to maintain administrative efficiency but in *State of UP* v. *Dr K U Ansari*[126] the Supreme Court reiterated that the expression efficiency includes all relevant matters necessary for discharging one's duties efficiently and satisfactorily. *Again in Anil Chandra* v. *Radha Krishnan Gaur*[127] the Supreme Court reiterated the essentiality of compelling reasons namely backwardness, inadequacy of representation and over all administrative efficiency to be essential requirement without which the structure of equality of opportunity under Article 16 will collapse. In a nutshell, the judicial approach has not been in response to the desired objective of the Parliament intended through adding proviso to Article 335 so as to benefit the Scheduled Castes and Scheduled Tribes promotees in services under the State.

6.3 Should Reservation for S.Cs/ S.Ts be ended?

In the above backdrop, time and again, voice is raised as to doing away with reservation itself. There are writers who argue that it is not intended to continue indefinitely. Dr D.D. Basu, the most voluminous writer on the Constitutional law[128] views that, "reservation can never be a substitute for the uplift of the weaker sections on the social and economic plane. Reservation was meaningful at the commencement of the Constitution as a temporary measure, at a time when the State was required and expected to promote with special care, the education and economic interests of the weaker sections of the people, and in particular the Scheduled Castes and Scheduled Tribes." He cites senior advocate P.P. Rao's article[129] and extract of passage from Justice Rangarajan's books[130] to establish that reservation was intended to be temporary phase measure and ultimately creates an atmosphere of discontent and frustration. He also cites[131] some writers to support time bound reservation. The matter is very serious.

The objectors are sometimes very crude. Sometimes very harsh and provoking. Some reactionary assessments are presented here. V. T. Rajshekhar Shetty presented very bad effect of Reservation to the humiliation of SCs/ STs but unwittingly undeserved reactions met by them, that is to say–

1. Constitutional reservations have reduced the mass of untouchables into beggars endlessly begging for the caste-Hindu crumbs of bread thrown at their whims and fancies,
2. The majority of caste Hindu grow increasingly jealous and curse the recipients "Government Brahmins" and the alleged rising number of atrocities against Harijans is an offshoot of this upper caste jealousy and prejudice against reservations;
3. Except producing some elite among Dalits, the system has done the greatest disservice to the Dalits as a whole."[132] Few view that reservation further stigmise and discredit Dalits. The upper caste

> employees treat them as trespasser coming into services at the expense of really deserving hands and recruited on the basis of 'birth' and not 'worth'. They are harshly treated by bosses. Some view that "educated untouchables are taunted and slighted and constantly reminded of the unfairness of their treatment. Thus, the negative viewer do not find any merit in reservational policy in favour of SCs/STs. They view negative impact of killing their initiative, drive and capacity[133] and argue that facilities and concessions make them idle and retard their initiative for hard labour because of which they are lagging behind."[134]

Be the sympathetic viewer of the constitutional scheme, be the reactionary evaluator, both have common design. The farmer view that since the commencement of the Constitution (26.1.1950) enough time has been given to SCs/STs to enjoy the fruit of constitutional policy of amelioration of their condition and end deprivation, the latter view cunningly negative impact, as if the scheme of reservation was exercise in futility by the framer of the Constitution. Their common design is to suggest the end of reservation policy in favour of such classes.

6.4 Has the Persecution of SCs/STs Ended

Any opposition to reservation in favour of S.Cs. and S.Ts. has to answer the serious questions. **First**, have the social disabilities of the Scheduled Castes and Scheduled Tribes on the basis of which reservation benefit was conceded to them been removed and are they allowed the equality in fact ?

The answer is obviously negative. As late as September 29, 1988, the Division Bench of Rajasthan High Court was to pronounce upon the legality of the practice of purification of Harijans by 'Gangajal' and 'Tulsidal' prior to entry in temple of 'Shri Shrinath ji' near Udaipur. J.S. Verma J. exposed the problem.

> "It is tragic that on the eve of Gandhi Jayanti we are debating a Harijans' right to enter a public temple for worship as an equal; and directions of the court be needed for enforcement of this right to equality. All men are born equal and the classification between them thereafter is man-made and artificial against the divine dictate. To present them as unequal before God is, therefore, injustice and insult to our Maker beside being contrary to the guarantee and mandate of equality in our Constitution and a basic human right. To name them 'Harijans' and then discriminate them for entry into a public temple to worship 'Hari' is not merely violation of a constitutional guarantee or insult to them

but sheer hypocrisy and insult to 'Hari' rendering their name a misnomer".

Even by 2015 there is no improvement. Schools are still discriminatory experimentations. Education is gateway in walks of life. But what psycho effect will it have if dalit children are discriminated on ground that they are Dalits ? the Indian Express visited schools across the country where lessons in caste difference start early. During the first and second weaks of November, 2015 the Indian express published a series of News item under caption, " Keeping Dalits Out – Caste in Class Room". It revealed startling facts even after the 68 years of the independence–

- Caste on Writ - green for Dalits, red for Thevars.[135]
- Caste in the Cradle: separate Aganwadis are for Dalit Children.[136]
- Since appointment of Dalit cook to prepare Mid day meal out of 118 students 100 students left Kagganahalli school in Kolar, Kernataka[137]
- Students of Rajikiya Ucch Madhyamik Vidyalaya in Benada village in Jaipur have often been threatened, "Sweep the the Floor or we'll give you a TC (Transfer Certificate)." Dalit students are forced to clean floor twice a day. They are not given marks easily.[138]
- In Vande Matram High School in Andara Gram Panchayat of coastal Kendrapara class X Dalit students decided to offer to scrape the tender coconut for Ganesh Puja and for this 21 students belonging to Dalit community were insulted faced casteist slurs, were barred from offering prayers, and kept locked in the school for five hours.[139]

Editorial of the Indian Express dated 12.11.2015 very aptly concludes after exposure of the earlier incidents of discrimination in the seat of learning, "Article 15 of the Constitution bars discrimination on the basis of caste and laws are in place to penalise it. If it still persists – and it does – that is due to lack of institutional vigilance and intervention."[140] No change of heart has taken place and the hope of the framers has gone frustrated. The seat of learning, teaching the first lesson of citizenship, are not exceptions but representative of the wider malaise.[141]

The disability attached to the depressed class persists and abolition of untouchability, declaration of its practice a criminal act and all such assurances to the depressed people appear to remain paper assurance unable to prohibit caste disability perpetuation in reality. And to an angry

Dalit Poet Yashwant Manohar God is helpless to answer his questions: Tell me truth: Did you create the earth ? Did you create Varna, Jati and Karma theory ? Put your hand on this revolutionary, Gita and tell me the truth". The God has nothing to say but to express his sorrowfulness that "They (caste people) created me for their selfish ends and made me speak what they wanted". Nathwara Temple incident is nothing but expression of this vested interest notion. Disability of S.Cs. has not gone, it is not likely to go unless the gap between the example and precept is filled in. It can be furnished only with Gandhian mission and Warrens spirit. We all know Gandhian way of assimilation and living with Harijans. So was feeling touch of Warren C.J., the declarer of the principle that "Separate can never be equal" in ***Brown v. Board of Education***.[142] On the first day asked about evening Chief Justice Warren by a businessman, "How do you like the new Chief-Justice", the Negro attendant's reply was, "in all the years I've been here, it is the first time, I have been treated like man". Have we been successful in inspiring such a feeling among our untouchable and depressed brethren ? It will not be out of place to tell the story of Pandit Govind Malviya, son of Mahamana Madan Mohan Malaviya and a former Vice-Chancellor of the Banaras Hindu University, who was seriously canvassing for a berth in Rajya Sabha before Shriman Narayan, General Secretary, A.I.C.C. In reply to the query of the letter that "there are charges that you still observe untouchability and are not prepared to take food along with Harijans" his explanation was that he was keen only observing hygienic rules strictly and did not believe in untouchability. When the matter was referred to Jagjivan Ram, Chairman of Disciplinary Action Committee of Congress at that time his prompt suggestion was: "Ask Malviyaji to dine with me today at my residence. You can also come with him". On communication of this suggestion Malviyaji disappeared from the residence of Shriman Narayan. This is the story of a staunch traditional Brahmin who did have genuine faith in such practices. There are still worse stories. Some caste Hindu perform the drama of drinking water from the hands of Harijans at the time of election without having any intention to mingle with them and they again practice untouchability after the election fever is gone.[143] Second, have the incidents of atrocities of Harijans and other Scheduled castes minimised in post independence era ? Have the benefits of reservations gone to those who were still at 'the rock-bottom levels of poverty' or 'poorest of the poor'? The answer is negative. In Andhra, despite the prohibition of untouchability on paper Harijans were neither allowed to draw water from public wells or enter temples nor could occupy the House sites allotted to them because landlords would not allow to occupy the plots. In one instance: a landlord hanged his Harijan servant in public for the alleged theft of a writ watch. In 1979, 213 cases of atrocities on Harijans were registered in Andhra Pradesh. On April 17, 1977 in reaction to the complaint of assault on a Harijan ryots imposed social boycott of the entire Harijan community in the village Muppala in Krishna district and they were prevented from drawing water from the village well and were denied employment. The massacre of Belchi village Harijans in Bihar on May 27, 1977 speaks of the ugly dance of caste hatred. On June 28, 1977, three Harijans of Salagre village in Maharashtra were mercilessly beaten up by police and one of them died whose dead body was thrown in a well nearby. The Belchi episode of mass killing of Harijans was again repeated in Pipara village of Bihar. Atrocities on Harijan are such that they know bounds and no occasions. Even during elections either Harijans are not allowed to caste their votes freely or if they try to cast their votes according to their choice they have to face consequences. During Ninth Lok Sabha Elections in 1990 victims of atrocities in Vaishali were mostly the Harijans. The death of Chandrika Mahato in firing a polling booth is a big question on our democracy. As early as 1976, Mr Justice Krishna Iyer, the Judge Supreme Court of India was provoked to say:

> "The Scheduled Castes and Scheduled Tribes are historically humble humans, and even currently, according to report of Parliament, horrid crimes are perpetrated on Harijans. And, men alienated and embittered for ages but no militantly aware, are an over-powering. They will breakout social barricades and then the barrels of guns cannot quell."

But the situation has not improved. Despite Untouchability Abolition Act and now Civil Rights Act atrocities on Harijan has not minimised. A very vivid picture has been presented by Dr Upendra Baxi in the following words:

> "Violence against untouchables, who constitute 15 per cent of Indian population, not on increase not just in levels of brutality. The period 1973 to 1978 according to one estimate, witnessed 62,295 violent incidents commonly called 'atrocities', against untouchables life and property. In 1977-78, 12,746 atrocities were registered involving 354 killings and 306 registered cases of rape. The very names – Kilvennmari, Belchi, Dharampur, Villipuram, Pantnagar, Mahathwada, Pipara – evoke a cluster of images of inhuman violence: huts set ablaze, people tied to trees and burned alive, people shot and point blank range or hacked to pieces, women raped and brutally killed, children bayoneted or burned alive. The gruesome story of genocidal violence against untouchables is not yet fully told. But what we know is already enough to strip away every pretence to tolerance and no violence from

the face of India and to reveal instead, a brutalised and brutalising society."

In most cases of atrocities on Harijans governmental machinery remains callous and maintains extreme indifference. As a matter of fact violence involving untouchables is direct attack on the authority of the State itself, but the government officials do not take in that challenging tone.

On February 13, 1990, the President of Akhil Bharatiya Bandhua Mazdoor Mukti Sangh met the Union Home Minister Mufti Mohammed Syeid and Union Labour Minister Ram Vilas Paswan to narrate the sufferings and constant threat to the lives of 60 Harijan labourers including women and children at the Nalagarh brick kilns in Solan, Himachal Pradesh. His version was that Harijan workers were denied wages, were given food only once a day by their employers and women including minors were being raped and men were beaten up at will. Between 1981 and 1986, 1,15,055 cases of atrocities on Harijans were registered and during 1989, 14,269 cases have been registered.

Barring a few instances of reservation riots in cities, violence against Harijans has been in rural areas resulting from its start in Godavari-Tungabhadra delta, Thanja, Vur Bihar and Punjab in form of untouchable resistance and consequent repression into the wide spread areas. To quote P. Seth, "the current conflicts... are neither local in implication nor sectional in interest, nor short-lived and transient", but they have:

> "remained confined neither to States which are supposed to have worked out in various crises of modernisation (Maharashtra) or those with strongholds of conservatism or backwardness (U.P., Bihar and M.P.) nor to the states where social reform movement favouring the backward castes had already occurred (Maharashtra, Tamil Nadu)".

The untouchables are vulnerable to repression not only from upper peasantry but also from the socially backward but 'economically aspiring and politically ascendants castes of lower peasantry' who in late seventies turned toward untouchables with ruthless "aggressiveness and ferocity".

The different studies conducted on Abolition of Untouchability and Untouchability Offences Act, 1955 and since 1976 Protection of Civil Rights Act, 1976, end with dissatisfactory note on effectiveness of the Act. The following Table 6 will show cases under PCRA, disposed off or pending.

The conviction rate under PCRA is considerably low than the conviction under the earlier Act. Marc Galanter expressed his puzzle on fact PCRA though more "comprehensive and apparently stronger Act was less used and led to inferior results". The puzzle of Marc Galanter is justified in the view of the outcome of cases falling under UDA between 1955 and 1976 and outcome of cases falling under PCRA. Table 6 has shown post PCRA position and the following Table 7 will show pre-PCRA position.

A comparative study of the two just succeeding Tables 7 and 8 show that under UOA the average conviction rate between 1955 and 1976 was 32.60 whereas under PCRA, it has fallen considerably low to 7.85. On the other hand, during 1955-76 acquittal rate was 17.35 whereas during 1977-82 it has gone upto 26.10. The tremendous downfall in the rate of conviction may be lamented as unsuccessfulness of PCRA to give justice expeditiously and not to allow the accused unpunished. A number of reasons may be attributed. ***First***, the officials – police and magistrates, on whose initiative anti-disabilities prosecution depend, have sympathetic attitude towards local dominant elements. Marc Galanter refers to one Untouchable Ph.D. succinctly putting "law means police and police means higher caste people." ***Second***, in most of the cases police are not aware of PCRA. ***Third***, the most of complaints end with compromise due to career pressure. Fourth, complainants and the witnesses, which are required to prove the cases are extremely vulnerable to intimidation and reprisals. The possibility of misuse of PCRA also cannot be ruled out altogether. The increase in acquittal rate in post-1976 period may give impression that the false complaints might have been engineered and PCRA might have been used for the end of victimisation of some caste people either by the S.Cs. themselves or on behalf of some dominant people. However, the study of atrocities on Harijans reveals that they are still vulnerable to repression and maltreatment.

The lower economic position remains to be curse for them. And, despite the different plan schemes economic inequalities have increased.

In 1976 UAO Act was renamed as PCRA (Protection of Civil Rights Act, 1955) but the fate of the poor implementations of this Act as well as SCs and STs (Prevention of Atrocities) Act, 1989 has not improved. Social status, money and muscle powers are the main reason for non-effective implementation of such laws. A very informative and realistic study has been conducted by A. Ramaiah of the views of different actors in Scheduled Castes and Scheduled Tribes atrocities.[141]

To cite a few examples views of one dominant caste (Thevar), common man. Speaking of untouchability in spite of the Constitution and different laws he talked of the general perception, "Eagle is always eagle and crow is always crow. These two cannot be equals. Can Tiger and Cat be equals?

Table 6.2: Table showing the Number and Percentage of Cases Disposed off by the Court and Pending Trial from 1977 to 1982

Sl. No.	*Years*	*Fresh cases challenged*	*Previous cases brought forward*	*Fresh plus prev. cases*	*Convicted*	*Percentage*	*Acquitted*	*Percentage*	*Pending*	*Percentage*
1.	1977	2,920	2,273	5,193	551	10.61	1,463	28.17	3,179	61.21
2.	1978	3,751	3,953	7,704	490	6.36	2,002	25.98	5,212	67.65
3.	1979	3,444	4,803	8,247	613	7.43	2,062	25	5,572	67.56
4.	1980	3,550	5,579	9,129	1,267	13.87	2,866	31.39	4,996	54.72
5.	1981	2,865	4,995	7,860	441	5.61	2,085	26.52	5,334	67.86
6.	1982	2,665	4,547	7,212	199	2.75	1,633	22.65	5,380	74.59
		19,195	26,150	45,345 7,557	3,561 593	7.85	1211 2,018	26.7	29,673 4,945	65.43

Table 6.3: Table showing Cases Pending and disposed under UOA, 1955 (1955-76)

Sr. No.	Years	Challaned	Convicted	Percentage	Acquitted	Percentage	Compounded	Percentage	Pending	Percentage
1.	1955	180	80	44.44	12	6.66	12	6.66	76	41.22
2.	1956	599	149	24.87	106	17.69	156	26.04	188	31.38
3.	1957	414	87	21.01	34	8.21	86	20.77	207	50
4.	1958	482	56	11.61	43	8.92	65	13.48	318	65.97
5.	1959	401	105	26.18	70	17.45	82	20.44	144	35.91
6.	1960	240	57	15.41	39	16.25	74	30.83	90	37.5
7.	1961	438	107	24.42	141	32.19	138	31.5	52	11.87
8.	1962	338	77	22.78	91	76.92	81	23.96	89	26.33
9.	1963	3[illegible]4	77	24.78	47	14.96	80	24.47	110	35.03
10.	1964	336	157	46.72	53	15.77	50	14.88	76	22.61
11.	1965	321	136	42.36	52	16.19	46	14.33	87	27.1
12.	1966	447	199	44.51	89	19.91	85	19.01	76	77
13.	1967	313	135	43.45	56	17.89	56	17.89	85	27.15
14.	1968	184	35	19.02	39	21.19	53	28.8	84	45.65
15.	1969	272	48	17.04	25	9.19	71	26.1	128	47.05
16.	1970	29[illegible]	50	17.18	59	20.27	107	36.76	75	25.77
17.	1971	439	91	20.72	96	21.88	138	31.43	114	25.96
18.	1972	1,416	631	44.54	253	17.86	233	16.45	299	21.11
19.	1973	2,356	1,207	51.23	312	13.25	388	32.14	449	19.05
20.	1974	1,588	669	42.12	247	15.55	288	18.13	384	24.18
21.	1975	2,588	936	36.16	480	18.52	611	23.6	561	21.67
22.	1976	4,427	925	20.89	867	19.58	341	7.7	2,564	57.01
		18,384	5,995	32.6	3,191	17.35	5,241	17.62	6,256	34.02
Average Per Year		835	272		145		147		284	

These people (SCs) simply make noise in the crowd. Can they come to our village with slippers? Can they first of all sit and have tea in our tea stalls? Can they first of all have tea in our village? Can they have tea in glass instead of **chateau** (coconut shell). If our people come to know that you are a Dalit SC person, your pant and shirt will be removed: they will beat you, abuse you saying......What can you do? What case? Let them give the case to the police. We will give Rupees 500 to the police and case will be withdrawn."[145] Even in case of rape followed by murder the relations of the deceased dare not to be witness. Police did not arrest culprits and demanded money to pursue the case. Witnesses are not to do anything in view of threatening from caste Hindus. In one case, the accused said, "They (Dalits) cannot do anything because the caste Hindus are together. We resolve our problem with the help of police. All money: everything is money, we have so much money because we are together. They have no money what case that we have not seen. The policemen are with us and so we have no problem."[146] One advocate associated with such case said, "the police officials in charge of implementing PCR and POA Acts, have made these laws as means of generating additional income for themselves. Whenever the victims goes to the police station, the police collect around Rupees 1000 from victim to file a case. Later they collect around Rupees 5000 from the accused to do the needful to acquit the case or for a compromise..... The police misuse the law, but they will say that the Dalit misuse the law. This is totally untrue."[147] NGO's researcher talked of Court, "The Court is not free from caste prejudice. The Magistrate seems to be more concerned with the accused rather than the victims."[148] The witness's statement is twisted. Typist does all this in knowledge of the judge. The conclusion of N.G.O. was that, "the biased attitude of the judges towards SCs is one of the few important reasons for the most PCR/POA cases ending in acquittal. Special Public Prosecutors have their own problems- cases not registered in proper sections; witnesses afraid of dire consequences; many duties burden; charge of many districts but no office or assistant.[149]

6.5 Position of SCs/STs in Government Services

Has the reservational benefit given to the members of Scheduled Castes and Scheduled Tribes in the State and Union services served any significant purpose in increasing the representation of such classes in services? Have the Scheduled Castes and the Scheduled Tribes secured due representation in University service and academic pursuits?

The answer of such questions would be negative. A former Minister, B.S. Murthy has given sombre picture of actual plights of Harijans. The figure presented by him, as on January 1, 1970 indicated that after the twenty years of reservational policy the percentage of Scheduled Castes and Scheduled Tribes was very meagre, i.e., in Class I, 0.40 per cent, in Class II, 1.47 per cent and in Class III and IV, 3.41 as against 22.5 per cent population of such classes. Iyer J. was prompt to comment on this unsatisfactory situation that "This was socio-economic democracy in reverse gear and a callous picture of under-representation in administration as if harijans and girijans were still untouchable and unapproachable, vis-à-vis services under the State".

The following Tables 6.4 and 6.5 show the position of S.Cs. and S.Ts. in different services in India and abroad.

Table 6.4: Table showing Percentage of Reservations in Favour of S.Cs. and S.Ts.* in Central Services

As on	*Class I*		*Class II*		*Class III*		*Class IV*	
	S.C.	*S.T.*	*S.C.*	*S.T.*	*S.C.*	*S.T.*	*S.C.*	*S.T.*
1.1.70	2.36	0.40	3.84	0.37	9.27	1.47	18.09	3.59
1.1.71	2.58	0.41	4.06	0.43	9.89	1.70	18.37	3.65
1.1.72	2.99	0.50	4.13	0.44	9.77	1.72	18.61	3.82
1.1.73	3.14	0.50	4.52	0.49	10.05	1.95	18.37	3.92
1.1.74	3.25	0.57	4.59	0.49	10.33	2.13	18.53	3.84
1.1.75	3.43	0.62	4.98	0.59	10.71	2.27	18.64	3.99
1.1.76	3.46	0.68	5.41	0.74	11.31	2.51	18.75	3.93
1.1.77	4.16	0.77	6.07	0.77	11.84	2.78	19.07	4.35
1.1.78	4.50	0.85	6.44	0.88	12.22	2.86	19.13	4.66
1.1.79	4.75	0.94	7.37	1.03	12.55	3.11	19.32	5.19
And as on 1.1.83	6.72	1.13	10.17	1.47	14.61	4.14	19.67 (excluding sweepers)	5.51

Table 6.5: And, in All-India Services as on 1.1.1983*

Services	*No. of Employees*	*Scheduled Castes*	*Per cent of total*	*Scheduled Tribes*	*Per cent of total*
IAS	4,236	401	9.54	181	4.27
IPS	2,198	330	10.40	77	3.50

* India, 1985, p. 183.

Source: Digest from the Reports of the commissioner for S.Cs. and S.Ts. shown in A.B.S. K.S.'s case (1981) 1 S.C.C. 246 at p. 284.

The rich have become richer and the poorer and benefit of protective discrimination has not reached to the bottom level and they have remained where they were with violence and victimisation.

In relation to other services too, the representation of Scheduled Castes is terribly low. The following Table 6.6 will show their proportion in Government Services, Public Undertakings and Nationalised Banks.

Table 6.6: Table showing Percentage of Scheduled Castes Employees in Various Categories of Services as on 1.1.1982

(Percentage)

	Central Govt. Services (56 Ministries/ Depart.)	*Public Undertaking (177 Enterprises) (a)*	*Nationalised Banks (20) as on 1.1.1981 (b)*
Group A	4.95	2.90	13.39 (Officers)
Group B	8.54	5.11	11.25 (Clerks)
Group C	13.44	18.11	20.36 (Sub-Staff)

*Source** Department of Personnel and Administrative Reforms, Ministry of Home Affairs.

(a) Bureau of Public Enterprises, Ministry of Finance.

(b) Department of Banking Division, Ministry of Finance.

The trend of the paucity of SCs representation at national level is also discernible in State and Union Territory services.

Inadequacy of representation of SCs is evident from the information collected about the representation of scheduled caste in different State/ UT Govt. services which is reproduced below:

Table 6.7: State/UTs-wise information about the representation of SCs in State/UTs Govt. Services

Sl. No.	Name of the State	Scheduled Castes	Per cent SC Population	Group A	Group B	Group C	Group D	Remarks
	INDIA	1665.76	16.20					
				Per cent of SC appoined	Per cent of SC appointed	Per cent of SC appointed	Per cent of SC appointed	
1.	Punjab	70.28	28.90	16	18.44	18.4	31.35	
2.	H.P.	15.02	24.70	10.83	18.94	18.14	26.89	
3.	W.B.	184.52	23.00	10.28	17.15	17.15	21.26	
4.	U.P.	351.48	21.2	12.17	15.03	17.77	37.95	As on 2004 (SC & ST combined)
5.	Haryana	40.91	19.40	3.77	10.93	17.19	3.75	
6.	Tamil Nadu	118.57	19.00	10	12	15	24	As on 1.1.2004
7.	Uttarakhand	15.17	17.90	23	16	14	15	As on 1.4.2009
8.	Chandigarh	1.57	17.50	9.06	7.29	12.97	14.18	
9.	Tripura	5.55	17.40	9.98	11.94	13.18	13.23	
10.	Rajasthan	96.64	17.20	12.53 (Gzetted)	-	16.40 (Non-Gazetted)	-	As on 31.3.2009
11.	Delhi NCT	23.43	16.90	-	22.99	16.88	-	
12.	Orissa	60.82	16.50	9.85	12.74	14.60	24.55	
13.	A.P.	123.39	16.20	14.83	-	15.87	32.77	Only gazetted, Non gazetted and group D posts as on 1.1.2007
14.	Karnataka	85.63	16.20	18.63	15.97	15.94	24.56	
15.	Puducherry	1.57	16.20	11.54	14.03	12.45	12.89	

(Contd...)

16.	Bihar	130.48	15.70	14.58	14.13	8.86	11.51	
17.	M.P.	91.55	15.20	12.31	16.19	15.91	24.03	
18.	Jharkhand	31.89	11.80	9.36	10.13	9.58	9.97	
19.	Chhattisgarh	24.18	11.60	11.02	12.58	13.19	22.11	
20.	Maharashtra	98.82	10.20	9.88	11.55	11.98	16.85	
21.	Kerala	31.23	9.80	11.43	-	9.42	10.47	No group B posts. As on 1.1.2008
22.	J.& K.	7.70	7.60	-	-	-	-	
23.	Gujarat	35.93	7.10	7.79	3.50	9.99	8.88	
24.	Assam	18.25	6.90	5.56	5.83	11.40	-	
25.	Sikkim	0.27	5.00	-	-	-	-	The Sikkim Govt. has given only SCs employees in position (exclude 6 Department) i.e. Group A 15, Group B 42, Group C 266 and Group D-134 as on 1.1.2010
26.	D & Diu (UT)	0.05	3.10					Representation of SC in Gr. B-04, & Gr. C-25 Total 26 strength of 27 employees has not been given
27.	Manipur	0.37	2.6	NA	NA	NA	NA	
28.	D & N Haveli (HT)	0.04	1.90	1.73	3.46	64.16	30.63	
29.	Goa	0.23	1.80	2.1	2.0	2.0	2.0	
30.	Arunachal Pradesh	0.06	0.60	NA	NA	NA	NA	
31.	Meghalaya	0.11	0.50	NA	NA	NA	NA	
32.	A & N Island (UT)	0.00	0.00	NA	NA	NA	NA	
33.	Lakshadweep	0.00	0.00	NA	NA	NA	NA	
34.	Mizoram	0.00	0.00	NA	NA	NA	NA	
35.	Nagaland	0.00	0.00	NA	NA	NA	NA	

The following Table 6.8 shows comparative position of S.Cs. and S.Ts. vis-à-vis other castes in Class I services in Central Government.

Table 6.8: Caste Composition of Class I Officers in Central Government (In percentage)

Caste Category	*Share*	*Population*
Upper Castes	89.63	25.34
Backward Castes	4.69	52.10
S.C./S.T.	5.68	22.60
Total	**100.00**	**100.00**

Source: Report of the Backward Class Commission, New Delhi, First Part, 1980, p. 92. Figure for U.C. is residual of B.C., S.C., and S.T.

Table 6.9: Caste Composition of Employees in High Commissions Abroad (In percentage)

Category	*U.C.*	*O.B.C.*	*S.C./S.T.*	*Total*
Class I	90.9	0.0	9.1	100.00
Class II	94.0	0.7	5.3	100.00
Class III	92.5	1.0	6.5	100.00
Class IV	91.8	0.4	7.8	100.00

U.C. = Upper Castes
O.B.C. = Other Backward Castes
S.C. = Scheduled Castes
S.T. = Scheduled Tribes

Source: Columns 3 and 4 are from Rajya Sabha Debates on September. 11, 1981, as quoted by Shri Karpoori Thakur in an 'Appeal'. Column 2 is residual of column 3 and 4.

The poor representation of S.Cs. and S.Ts. may also be visible in social composition of managerial posts given in the following Table 6.10.

Tables 10 to 12 show that barring the Class III and Class IV services the Scheduled Castes representation in services has not been up to mark. Even in these services the representation of Scheduled Tribes is not in proportion to their reserved quota, i.e., the highest percentage in Class III in 1983 was 4.14, as against 7.5 per cent quota and in Class IV services were 5.51 as against 7.5 per cent quota. In relation to Class I and Class II services, S.T. seats were 1.43 and 1.47 respectively in 1983 as against

7.5 per cent quota, i.e., about 20 per cent of the reserved quota. A little improvement was shown in the Scheduled Castes position whose highest percentage in Class I in 1983 was 6.72 and in Class II was 10.17 as against 15 per cent quota of reserved seats, i.e., in relation to Class I only 45 per cent of the reserved seats were filled in and in relation to Class II services about 66.6 per cent of the reserved seats could be filled in. Likewise in IAS, only 9.54 per cent and in IPS only 10.40 per cent seats of Scheduled Castes candidates were filled in as against 15 per cent of their reserved quotas. And only 4.27 of seats were filled in IAS in 1983 as against 7.5 per cent reserved seats for S.Ts. and only 3.50 per cent seats were filled in IPS in 1983 as against 7.5 per cent reserved seats for them.

Table 6.10: Social Composition of Managerial Posts

Sl. No.	*Category*	*Per cent*
1.	Brahmin	41.4
2.	Business castes like Bania, Arora, etc.	43.1
3.	Cultivators like Jat, Patel, etc.	14.3
4.	Other Lower Castes	00.8
5.	Scheduled Castes	00.4

Source: Dynamics of Reservation Policy, Patriot Publishers, New Delhi, 1985, as given in Prasad, Ishwari, Reservation: Action for Social Equality (New Delhi: Criterion Publications), 1986, p. 136.

What is reason for leaving reserved seats upfilled ? Is it always non-availability of S.C. and S.T. candidates with minimum prescribed qualifications ? The answer of Ghanshyam Shah is "more often than not, it is because of the prejudices of the recruiting authority against S.C. and S.T. candidates that operate against their interest." The Commissioner for S.C. and S.T. noted that out of 1515 Scheduled Tribe vacancies proposed for dereservation in 1974, the S.T. candidates were available for 254 vacancies in Class III services but they were declared unsuitable for appointment. The Commissioner express anguish and despair:

> "It is strange that this should happen in the case of Class III vacancies to fill when there are special instructions that the candidates belonging to Scheduled Castes/Scheduled Tribes are to be judged by relaxed standard. In this category, most of the posts are non-technical or quasi-technical for which there is an additional provision to the effect that if Scheduled Castes/Scheduled Tribes candidates are not available to utilise fully the vacancies reserved for them in the direct recruitment

quota even by relaxed standards, the best them fulfilling the minimum educational qualifications are to be selected for appointment to the extent of vacancies reserved for them. In order to bring such candidates to the minimum standards necessary for the maintenance of efficiency of administration, they are to be given in service training. It is indeed a pity that the Scheduled Tribe candidates possessing the minimum qualifications laid down for the posts, should be deemed as unsuitable for appointment to Class III posts inspite of the above provisions."

Thus, the recruitment to the services is procedurally legal, but socially outmoted. There is collusion between the top bureaucracy and white collar professionals "deliberately so recruited, through a specially designed examination, as to share similar cultural backgrounds, style of life and set of loyalties." To get a job 'influence' and 'connection' have become more important than talent and skill. The lot of Scheduled Castes and Scheduled Tribes has become victim of Class bias. The officers incharge delay the implementation of the government orders regarding recruitment or promotion of S.Cs. and S.Ts. In number of cases court process is invoked to delay the reservation at promotional stage. And, sometime, decision-makers dereserve certain posts on one pretext or the other.

6.5.1 Position of SCs/STs in Educational Institutions

The position in the Universities is in no way different. In respect of teaching jobs two considerations are said to govern the appointments– the need of highly quailed teachers with a view to ensure teaching standards and that qualified candidates are not available from among the Scheduled Castes. And these considerations did not allow the implementation of reservation policy in University appointments to the reaching posts. However, in Karnataka, the reservation policy of filling 15 per cent of seats by the Scheduled Castes has been adopted by the Universities since 1976. But the case study of four Karnataka Universities as to teaching posts appointments gives totally unsatisfactory picture of Scheduled Castes appointments. Thus, in Bangalore University, percentage of S.C. teachers is 2 per cent, in Mysore 2.6 per cent, in Karnataka 0.8 per cent and in Agricultural University 0.6 per cent. The following Table 6.11 shows the meagre percentage of S.C. teachers.

The Table 6.12 shows that out of 275 Professors only 4 Scheduled Castes Professors were appointed, out of 447 Associate Professors, only 6 Scheduled Castes and out of 1,421 Assistant Professors only 17 Scheduled

Castes persons were appointed. The technical answer of the negligible percentage is that qualified Scheduled Castes candidates are generally not available. But reasons are much deeper. Five reasons were shown in Karnataka study: hostile selection committees, indifference of employers, non-availability of qualified candidates, corrupt practices and the roster system. However, two factors are dominant- the indifference of the employers and hostile selection committees. Vice-Chancellors do not evince keen interest in safeguarding the interests of the S.C. candidates as they would be less helpful in political battle in the temple of the learning. V. Cs. Act according to the tune of teacher politicians of influential group and compose the Selection Committees accordingly. The survey of the Kakatiya University and Rajasthan University tell the same story. In the former teaching staff position was like this: Out of 165 teachers, 126 belonged to Forward Castes/Classes, 36 belonged to Backward Classes and only 3 belonged to the Scheduled Castes. Thus, the percentage of Scheduled Castes teachers was 1.82 per cent. The position of Rajasthan University was still worse.

Table 6.11: The following Table 15 indicates the caste background of the Rajasthan University teachers during 1961-70

Position	*Mysore*			*Bangalore*			*Karnataka*			*Agr. University*		
	Total No.	*Scheduled Castes*		*Total No.*	*Scheduled Castes*		*Total No.*	*Scheduled Castes*		*Total No.*	*Scheduled Castes*	
		N	*Per cent*		*N*	*Per cent*		*N*	*Per cent*		*N*	*Per cent*
Professors	69	1	1.4	57	3	5.2	72	-	-	77	-	-
Associate Professors	90	4	4.4	-	-	-	160	-	-	197	2	1
Assistant Professors	288	4	1.4	251	5	2	371	5	1.4	511	3	0.6
Total	**477**	**9**	**2**	**308**	**8**	**2.6**	**603**	**5**	**0.8**	**785**	**5**	**0.6**

The following Table 6.12 indicates the caste background of the Rajasthan University teachers during 1961-70.

Table 6.12: Caste Background of University (Rajasthan) Teachers*
(In percentage)

Caste Category	*Natural Sciences*	*Social Sciences*	*Total*
Upper Castes	88.3	81.5	84.3
Intermediate Castes	1.7	5.7	4.0
Lower Castes	Nil	0.7	0.4
Muslims and Christian	1.7	0.7	1.2
No Response	8.3	11.4	10.1

* The Survey was conducted by Yogendra Singh, a renowned Professor of Sociology during 1969-70.

The above survey reveals that Scheduled Castes are negligible in University teaching profession. Though non-availability of the qualified candidates cannot be ruled out still the working of selection system and determination of yardstick of qualification is not beyond manipulative reach. Mumtaj Ali Khan very nicely exposes the practice behind the scene: "Quite often the qualifications are fixed in such a manner that no Scheduled Caste candidate is available; though relaxation can be done in their case, it is generally observed in the case of the caste Hindu candidates. Even when qualified candidates are available, relaxation is made in the case of the caste Hindus on some ground or the other."

The discriminatory policy and the ways in which unwritten reservations work are very horrifying. The selection of a candidate does not necessarily indicate the non-availability of better candidates than the candidate chosen, but on invisible and untold reservation usurped in favour of dominant class. Any objection of reservation against Scheduled Castes and Scheduled Tribes cannot shut eyes on these inner stories of frustrating the cause of S.Cs. and S.Ts. and grabbing all benefits on the basis of untellable and invisible reservations. This is the mind set by which not only the cause of SC/ST is suffering but also the cause of learning is badly threatened.

SC/ST seats are not filled in. An RTI information sought by Mr Mahendra Pratap Singh revealed that there was no SC/ST Professor in 4 Central Universities – JNU, Delhi University, B.H.U. and Allahabad[150].

The following is the overall figure of sanctioned and filled in posts:

Table 6.13

University	*Sanctioned Post for S.C.*	*Filled in*	*Sanctioned Post for ST*	*Filled in*
AMU	283	1	142	0
DU	255	44	128	14
JNU	109	24	55	9
BHU	362	115	181	30

There is general antipathy in not providing reservational benefits to SCs/STs. Even after 18 years of its existence, NHAI/did not extend any reservational benefit to SCs/STs employees which caused flood of representation and petitions from such employees. Taking cognisance of massive irregularities in reservation roaster points in NHAI, the National Commission for Scheduled Castes sought detailed information and Lok Sabha M.P. Pradeep Tamta expressed grave concern. He said, "It is surprising to note that whereas government has directed to the officers including attached offices to implement the reservation roaster under the Reservation Policy of the Government and also issued instructions from time to time to take special measures/recruitment drive for this under represented section in all organisations, the blatant violation of the same is of grave concern."[151]

In another incident The National Commission of Scheduled Castes (NCSC) had to issue arrest warrant against HRD Secretary who failed to appear before Commission at the date of hearing fixed to hear the complaint of Indu Chaudhary, General Secretary of SC/ST Employees Welfare of B.H.U. The complaint was that, "the University authorities have been ignoring the reservation policy while filling up vacant posts, promotions and other benefits". When complained about it, the University with a view to teach her lesson wrongfully deducted Rs 27,000 from her salary and framed a vigilance case against her.[152]

Overall assessment of the poor, vulnerable and deplorable condition of SCs/STs is that their lot has not improved significantly. Social more still continues to despise them and exploit them too. They are still attacked, raped, denied access to places of worship, common water sources, education, dignified jobs and other rights. In spite of untouchability being abolished and its observance in any form made punishable under P.C.R. Act, 1955 (before its renaming in 1976, Untouchability Offences Act) and SC/ST

(POA) Act, 1989 the position is what Apex Court observed in *Arumugam Servai v. State of Tamil Nadu*[153]: "In some places in Tamil Nadu there are separate tumblers in hotels for serving etc. to SCs and non-SC persons and a large section of Indian Society still regards a section of its own countrymen as inferior which is one of the main causes holding up the country's progress and this mental attitude is unacceptable in modern age". Article 25(b) provides constitutional guarantee of "the throwing open of Hindu religious institutions of a public character to all classes and sections of Hindus" and SCs are no other than Hindus. But, as late as September 2015 the news appeared in a national daily newspaper that four women belonging to the SCs were thrown out of temple, beaten and the village panchayat imposed Rs 1000 fine and performed purification of the temple premises.[154]

Still, more importantly, the situation of education laughs at controversy as to abolition of reservation for SCs/STs. There is constitutional guarantee under Article 21-A of the Constitution of the free and compulsory education to all children of the age of six to fourteen years; one of the fundamental duties of the citizens is to provide opportunities for education to their children between the age of six and fourteen years; there is Right to Education Act[155] and so on. Agreeing that all these commitment is fulfilled, the most question is: Where will the children of poor SCs be provided facilities to get education? The decision of ***Sudhir Agrawal J. in Shiv Kumar Pathak and 11 Others v. State of U.P.***[156]delivered on 18.08.2015 speaks a volume on the condition where the poor (mainly SCs/STs) children would be taught. There are three kinds of Schools, (i) **Elite School**[157] where the children of highly rich people, high class bureaucrats, ministers, M.Ps, M.L.As and high middle class people are educated. These schools have best kind of infrastructures, tutorial staff and all modern amenities (ii) **Semi-Elite School's**[158] which are not of that rank but are good with infrastructure and teaching staff; and (iii) **Common men's Schools**[159] where Schools struggle for basic amenities for children, coming thereat, like drinking water, space for natural calls etc. "Even classrooms are in extremely shabby and bad conditions. At many places, classes are being run in open space. The structure, if any, is in dilapidated condition". In U.P. itself 2.70 lacs posts of Assistant Teachers in Primary Schools run by Board were found vacant by the High Court. Students are taught by sub-standard low paid Shiksha Mitra, Aganbari Karya Katri etc. The third category Schools are meant for most of the SCs.[160]

Compare and Contrast: Elite children study with all facilities in elite schools and the SC/ST children have to depend on government run schools. The conditions and standard of teaching in such government schools is reported to be horrible. In 2014 the National Council of Educational Research and Training (NCERT) had stated in its National Achievement Survey 2014 that the performance of the class III and class V students of the city government schools was much lower than the national average when they were asked to recognise a simple text, or do simple addition or subtraction.

On 22.09.2015 in Indian Express Chandigarh News Line at P. 1 a study of 22 City Government Schools was published with caption "Student of Class III and V can't solve simple math problems – Study". Illustrations reveal vulnerable position and most poor standard in all subjects – English, Hindi, Maths, EVs.[161] The condition of rural government Schools may be easily understood.

6.6 Misuse of SC/ST Certificate to the Detriment of SC/ST Claims

The misuse of Caste certificate in relation to SEBCs has already been discussed in Book-2. The misuse of caste certificates against SCs/STs is presented here.

The benefit of SC/ST has prompted many others to deprive the genuine SC/ST of their rightful claim and grave benefit by false certificate. In *Kumari Madhuri Patil* v. *Addl. Commissioner*, Tribal Development[162] the division bench of K. Ramaswamy and N. Venkatachala JJ was confronted with the complicated and complex issue of wrong caste certificate of 'Mahadeo Koli' ST caste grabbed by 'Koli' girls which is a other Backward class. Due to delay in scrutiny committee process the elder sister had reached in last year examination of medical study. They allowed her to appear in the final examination. But ordered that "*she will not be entitled in future to any benefits* on the basis of the fraudulent social status as Mahadeo Koli. K. Ramaswamy J. also ruled that direction would not be treated and used as a precedent in future cases as it would defeat the constitutional goal. The younger sister was in midway in BDS i.e. in the end of second year. The Court ruled that "she cannot continue her studies with her social status of 'Mahadeo Koli', a scheduled tribe and the concessions which she might have got on that account."[163] The cancellation and confiscation of such certificate was upheld. The facts show that their father had taken benefit of such fraudulent certificates, as his service record showed him ST Mahadeo Koli. The fraud was unearthed on verification of their school entry of father's caste. K. Ramaswamy J. exposed the danger of such fraudulent activities. Said, the learned judge:

"The admission wrongly granted or appointment wrongly obtained on the basis of false social status certificate necessarily has the effect of depriving the genuine Scheduled Castes or Scheduled Tribes or OBC candidates as enjoined in the constitution of the benefits conferred on them by the Constitution."[164]

Again in *Director of Tribal Welfare Government of A.P.* v. *Laveti Giri*[165] the same bench had to deal with the issuance of false certificate from the Tehsildar of another area (area other than native one) as Kondakapa tribe a S.T. The service record of the government servant father also showed the same. But the School Certificate of father showed that he was 'Kapu' a non-S.T. Director did not allow that status while the respondent was pursuing B.E. first year course. The Court reverse the decision of the Director. The Supreme Court took notice of the fact that father never appeared and deposed. On the basis of High Court order the respondent had completed B.E. Course. The Supreme Court only declared that (i) *he did not belong to ST and* (ii) *was not entitled to any employment on that basis*.

K. Ramaswamy J. speaking for the Court reiterated the guideline issued by the Supreme Court in *Madhuri Patil* case for issuance of caste certificate made a good and timely suggestion that "the Government of India should have the matter examined in greater detail and bring about a uniform legislation with necessary guidelines and rules prescribing penal consequences on person who flout the Constitution and corner the benefits reserved for the real tribals etc., so that the menace of fabricating the false records and to gain unconstitutional advantage by plain/spurious persons could be prevented, lest they would defeat the unconstitutional objective of rendering socio-economic justice envisaged under the Preamble and Articles of 46, 14, 15, 16, 38 and 39."[166]

Consonance with the message of above cases the division bench of Ramaswamy and G.T. Nanavati JJ ruled out any estoppel in State of *Tamil Nadu* v. *A. Gurusamy*.[167] It was a peculiar case - an S.C. claimed S.T. benefit, when respondent was studying in School he was described as a member of "Thotti" community which as per Presidential Notification item 67 was a S.C. Subsequently, in 1970, the respondent obtained a certificate from the Revenue Divisional Officer indicating him to be "Kattunaicken" which was S.T. in ST List for Tamil Nadu at item No. 9. Both the orders were passed by the President of India under Article 341(1) read with Article 366(24) and under Article 342(1) read with Article 366(25) respectively for SCs and STs. Respondent applied for permanent certificate for S.T. On enquiry it was found that he was not a S.T. and his certificate issued by Revenue Divisional Officer was cancelled. He filed a civil suit for declaration that he is 'Kattunaicken', a S.T. Civil Court granted and affirmed by appellate Court. The Supreme Court ruled that Presidential order under Articles 341 and 342 is conclusive and alterable only by Parliament under Articles 341 (2) and 342(2). Thus, by implication civil court jurisdiction is prohibited. The plea of estoppel was rejected. The Court classified that, "It is a fraud played on the Constitution. A person who plays fraud and obtains a false certificate can not plead estoppel. The Court ruled that appellant was liable for prosecution and said, "the Courts would not lend assistance to perpetuate fraud on the Constitution and he cannot be allowed to get the benefit of the fraudulent certificate obtained from authority."[168]

The judiciary has maintained a distinction between education pursuing and jobs. In the former it has taken somewhat lenient view not to disturb degree but no benefit to be sought as SC/ST on that count. In the latter it has taken touch attitude. Thus, in *R. Vishwanath Pillai* v. *State of Kerala* and *Vimal Ghosh* v. *State of Kerala* vide order passed on 7.1.2004.[169] The dealing with two different civil appeals on the issue of false caste certificates, the Apex Court showed its anxiety on snatching of SC/ST claims by forward class people by procuring/manipulating caste certificate. In *R. Vishwanath Pillai's* case, the appellant belonged to the forward caste as per school record. Later on he managed a S.C. Certificate and on that basis he was selected as a direct recruit to the post of Deputy Superintendent of Police against a post reserved for Scheduled Caste. He got promotion as I.P.S. He had completed long 27 years service when the complaint was made as to the falsity of his caste certificate. On inquiry conducted by the Kerala government it was revealed that the appellant did not belong to SC category. Consequently the Kerala government dismissed the appellant from the service. He filed appeal in the Supreme Court by S.L.P. under Article 136 of the Constitution. One of the pray of the appellant was that the order of dismissal be substituted by order of compulsory retirement or an order of removal from service to protect his pensionary benefits in view of 27 long years service tendered by him.

A three judge bench consisting of V.N. Khare C.J. and Ashok Bhan and Dr A.R. Lakshamanon JJ rejected his plea and upheld the dismissal order. The apex Court explained:

"The appellant obtained the appointment in the service on the basis that he belonged to a Scheduled Caste Community. When it was found by the scrutiny committee that he did not belong to the scheduled caste community, the very basis of his appointment was taken away, His appointment was no appointment in the eye of the law. He cannot claim a right to the post as he had usurped the post meant for a reserved category candidate by playing a fraud and producing a false caste certificate. Unless the appellant can lay a claim to the post on the basis of his appointment, he cannot claim the institutional guarantee given under Article 311 and cannot be considered to be a person who holds a post within the meaning of Article 311. Where an appointment in a service has been acquired by practicing fraud or deceit, such an appointment is no appointment is law, in service and in such situation Article 311 of the Constitution is not attracted at all."[170]

Rejecting the plea to substitute the order of dismissal by an order or compulsory retirement or removal from service, the Court observed:

"The consequential right of pension and monetary benefits can be given only if the appointment was valid and legal. Such benefits cannot be given in a case where the appointment was found to have been obtained fraudulently and rested on the false caste certificate."

The hon'ble Court also explained the ill consequence of such fraudulent acts attracting no sympathy. Said, the Court, "A person who entered the service by producing a false caste certificate and obtained appointment for the post meant for a Scheduled Caste, *thus depriving the genuine Schedule Caste candidate of appointment to that post*, does not deserve any sympathy or indulgence of the Supreme Court." The Court ruled out any sympathy on the basis of equity as one who seeks equity must come with clean hands and that was not the case of the appellant.

In Vimal Ghosh case the Court took a somewhat lenient view about retention of degree which he had obtained after pursuing study on the basis of different interim order of the High Court. Though fraud in this case appeared to be committed from quite earlier time. The School record showed the appellant's caste as a Scheduled Caste. On that basis he obtained admission to the Regional Engineering College at Calicut against a seat reserved for a Scheduled Caste candidate. On complaint, scrutiny committee found that his father did not belong to a Scheduled Caste. Consequently his admission was cancelled, but he got interim orders from the High Court and pursued study and appeared in the examination with condition of the result declaration subject to the further order of the Court. The Supreme Court found that the appellant had pursued engineering study from 1992 to 1996 under the interim orders of the High Court. The Court allowed the degree to be retained with condition that he would not be treated as a Scheduled Caste candidate in future either in obtaining service or any other benefits from caste certificate. His caste certificate was ordered to be cancelled.

The leniency of the Court to allow the retention of degree by the appellant in *Vimal Ghosh case* on the consideration that no purpose would be served in withholding the declaration of result, it is submitted, would not have been conceded as it exposes that the Court process may unwittingly serve as perpetuation of fraudulent act and thereby injustice. It does not do justice with SCs/STs who claim of a seat in admission was usurped by foul means by an undeserving candidate. In order to have deterrent effect for future even that much concession should not have been conceded - as the appellant has sow, so he would have been allowed to reap. The authors agree with a researcher from the Scheduled Caste itself - only the wearer knows where the shoe pinches. Thus, Dr Ram Samujh comments, "every case of false caste certificate should be dealt rigorously by all means. It will create a deterrent impact on the false caste certificate users and on the other hand, it would protect the interest of deprived classes."[171]

It is so because these are symptoms not the whole of fraudulent activities which remain unearthed due lack of courage on affected SCs/STs to challenge and united efforts of power that be of the forward caste if some challenge comes on the fore. Even in same case proper issue is not raised on technicalities the benefited is conceded to some persons. The decision of S. Ranganathan J. in *Khazan Singh* v. *Union of India*[172] is glaring example. A 21 years old Khazan Singh was adopted by a Kishan Lal Julaha, Kabirpanthi belonging to S.C. community in 1969 (adoption was executed on 5.1.1969 on a stamp paper of Rs 25). Intending to enter in police service he applied to Dy. Commissioner, Delhi for S.C. Certificate in 1970. He was appointed to the post of Sub-Inspector in Delhi Police on the basis of Deputy Commissioner's Certificate under the S.C. category. On complaint Assistant I.G. terminated his services. The issue raised was that adoption was not valid within the meaning of Section 10 of the Hindu Adoption Act which requires that normally a body adopted should not have completed 15 years. The Court ruled that it was relaxable in view of custom and no opportunity of being heard was given. However, the issue never arose: could a 21 year old boy having enjoyed all privileges of Jat community could be given benefits of reservation under the S.C. category ?

In *Union of India* v. *S. Krishnan*[173] the Supreme Court a definite view that a case certificate found to be fake, even though issued on the authority of some letter issued by some officers like Director of District Welfare, will not be honoured. On the basis of procuring false S.T. certificate of a member of Malayalee community got employment. On verification his certificate was found to be fake and therefore, after holding the departmental enquiry he was compulsorily retired. Later on he contended that he was

Lambadi, a member of S.T. Community in the State of Tamil Nadu. The High Court relying on the letter from Director of District Welfare held him to belong to S.T. The Supreme Court did not agree with the High Court as the letter of the Director was not relatable to entries in the Presidential constitutional order and upheld the order of the State government issued on the basis of entries in the Presidential order that Lambadi was not an S.T. in Tamil Nadu. Thus, it declared the caste certificate fake and upheld the consequent compulsory retirement of the respondent.

In *Raju Ram Singh Vasave* v. *Mahesh Deorao*[174], the apex Court ruled that inspite of the High Court order to contrary in light of the further development warranting reconsideration the S.T. status of the claimant can be reopened.

In backdrop of the above situation, prevailing conditions and social mores will it be advisable or wise step in overall national interest to shunt off reservation in favour of SCs and STs or some rationalisation needs so that the benefit of reservation reaches to the real claimant among SCs and STs?

References

1. A.I.R. 1962 S.C. 36.
2. The Railway Board Circular dated April 27. 1959.
3. *Ibid.*, p. 595.
4. *Ibid.*
5. *Ibid.*, p. 601.
6. *Ibid.*, p. 605.
7. *Ibid.*, p. 605.
8. *Ibid.*, p. 610 (Wanchoo, J.).
9. *Ibid.*
10. *Ibid.*
11. *Ibid*, p. 617 (Ayyangar, J.).
12. *Ibid.*
13. *Ibid.*, 618.
14. *Ibid.*, 617.
15. *Ibid.*
16. A.I.R. 1957 Pat. 617.
17. A.I.R. 1959, Bom. 134.
18. A.I.R. 1960, All. 484.
19. A.I.R. 1969 Cal. 576.
20. A.I.R. 1970 Ori. 224.

21. A.I.R. 1971, S.C. 1977.
22. A.I.R. 1976 S.C., 490.
23. *Ibid.*, p. 498 (para 29).
24. *Ibid.*
25. *Ibid.*, pp. 506 and 511-12 (Khanna, J.); pp. 512 and 520 (Mathew, J.), p. 141 (Gupta, J.): pp. 550-51, 553-54 (Fazl Ali, J.)
26. *Ibid.*, pp. 521-22 (Beg, J.).
27. (1981) I.S.C.C. 246.
28. *Ibid.*, p. 296.
29. *Ibid.*, pp. 296-297.
30. *Ibid.*, p. 274.
31. *Ibid.*
32. *Ibid.*, p. 297
33. *Ibid.*
34. *Ibid.*
35. A.I.R. 1981 S.C. 558.
36. A.I.R. 1986 Pat. 124.
37. (1986) 2 S.C.C. 679 at p. 694 (para 92).
38. (1962) 2 S.C.R. 586 at p. 600.
39. *Ibid.*
40. *Ibid.*
41. *Ibid*, p. 606.
42. *Ibid*, p. 613.
43. *Ibid.*, p. 612.
44. *Ibid.*, p. 603.
45. Edward, H.T. and Zaretsaky, B.L. "Preferential Remedies for Employment Discrimination", 74, M.L.R.I. 40 (Nov. 1975).
46. Wright, J.S., "Colour Blind Theories", 47 Univ. of Ch. L.R. 213, 219 (Winter, 1980).
47. Chitnis, Suma, A long way to Go, 1977, p. 210 Cited from Marc Galanter, Competing Equalities, p. 77.
48. Carl Cohen, "Why Racial Preference is Immoral and Illegal", Commentary, 40, 51 (June) 1979.
49. See RCSCST, 17th Report (1967-68), para 2.5.
50. The Times of India, 14.5.1981 (Justices R.N. Mishra expressed the views at a symposium).
51. A.I.R. 1978 S.C. 597.
52. See Goldman, Justice and Reserve Discrimination (Princeton Uni., 1979); Posner, R.A., "Recent Development – The Parados of Preferential Treatment- Reverse Discrimination", 53 W.L.R. 170: "The Unresolved Problems of Reverse Discrimination", 67 C.L.R. 87 (January. 1979; Husk, D.N., "Preferential Hiring

and Reverse Discrimination in Favour of Balcks: A Moral Analysis", 23 A.J.J. 143 (1978) Ely. Sir John Hart "The Constitutionality of Reverse Racial Discrimination", 41 Uni. Chi. L. Rev. 723 (1974).

53. 482 F. end. 1333.
54. *Ibid.*
55. (1992) S.C.C. (L. and S.) Supp. 1 at p. (para 821).
56. *Ibid.*, p. 160 (para 300).
57. *Ibid.*, p. 265 (para 538).
58. *Ibid.*, p. 445 (para 820).
59. *Ibid.*, p. 268 para 538.
60. *Ibid.*
61. *Ibid.*, p. 273 (para 552).
62. *Ibid.*, p. 160 (para 300).
63. *Ibid.*, p. 445 (para 820).
64. General Manager Souther Railway v. Rangachari, (1962) 2 S.C.R. 586.
65. Mandal case p. 449 (para 827).
66. *Ibid.*, p. 450 (para 828).
67. *Ibid.*, p. 450.
68. *Ibid.*
69. *Ibid.*, p. 451 (para 828).
70. 1992 Supp. 1 S.C.C. 594.
71. *Ibid.*, p. 160 (para 301).
72. *Ibid.*, pp. 160-161 (para 302).
73. *Ibid*, p. 161 (para 304).
74. *Ibid.*, pp. 192-193 (para 376).
75. *Ibid*, p. 194 (para 379).
76. *Ibid.*, p. 267 (para 543).
77. *Ibid.*, p. 452 (para 831).
78. *Ibid.*
79. *Ibid.*, p. 131 (para 240).
80. *Ibid.*, p. 163 (para 311).
81. *Ibid.*, p. 269 (para 548).
82. *Ibid.*, p. 131 (para 242).
83. G.M.S. Rly. V. Rangachari, (1962) 2 S.C.R. 586 at p. 596.
84. *Ibid.*, p. 604.
85. *Ibid.*
86. *Ibid.*, p. 606.
87. P.K. Dave, 'Promotion and Incentives in Public Services' (12), Indian Journal of Public Administration, 1966, pp. 533-543 at p. 536.
88. Department of Social Welfare, 1969, p. 278.
89. RCSCST 1975-77, Vol. I, pp. 43-47.
90. For detail see, Marc Galanter, Competing Equalities (1984), pp. 100-101.

91. Mandal Case (1992) S.C.C. (I. and S.) Supp. 1 at p. 269 (para 548).
92. See, Marc Galanter, 'Competing Equalities' (1984) p. 105.
93. *Ibid.*
94. (1997) 5 SCC 201.
95. *Ibid.* p. 238 (para 42).
96. *Ibid.* p. 239 (para 43). See also Commissioner of Commercial taxes, A.P. v. G. Sethumadhava Rao (1996) 7 SCC 512. A three judge bench of the apex court ruled that the intention behind introduction of Article 16(4-A) was to remove the defect pointed out by the Supreme Court in Mandal case.
97. (1992) Supp (3) SCC 217.
98. (1996) 6 SCC 684.
99. *Ibid.* p. 701 (para 24).
100. (1996) 2 SCC 715.
101. *Ibid.* p. 735 para (16).
102. (1999) 7 SCC 209.
103. (2000) 1 SCC 430. Ajit Singh II was also reiterated in M.G. Vadappanavar v. State of Karnataka (2001) 2 SCC 666.
104. (2003) 5 SCC 604.
105. (2006) 8 SCC 212.
106. Ajit Singh, State of Punjab (1996) 1 SCC 715; Ajit Singh II v. State of Punjab (1999) 7 SCC 209; and Ajit Singh III v. State of Punjab (2008) 1 SCC 430. See also *M.G. Badappanvar v. State of Karnataka* (2001) 2 SCC 666 wherein the Supreme Court followed Ajit Singh cases and Virpal Singh case to the effect that if promotion is obtained by way of reservation, the consequential seniority will not be counted.
107. (2006) 8 SCC 212 at p. 278.
108. (2008) 6 SCC 1.
109. (2001) 1 SCC 467.
110. *Suraj Bhan Meena v. State of Rajasthan* (2011) 1 SCC 467 at pp. (483-484) (para 65).
111. *Ibid.* p. 484 (para 66).
112. (2012) 7 SCC 1 (d/April 27, 2012).
113. *Ibid.* p. 22 (para 35).
114. (2006) 8 SCC 212.
115. (2012) 7 SCC 1 p. 32 (para 72).
116. (2012) 10 SCC 235.
117. *Ibid.* p. 460 (para 17).
118. The Times of India, 12.3.2016 p. 10.
119. *Ibid.*
120. (1996) 6 SCC 580.
121. AIR 1993 SC 477 : 1992 Supp (3) SCC 217.
122. (2006) 8 SCC 212.

123. (2002) 4 SCC 34.
124. *Ibid.*
125. AIR 1978 SC 490.
126. (2002) 1 SCC 616.
127. (2009) 9 SCC 454.
128. D.D. Basu, Commentary on the Constitution of India in 10 volumes covering more than12000 pages. See Basu, Vol. 2 pp. 1823-1824.
129. P.P. Rao Right to Equality And The Reservation Policy, 42 Journal of The Indian Law Institute (2000).
130. J. Rangrajan, Constitution of India – Five Decades p. 312.
131. Jyotica Pragya Kumar, Policy of Reservation – Its Envisioned Perspective 39, Journal of Indian Law Institute (1997) and C. M. Jariwala, Reservation in Admission to Higher Education, 42 Journal of the Indian Law Institute (2000).
132. 'Reservation Blessing or Curse', Sunday Statesman Magazine (19.2.1978).
133. Pratap C Agrawal, Half Way to Equality.
134. Bhardwaj, Problems of Scheduled Castes and Scheduled Tribes in India (1979), p. 90.
135. In the Schools of Tirunelveli in Chennai different caste students come in different shades of red, yellow, green and saffron by wearing on their writs, on their foreheads, around their necks and under their shirts, so that they may be identified who they are. The Indian Express 4.11.2015 pp. 1-2.
136. What a heart touching expression was found when a Chamar girl Manavi went to meet her friend Suhani Patel in Aganwadi No. 160 and was stopped and asked to go to Aganwadi No. 159 which was meant for Chamars (Dalits), her mother observed, "She came home and asked me why she could not go to No. 160 and I did not know what to say". The Indian Express 5.11.2015 pp. 1-2.
137. After publication of this news on 6.11.2015, the administration became alert and after 5 months of boycott students ate mid-day meal. The Indian Express 10.11.2015 pp. 1-2.
138. The Indian Express, 6.11.2015, p. 1.
139. See Indian Express 7.11.2015, p. 1 column, "*Sir said I was a Dalit so could not be part of Punja.*"
140. The Indian Express, 15.11.2015, p. 8.
141. *Ibid.*
142. 347 U.S. 483 (1954).
143. There is a story written by well known Hindi Professor in which he narrates how a election seeker Brahmin reached for canvassing in a Harijan Basti. Asked for water. The pot (Lota) was rubbed with sand-water was presented. He poured pretending to touch by lip and did not drink a drop of that.
144. A. Ramaiah, Laws for Dalit Rights and Dignity, Rawat Publications, 2007.
145. *Ibid.* p. 200.
146. *Ibid.* p. 104.
147. *Ibid.* p.116.

148. *Ibid.* p. 119.
149. *Ibid.* p. 167.
150. http.//khabar.ibnlive.in.com/news/81410/1
151. http.//www.dailypioneer.cm/nation/ncse-seeks-18-yr-details-ofquota-irregularities.html
152. http.//www.thehindu.com/todays/tp-national/arrest-warant-against-hrdsecretary/article575499.ece.
153. (2011) 6 SCC 405.
154. The Hindu 07.09.2015, p. 9. The Temple had been constructed out of public money including the contribution of M.P. Local Area Development Fund by the former Prime Minister H.D. Dev Gowda.
155. R.T.E. Act.
156. Decision was delivered on 18.08.2015.
157. *Ibid.*, para 81.
158. *Ibid.*, para 82.
159. *Ibid.*, para 83.
160. *Ibid.*, para 84. In his decision dated 18.08.2015, Sudhir Agrawal J. directed that it must be insured that the Children / wards of Government servants, semi-government servants, local bodies, representative of people, Judiciary and all such persons who receive any perk, benefit or salary etc. from State exchequer or public fund send their children / wards to the Board run Primary Schools. The worst part is that the teacher who filed the petition was tacked. The Hindu Column, "Teacher Who Filed PIL on Primary Schools Sacked", 28.08.2015, p.1.
161. Indian Express Chandigarh News Line at p. 1, dated 22.09.2015.
162. (1994) 65 CC241 (D/Sept. 2, 1994).
163. *Ibid*, p. 254.
164. *Ibid.*
165. (1995) 4 SCC32. (dt. April 18, 1995).
166. *Ibid*, p. 41 (para 8).
167. (1997) 3 SCC 541.
168. *Ibid* 545.
169. (2004) 4 SCC (L and S) 350.
170. *Ibid*, p. 352.
171. Dr Ram Samujh, Reservation Policy - Its Relevance in Modern India, Samrudh Bharat Publication, Mumbai, 2005, p. 124.
172. A.I.R. 1986 Del. 60 (S. Ranganathan J.).
173. (2008) 3 SCC 177.
174. (2008) 9 SCC 54.

Chapter - 7

Ressentiment: Spontaneous, Preemptive and Violent

Man by nature wants to live a happy civil life with dignity. Any sort of indignation invites natural revolt from within. Human urge for respect and equal treatment breeds the desire to be free from domination of others. Edgar Bodenheimer expresses this natural inclination when he says, "the sense of injustice revolts against whatever is unequal by caprice"[1]. The American Civil War (1861-1868) was a revolt against human indignation through slavery. So was the case of the French Revolution. It was waged against discrimination by feudal class against the middle classes.

Democracy breeds discrepancies in status, wealth, and power. Daniel Bell rightly points out, "when one is barred from modifying these discrepancies, the result is often – in Nietzsche's term – resentment, or envy, anger and hatred at the top."[2] Alexis de Tocqueville very well narrated the cause of resentment in a democracy.[3] The natural consequence of a civil society is that "the interest of the excluded is always in danger of being overlooked" and ressentiment, "is the chief psychological fuel of disruption and conflict." The problem both in U.S. and India (as well as elsewhere) is how to reduce it. The problem is perennial. As Tocqueville viewed "democratic institutions successfully develop sentiments of envy in the human heart." Where superiority – inferiority are deep-rooted the chances of the ressentiment is more likely. The ressentiment can find expression in two ways – the *first* is the natural reaction of oppressed, depressed, humiliated and discriminated and *second*, under Tocqueville effect i.e. people may suffer less but these sensibility is exacerbated.[4] To these two, a third and the most dangerous way of ressentiment may be apprehension of threat to status quoists privileges due to reform measures.

The French pronounciation of ressentiment is [rjjatima]. It is made out of Latin sentir by pre fixing re. Sentir means to feel. The French ressentiment is conveniently used in English as resentment allowing hostility towards people who frustrate one's expectations. Ressentiment was first introduced as a philosophical/ psychological term by the nineteenth century philosopher Soren Kier Kegaard.[5] Later on Nietzsche expanded it in Germany.[6] It related to the psychology of master slave question and consequent birth of morality. Hong translated ressentiment as envy[7].

7.1 Different Kinds of Resentments

There are different explanations for ressentiment provided by Kier Keggard, Nietzsche, Scheler, Weber and Sartre. The analysis of Max Weber is more nearer to our present study.[8] Relating ressentiment to Judaism, he suggests ethical salvation religion of a 'pariah people'. Weber defines ressentiment as "a concomitant of that particular religious ethic of the disprivileged which in the sense expounded by Nietzsche and in direct inversion of the ancient belief, teaches that the unequal distribution of mundane goods is caused by the sinfulness and the illegality of the privileged and that sooner or later God's wrath will overtake them."[9]

Resentment[10] in context of positive action or compensatory discrimination may take different forms. **First**, spontaneous, natural and more commendable and less objectionable resentment relates to the targets of social exclusion and marginalisation resulting into social disadvantage and relegations to the fringe of society. But such resentment and outburst does not remain approval so it crosses the boundary of genuine grievance redressal like Gandhian way adopted by leaders like Nelson Mandela in the South Africa and Martin Luther King Jr. in the United States of America. Since man is a social animal, he wants to live amicably in the society of the others. Social exclusion marginalises some people for none of their fault but for their helplessness to get birth in a particular caste and creed. "Social exclusion" is explained as "the process in which individuals or entire communities of people are systematically blocked from (or denied full access to) various rights, opportunities and resources that are normally available to members of a different group."[11] It is a multidimensional process of progressive social rupture, detaching groups and individuals from social relations and institutions and preventing them from full participation in the normal, normatively prescribed activities of the society in which they live.[12] The area of social exclusion is varied, e.g., housing, employment, healthcare, civil engagement, democratic participation and due process. Resentment of this kind may be recourse to judicial process like Dred ***Scott v. Sanford***[13] claiming right to sue for getting relieved from slavery or ***Brown v. Board of Education***[14] claiming desegregation of black and white children in Schools or protest procession of Dr Ambedkar for equal right of Mahars to use the water of pond and entry in Mandir or various demonstrations organised by Ramaswami Naykar under the banner of 'Self Respect Movement' in South India or by Martin Luther King, Jr. in America claiming civil rights of Negroes.

The natural expression of resentment may be observe in the following two poems:

> This country which demands
> A pot of blood,
> For a swallow of water,
> How can be it mine
> Though give the world
> The (empty) advice of peace"[15]
> Prahlad Chandrawankar

The Agony and Anguish of the Dalits

> We assist you in your birth pangs
> We bring forth your children
> We wash your linen
> We clean/scrub your utensils
> Yet we remain 'achuth'.
> We plough your field
> We fill your large godowns
> But, you in turn, starve us.
>
> We cremate your ancestors
> We do mundanc for the clan
> So that you can mourn the dead
> Is this why you burn us alive ?
> As the lamentation were going on
> I smelt the burning of flesh, which echoed:
> Woe to you the touchables,
> You burnt us alive,
> Woe to you the zamindars,

The land that you grabbed from us
Will be confiscated and distributed.
Woe to you the politicians
You sided with the dominant castes
Your power will be curtailed
Woe to you the police
You harassed us unnecessarily
You will be buried alive.
Woe to you the dalit leaders
You sold us for your survival
Your security will be shattered.
Slowly the woe turned into blessings
Blessed are the bhandhua-mazdur
For you will break out from the
Perpetual bondage.
Blessed are the Dalit women
For you will mother the
Martyrs of Dalitsthan.
Blessed are you the activists
You shall be rewarded for
Your commitment.
Blessed are the Dalits
For you will create a Dalitsthan
From your burnt ashes.[16]

Second, the second category of resentment relates to prejudice, hate and inherent despise against the unfortunate depressed and socially excluded persons. Caste people do not tolerate if a dalit wears clean cloths, makes a house with roof, he sends his children to good schools, uses good names for children. They resent, beat and torture. In his poem, **'Hindus and War of Public Conscience'**, Dr Ambedkar narrates how violent incidents occur if dalits struggle for their liberation, demonstrate, wear gold and silver ornaments, fetch water from clean well etc. Dalits actions are not against caste Hindus. Still they are tortured. In his poem, A way From the Hindus, Dr Ambedkar points out that untouchables may ask many questions from Hindu leaders: does Hindutva accept them as human being ? does it consider equality for them ? does it increase fraternity for them ? does it treat them as part of Hindus ? Does it denounce barbarism with dalits as sin ? Does it assure justice, humane condition, love, discriminationless human value for them ? If they do not accept all these for dalits how they expect dalits to remain with them. The dalits' progress, well living and healthy way of life do not affect Upper Caste people, still they resent and inflict maltreatment.

The sense of ego crosses limit of all propriety and good sense when caste people do not tolerate even slightest departure of behaviour of dalits from their ego inflated expectations[17]. So-

- Dalit leader abused for daring to sit on a chair;
- Dalit worker beaten on suspicion of theft;
- Dalit lynched while gathering grain from some one's field;
- Dalit beaten for riding on bi-cycle through caste inhabitancy;
- Dalit groom beaten for riding on horse in his marriage; procession;
- U.P. Dalit girl resists rape, loses arms as a result;
- Dalit tries to fetch water beaten to death.

Third, the category of resentment relates affecting of economic interests of the upper caste people by the dalits.

- The refusal of a dalit to sell bidis (hand-rolled cigarettes) on credit to the nephew of a upper caste chief, he met with retaliatory actions from that family by forcibly piercing his mostril, drawing a sting through his nose, parading him around the village and tying him to a cattle post.[18]
- Dalits demand to participate in a government public auction of common properties attracted attack on their colony by seven caste Hindu families and destroying 400 huts, attacking women, children and the elderly and displacing 700 dalit families.[19]
- In Bihar, the surplus land acquired under ceiling law and land available under voluntary surrender scheme were distributed among agricultural workers. Workers were awarded arrears of one crore rupees as arrear of minimum wages and indebtedness. Such measures coupled with "socio-psychological propaganda accentuated", antagonism between "agricultural proletariat and the landlords" and during 1975-1977 emergency it led to murders of and brutal assaults against untouchables.[20] In post-emergency period workers claim to wages and refusal to pay cancelled debts resulted in feudal anger and large scale massacres.[21]
- A dalit community was attacked by acid on the 24th Oct. 2000 in Barabanki as dominant caste Thakur could not tolerate the loss of

tender of fishing right in a nearby pond due to challenge of hegemony and monopoly by Thakurs.[22]

Fourth, the category of resentment and outburst by upper caste people has been when dalit took recourse to enforce their right through legal process. Thus,

- Dalits lodged F.I.R. against Rajputs and in retaliation five dalits were beaten to death by Rajputs in Hasanpur village of Varanasi district.[23]
- A Dalit woman rape victim had filed F.I.R. against the rapist who retaliated by pouring kerosene on her and setting her on fire.[24]

The most condemnable outburst in the form of upper caste/white resentment resulting into brutal violence and killing is the apprehension to shake status quoists privileged position by persons whosoever they are. The blind resentment of white or caste people makes target to even their own class people. The examples of the assassination of Abraham Lincoln in retaliation of the abolition of slavery and affirmative action order of Kennedy led to shoot him. Both had earned deadly reputation of being NEGRO SYMPATHISERS. President Abraham Lincoln had made efforts to ensure only minimal rights concerning life, liberty and fruits of labour and not political and civil rights for Negroes. But, even that much was not tolerated by vested interest whites and Lincoln sacrificed his life to quench the blood thirsty whites. So was the fate of President. On murder of President Kennedy Martin Luther King, Jr. lamented, "Our late President was assassinated by a morally inclement climate"[25] the virus of hate which had seeped into the veins of American nation. The apostle of non-violence, a drum major for justice, noble laurels for peace and the great son of humanity, Martin Luther King became prey of the same hate. King tried to pacify rebellious Negroes on note: " Don't get panicky…we are not advocating violence…We must love our white brothers. If I am stopped, this movement will not stop. What we are doing is just…"[26] But the hate heated racist did not spare him.

All dreams of King, "the rough places will be made plain and the crooked places…straight"; that the night of racism would give way before the morning of brotherhood" was broken and on assassination of President Kennedy and earlier bombing on Sept. 15, 1963 by racists of Birmingham of a Sunday Black school and killing of four little black girls and another black child being killed by white policeman on the same bloody Sunday and yet another black teenager peacefully riding his bicycle being killed by white hooligans, King's heart was broken. On the killing of six innocent black children King's reaction was, "honor and decency were also interred."[27] On President Kennedy's assassination he became apprehensive of bad days and warned if virus of hate seeped into the veins of the nation remained unchecked, will lead "inevitably to our moral and spiritual doom."[28] He also said remorsefully, "This is what is going to happen to me also. I keep telling you, this is a sick society."[29] The sickness of American society still continues. A very indepth and informative study on new faces of racism is presented by four learned writers published in Research in Political Sociology, Vol. 12.[30] They prophecy how the "white" group will

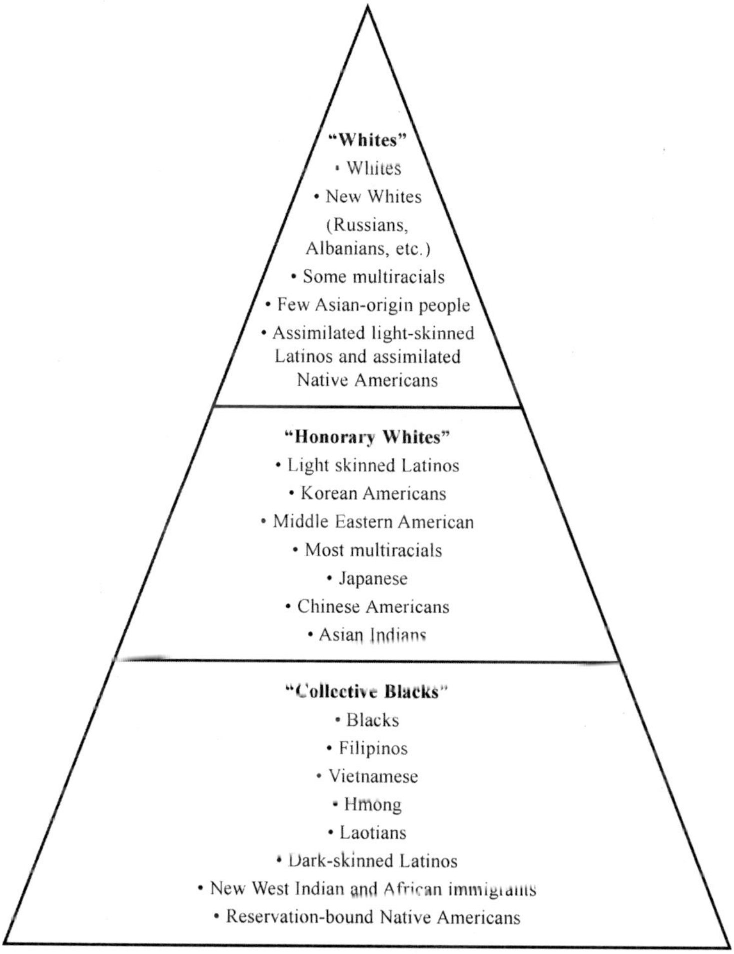

Fig. Preliminary Map of Tri-Racial System in the USA.

include groups such as traditional whites, new "white" immigrants and, in the near future, assimilated light-skinned Latinos. We predict the intermediate racial group or "honorary whites" will include groups such as most light-skinned Latinos (e.g. most Cubans and segments of the Mexican and Puerto Rican communities), Japanese Americans, Korean Americans, Asian Indians, Chinese Americans, and may be Middle Eastern Americans. Finally, the "collective black" will include groups such as blacks, dark-skinned Latinos. Vietnamese, Cambodians, Laotians, and possibly Filipinos.

The Indian caste ridden society is still worse with more subtle and cunning ways and means to serve the cause of status quoist hierarchical society. The study hereafter reveal that it has searched a new way to frustrate any reformative or protective attempt and that is addition in reactions similar to Americans - a weapon of self-immolation.

In most of the cases of the violent incidents victims are vulnerable and economically poor downtrodden untouchables. Dr Upendra Buxi presents the picture: "The period of 1973 to 1978 according to one estimate witnessed 62,295 violent incidents, commonly called "atrocities" against untouchable life and property. In 1977-78, 12746 atrocities were registered involving 354 killing and 306 registered cases of rape. The very names- Kilvennmani, Belchi, Dharampur, Villipuram, Pantnagar, Marathawada, Pipra – evoke cluster of images of inhuman violence: huts set ablaze, people tied to trees and burned alive, people shot at point of blank range or hacked to pieces women raped and brutally killed, children bayoneted or burnt alive."[31] Dr Buxi rightly comments, "the gruesome story of genocidal violence against untouchables is not yet fully told. But what we know is already enough to strip away every pretence of tolerance and non-violence from the face of India and to reveal instead, a brutalised and brutalising society."[32]

Sometimes caste hatred outburst even when nobody's interest is hurt and some prestige's is awarded to Dalit leaders. The attempt of Maharashtra Legislative Assembly through unanimous Resolution of the Assembly to rename Marathawada University to Ambedkar University was frustrated by Marathawada riots as caste Hindus raised a campaign of violence lasting 67 days over 1200 villages.[33] Republican Sena President Anandraj Ambedkar, a grandson of Dr B.R. Ambedkar was attacked on 16.6.2015 by Shiv Sena activists because of his leading a agitation demanding a memorial to the principal architect of the Indian Constitution and Dalit icon Dr B.R. Ambedkar at Dadar in Mumbai.[34]

7.2 Violent Reaction Against Dalit Uprise

The position of Dalits – SCs and STs, has been and still is most vulnerable in the Indian society. They have been and are still easy targets. They incur not only ill-treatment but also brutal repression, as upper caste people are not in a position to digest and easily tolerate their social uprise and improving conditions. In some cases economic interests of the upper caste people also comes into conflict which they are quite unwilling to tolerate. Discussion through examples, facts and datas have been presented throughout the study in the book to bring the vulnerability of Dalits. Here one of the reasons of reaction against Dalits i.e. indigestibility of Dalit's rise among the upper castes is dealt with.

For dalits all except them are upper castes – what to say of Brahmins, Kshatriyas or Banias, even well to do Shudras enjoying the status of peasantry backward castes also ill-treat SCs and STs. In most of the cases in villages and rural areas the represser are Jats, Yadavas, Kurmis and so on. It was very aptly pointed out by Yogendra Yadava, a sociologist that "questioning of *status quo* is the trigger and oppressor changes with the turf, it could be Jats in Rohtak, Yadavas in Mahendragarh, Rajputs and OBCs of Rors in Yamunanagar." There are many reasons for brutal reactions – Jobs and small business raising the status, vehicles and good houses in neighbourhood of other castes people and in some cases refusal of Dalits to work in fields of landlords.

A very informative report was published by Subodh Ghildiyal in Times of India, 24.10.2015 under caption "Dalit's Rise is Upper Castes' Envy-Dominent Class Unable Accept Changed Social Order." The following data compiled by NCRB shows the rise in violent reactions against dalits has a rising trend inspite of the two Parliamentary laws – Protection of Civil Rights Act, 1955 (before 1976 known as Untouchability Offences Act) and Scheduled Castes and Scheduled Tribes (Prevention of Atrocities) Act, 1989, to deal with crimes against the Scheduled Castes and Scheduled Tribes.

Table 7.1

Crimes Against SCs (Worst 15 States)			*Crimes Against STs (States with Over 100 Incidents in 2014)*		
	Incidents	*Rate*		*Incidents*	*Rate*
Uttar Pradesh	8,075	9.5	Rajasthan	3,952	42.8
Rajasthan	8,028	65.7	Madhya Pradesh	2,279	14.9
Bihar	7,893	47.6	Odisha	1,259	13.1
Madhya Pradesh	4,151	36.6	Chhatisgarh	721	9.2
Andhra Pradesh	4,114	48.7	Andhra Pradesh	627	23.8
Odisha	2,266	31.5	Telangana	569	17.3
Karnataka	2,138	20.4	Karnataka	487	11.5
Maharashtra	1,768	13.3	Maharashtra	443	4.2
Telangana	1,694	31.2	Jharkhand	432	5.0
Tamil Nadu	1,546	10.7	Gujarat	229	2.6
Gujarat	1,130	27.7	West Bengal	141	2.7
Chhatisgarh	1,066	32.6	Kerala	135	27.8
Jharkhand	903	22.7			
Haryana	830	16.2			
Kerala	816	26.8			
India Total	**47,065**	**23.4 All India**	**India Total**	**11,451**	**11.0 All India**

References

1. Jurisprudence, p. 232.
2. The Coming of Post-Industrial Society – A Venture in Social Forecasting Arnold Heinemann Publishing (India) Pvt. Ltd., 1974, p. 436.
3. "one must not blind himself to the fact that democratic institutions most successfully develop sentiments of envy in the human heart. This is not because they provide the means for everybody to rise to the level of everybody else but because these means are constantly proving inadequate in the hands of those using them. Democratic institutions awaken and flatter the passion for equality without ever being able to satisfy it entirely. This complete equality is always slipping through the people's fingers at the moment when they think to grasp it, fleeing as Pascal says is an eternal flight. The people grow heated in search of this blessing, all the more precious because it is near enough to be seen but too far off to be tasted. They are excited by the chance and irritated by the uncertainty of success, the excitement is followed by weariness and then by bitterness. In that state anything which in any way transcends people seems an obstacle to their desires and they are tired by the sight of any superiority, however legitimate." Alexis de Tocqueville, Democracy in America, p. 181.
4. Daniel Bell, The Coming of Post Industrial Society, p. 451.
5. Poole, Roger, Kier Kegaard, University of Virginia Press, 1993, pp. 226-228.
6. Kaufman, Walter, Editor's Introduction, Section 3 "On the Genealogy of Morals (in) Nietzsche : Basic Writings"; Kaufman trans., New York : The Modern Library, 1967.

7. Hong's translation of Two Ages : A Literary Review, pp. 81-87.
8. Max Weber, The Sociology of Religion (Boston : Beacon Press, 1993), KierKegaard views ressentiment as the constituent principle of the want of character, which from utter wretchedness tries to sneak itself a position. It is a process of leveling. The Present Age (Alexander Dru tr., 1962) Friedrich Nietzsche points out ressentiment as expression of one' own failure/ inferiority (On the Genelogy of Morality). So does Jean-Paul Sartre.
9. Max Weber, The Sociology of Religion. Boston : Beacon Press, 1993, p. 110.
10. Resentment is preferred in English and Indian Juridical thought on Compensatory discrimination.
11. Adler School of Personal Psychology (http://www.adler.edu/page/institute-on-social-exclusion/ about)
12. Hillery Silver. Social Exclusion : Comparative Analysis of Europe and Middle East Youth Initiative Working Paper (September, 2007) p. 15 (http:// www.shababinclusion.org/content/document/detail /558/1)
13. 60 U.S. (19 How.) 393 (1857).
14. 349 U.S. 294 decided on May 17, 1954.
15. Quoted from MulkrajAnand and Eleanor Zelliot (ed). Anthropology of Dalit Literature, Gyan Publishing House, New Delhi, 1992, p. 37.
16. Prakash Louis, Political Sociology of Dalits Assertion, Gyan Publishing House, New Delhi, 2003 pp. 9-10. Prakash Louis has also contributed a book titled, casteism is more Horendous than Racism."
17. Survey of media in 2006, see Rakesh K. Sinha, Dalits and Human Rights, Mohit Publications, New Delhi, 2010 p. 124.
18. *Ibid.* 125.
19. *Ibid.*
20. Upendra Buxi, Violence, Dissent and Development (in) Robert F. Meagher (ed.) Law and Social Change – Indo-American Reflections, N.M. Tripathi Pvt. Ltd., Bombay, 1988, pp. 72-93 at p. 84.
21. A. Sinha, "Class War, Not 'Atrocities' Against Harijans" Journal of Peasant Studies, 148 (1982).
22. Prakash Louis, Political Sociology of Dalit Assertion, Gyan Publishing House, 2003, p. 17.
23. Anand Swarup Varma, Hindutva Ki Rajniti Ka Sawaranprakar, Jansatta, 1.7.2001, p. 6.
24. Rakesh K. Sinha, Dalits and Human Rights, Mohit Publication, 2010, p. 125.
25. Stanislav KONDRASHOV, Martin Luther King, Novosti Press Agency Publishing House, Moscow, 1988, p. 41.
26. *Ibid.* 13.
27. *Ibid.* p. 40.
28. *Ibid.* p. 41.
29. *Ibid* p. 41.

30. Eduardo Bonilla- Silva, Tyrone A. Forman, Amanda E. Lewis and David G. Embrick, "IT WAS N'T ME" : HOW WILL RACE AND RACISM WORK IN twenty first Century AMERICA (in) Betty A Dobratz, Lisa K. Waldner, Timotty Buzzel (ed.) Political Sociology For The twenty first Century, JAI, An Imrint of Elsevier Science (2003), pp. 131-134.
31. Upendra Buxi, Violence, Dissent And Development (in) Robert F. Meagher (ed.) Law And Social Change :Indo American Reflection, N.M.T., Pvt. Ltd. Bombay, 1988 pp. 72-93 at p. 83.
32. *Ibid.*
33. *Ibid.* p. 85.
34. Hindustan Times (Lucknow ed.) 17.6.2015, p. 5.

Chapter - 8

Circumvention of and Resistance Against Reservation Policy

8.1 Restrictive Interpretation of Roster Rule etc. (Triumph of Status Quoism)

What the Roster is ?

With a view to give proper effect to the reservations prescribed, every appointing authority is expected to treat vacancies as 'reserved' or 'unreserved' according to model roster. Model roster is made by keeping hundred posts as component unit. Before 1990 there were only reservations for SCs/STs and Chapter IV of Constitutional and Other Miscellaneous provisions concerning to SCs and STs issued by Government of India on Feb. 5th, 1978 provided for model rosters each of 40/100 points. Now reservation is made for OBCs also. Keeping in view 100 posts roster is prepared. The U.P. Governor in exercise of his powers under section 2(5) of the U.P. Public Service (SCs/STs and OBCs) Reservation Act, 1994 issued the model roster which was notified by Personal Section of U.P. Government vide Notification No. 481/Personal-1/94-1/1994, Lucknow, dated March 29, 1994. It provides the roster as follow:

Table 8.1

1.	Scheduled castes	5.	Scheduled castes
2.	Unreserved	6.	Unreserved
3.	Other Backward classes	7.	Other Backward classes
4.	Unreserved	8.	Unreserved

(Contd...)

9. Scheduled castes
10. Unreserved
11. Other Backward classes
12. Unreserved
13. Other Backward classes
14. Unreserved
15. Scheduled castes
16. Unreserved
17. Other Backward classes
18. Unreserved
19. Other Backward classes
20. Unreserved
21. Scheduled castes
22. Unreserved
23. Other Backward classes
24. Unreserved
25. Scheduled castes
26. Unreserved
27. Other Backward classes
28. Unreserved
29. Other Backward classes
30. Unreserved
31. Scheduled castes
32. Unreserved
33. Other Backward classes
34. Unreserved
35. Scheduled castes
36. Unreserved
37. Other Backward classes
38. Unreserved
39. Other Backward classes
40. Unreserved
41. Scheduled castes
42. Unreserved
43. Other Backward classes
44. Unreserved
45. Scheduled castes
46. Unreserved
47. Scheduled castes
48. Unreserved
49. Scheduled castes
50. Unreserved
51. Other Backward classes
52. Unreserved
53. Scheduled castes
54. Unreserved
55. Other Backward classes
56. Unreserved
57. Other Backward classes
58. Unreserved
59. Scheduled castes
60. Unreserved
61. Other Backward classes
62. Unreserved
63. Scheduled castes
64. Unreserved
65. Other Backward classes
66. Unreserved
67. Other Backward classes
68. Unreserved
69. Scheduled castes
70. Unreserved
71. Other Backward classes
72. Unreserved
73. Scheduled castes
74. Unreserved
75. Other Backward classes
76. Unreserved
77. Other Backward classes
78. Unreserved
79. Scheduled castes
80. Unreserved
81. Other Backward classes
82. Unreserved
83. Scheduled castes
84. Unreserved
85. Other Backward classes
86. Unreserved

(*Contd...*)

87. Other Backward classes	94. Unreserved
88. Unreserved	95. Other Backward classes
89. Scheduled castes	96. Unreserved
90. Unreserved	97. Scheduled castes
91. Other Backward classes	98. Unreserved
92. Unreserved	99. Scheduled castes
93. Scheduled castes	100. Unreserved

The rosters for posts filled by direct recruitment are required to be maintained as follows:[1]

(i) A common roster should be maintained for permanent appointments and temporary appointments likely to become permanent or to continue indefinitely.

(ii) A separate roster should be maintained for purely temporary appointments of 45 days or more but which have no chance whatever of becoming permanent or continuing indefinitely.

(iii) A temporary post included in roster at the time of initial appointment when converted into a permanent post later will not after such conversion, be shown again in that roster but will be treated as reserved or unreserved according to the point at which it fell when it was initially filled.

(iv) Permanent vacancies which occur due to death, retirement, resignation or for any other reason and which are also physical vacancies will be shown in the roster at (i) above and reservation determined accordingly.

Separate rosters are to be maintained for determining the number of reservations in appointments made by direct recruitment and promotion (with separate rosters for each mode of promotion, viz. limited competitive examinations, selection, seniority-cum-fitness, etc.)[2]

The roster is to be used as an aid to determining the number of vacancies to be reserved and are not meant for determining the order of appointment or seniority.[3]

Restrictive Judicial Interpretation of Roster Rule

The Courts have given strict construction to the roster rule.

Recycled Roster in Retrenchment cases

In Government of A.P. and Others v. Bala Musalaiah and others.[4]

Division Bench of the Supreme Court of India speaking through B.L. Hansaria, J. insisted on operating backwards or recycling the roster while effecting retrenchment. The Government of Andhra Pradesh issued an order under Article 3.9 prohibiting the termination of reserved category candidates following normal rule in such cases. The G.O. spelled out the order of retrenchment of temporary employees as follows:

"*First*, Persons, other than those belonging to the Scheduled Castes, and the Scheduled Tribes, appointed temporarily, in the order of juniority;

Second, Probationers, other than those belonging to the Scheduled Castes and the Scheduled Tribes in order of juniority;

Third, Approved probationers, other than those belonging to the Scheduled Castes and the Scheduled Tribes, appointed temporarily in the order of juniority;

Fourth, Persons belonging to the Scheduled Castes and the Scheduled Tribes, appointed temporarily in the order of juniority;

Fifth, Probationers belonging to the Scheduled Castes and the Scheduled Tribes, in the order of juniority; and

Sixth, Approved probationers belonging to the Scheduled Castes and the Scheduled Tribes, in the order of juniority.

The court found it arbitrary on face of it as it required retrenchment of approved probationers of general category even before even temporary incumbents belonging to the Scheduled Castes and Scheduled Tribes could be retrenched. It was declared violative of Article 16(1) which was nothing but a facet of equality enshrined in Article 14. It relied on *Indra Sawhney's case*[5] that though Article 16(1) permits affirmative action it could not fly in face of Article 14. The Court ruled that the principle and policy behind the reservation would be adequately met and would receive constitutional approval, if while retrenching employee, the roster followed making appointments is adhered to. The court explained:

> "If the roster is operated backwards (recycled) and if the employee be retrenched as per normal principle be on a non-reserved point, reserved category candidate would not be retrenched, even if as per general rule of 'Last in, first out' he would have been required to be retrenched."[6]

The Court further clarified:

> "A reserved category candidate would be retrenched only when on the recycled path the reserved point is reached."[7]

The plus point of this mode of roster is that it would adequately protect the reserved category candidates inasmuch as their percentage in the service or cadre would remain as it came to be when appointments were made.[8] Hansaria, J. explained it again: "if in the cadre or service reserved category candidates were holding, say seven posts and seven persons are required to be retrenched; the reserved category employees would not be retrenched even when they be the last seven as per the seniority list, which would have otherwise happened on following the normal principle. Instead of the seven reserved category candidates being retrenched as per the normal principle, the reserved category candidate on the recycled roster point alone would be retrenched because of which the percentage of representation of such candidates in the service, as it got reflected in appointments made following the roster, would remain unaffected."[9]

The recycled roster was preferred on the view that "the reservation in appointment, to effectuate which roster is prepared, makes an incumbent of the reserved category senior to the general category incumbent, as though lower in merit the former gets appointed earlier as per roster point. This in itself protects to some extent the interest of the listed category candidates, as under the normal rule, the retrenchment starts from the juniormost employee and it travels back step by step."[10] The court declared the G.O. inoperative but in view of three decade operation since 3.8.1967, the decision was given only a prospective effect.

Anyway the Court took restricted view of reservational benefit. If in its good judgement government decides to give some special treatment to SCs and STs or say OBCs in cases of retrenchment it would have been allowed in view of Article 16(4) allowing benefits short of reservations and would not have tested its validity on touchstone of Article 16(1) read with Article 14.

In an earlier decision the division bench consisting of K Ramaswamy and Venkatachaliah, JJ. Had taken a practical and somewhat liberal view of reservational benefits to the backward classes in ***Vishwa Anna Sawant v. Municipal Corporation of Greater Bombay***.[11] In this case the Supreme Court followed its earlier decision in ***Municipal Corporation of Greater Bombay v. Mrs. Kalpna Sadhu Kamble***[12] wherein the court had allowed rule of reservation in promotion that names of the candidates belonging to backward classes who became eligible for promotion should be included in the deemed select list as per rules after they were declared fit for promotion by the Selection Committee by screening confidential history sheets of the respective employees, if they were not already declared fit by the promotion committee. In ***Jai Narain Ram v. State of U.P.***[13] the

Supreme Court of India ruled that where candidates duly selected under reserved quota opted not to join service others qualified candidates standing in merit should be given the chance to join irrespective of the fact that Commission was not requisitioned to prepare waiting list.

In pursuance of reservation policy for backward classes corporation prepared senioritywise list of backward classes employees considered fit for promotion to the post of Assistant Engineers and gave the fitment in the vacancies available to them at the respective dates in the roster, but they were not given promotion. One member Mr Mane filed a contempt petition in High Court and he was given promotion but others were not given promotions. It resulted into special leave petition in the Supreme Court in *Vishwa Anna Samant's case*. The division bench of the Supreme Court declared that reserved category candidates have the fundamental right to be considered for promotion under Article 16. The Court ruled that even where the claims of candidates of reserved categories were rejected on the basis of results of interview conducted for that purpose and subsequently the courts held that the seniority subject to fitness and not interview was proper procedure; the employer was duty bound to reconsider the past cases on the basis of seniority subject to fitness and claims of eligible reserved employees could not be rejected on the basis of the past interview. The Court ruled that the cases of such candidates ought to have been considered independently by a promotion committee or a competent Officer. The Court also made clear that when a writ petition of reserved category of employee filed in a representative capacity seeking benefit of promotion was allowed by the High Court, the employer could not deny such benefit to other employees who stood on a par with the writ petitioner.

The strict construction of Court was again to be found in ***Karnataka State Road Transport Corporation v. B.K. Doreswamy***[14], the three-judge Bench of Supreme Court consisting of Kuldip Singh, M.M. Punchi and K. Ramaswamy, JJ. Ruled that in absence of any provision to the effect that when a person belonging to a reserve class is not available vacancy should be filled by another class, the government was within power to fill the first vacancy on the basis of general merit. In this case rotation of vacancies for open competition/ backward classes/ Scheduled Castes and Scheduled Tribes was fixed by Karnataka government's instructions dated 6.9.1969 as follow:

1. Scheduled Tribes
2. Scheduled Castes.
3. Backward classes.
4. Open competition.

Para (b) of the Instruction read: "When a person belonging to Scheduled Tribes, the Scheduled Castes or other backward classes is not available for being selected for a vacancy reserved for such class, such vacancy shall be filled by selection on the basis of general merit."

The claim of petitioner was that since the Scheduled Tribe candidate was not available for the first vacancy. The vacancy would have been filled by him, as being member of a Scheduled Caste he was entitled to be appointed against the first vacancy. Speaking through Kuldip Singh, J. the court did not allow the claim of petitioner and declared filling of vacancy by the candidate of general merit valid.

In Union of India and others v. Rajiv Yadav, IAS and others[15] the Government of India explained 'roster system' vide letter of Ministry or Personnel dated 31.5.1985 that while allocating the Scheduled Castes/ Scheduled Tribes candidates to their Home States (insiders) vacancy shall be reserved for them in various cadres to the extent reservation percentage had been provided in direct recruitment to the IAS. The Supreme Court ruled that a selected candidate has a right to be considered for appointment to the IAS but has no such right to be allocated to cadre of his choice or to his Home State.[16] The Supreme Court made it clear that allotment of cadre is an incidence of service and therefore a member of an all-India Services bears liability to serve in any part of India.[17] Dealing with the principles of allocation as contained in Clause (2) of the letter dated 31.5.1985 where in preference was given to a SC/ST candidate for allocation to his home state, the court expressed the view that they "do not provide for reservation of appointments or posts and as such the question of testing the said principles on the anvil of Article 16(4) of the Constitution does not arise."[18] Kuldip Singh, J. speaking for the Court illustrated the virtue of roster system.[19]

(1) "It is common knowledge that the scheduled caste/scheduled tribe candidates are normally much below in the merit list and as such are not in a position to compete with the general category candidates. The 'roster system' ensures, equitable treatment of both the general candidates and the reserved categories. In compliance with the statutory requirement and in terms of Article 16(4) of the Constitution of India 22½ per cent reserved category candidates are recruited to I.A.S. Having done both the categories are to be justly distributed among all the cadres."[20]

The Supreme Court allowed the appeal of the Union and set aside the judgment of Tribunal and disallowed the claim of Rajiv Yadav to be treated as Union Territory cadre. Though the claim of Rajiv Yadav was disallowed, but keeping in view the fact that he had undertaken training in the Union Territory cadre in Hindi, the court directed that Rajiv Yadav shall be treated to be allocated to the Union Territories. The Court also conceded power of the Government to further transferring him from one cadre to another. The principle in Rajiv Yadav was applied in nine other cases[21] but in all cases the Court took note of special situations like training of the Officer in Hindi and therefore, directed their adjustment either in Home state or Hindi speaking belt subject to power of the Union to transfer them from one cadre to the other. In essence the court conceded their claim, by allowing Anil Kumar and Anju Gupta to continue in U.P. cadre, and taking practical note in other cases. What it refused to recognise was its recognition as matter of right. What the Court did was to upheld the validity of principles of "cadre allocation". It is submitted that the Court could have taken note of *Mandal case*, which it did not mention even, to arrive at conclusion that Article 16(4) does not deal with reservation only but to benefits short of reservation also. And, it is matter of policy whether SCs/STs should be given preferential allotment to the Home State cadre and in such case SCs/STs language may be one of the considerations for allocating Home state.

Running Account Roster System

The Supreme Court's Constitution Bench consisting of Kuldip Singh, S. Mohan, M. K. Mukerjii, B. L. Hansaria and S. B. Manjumdar, JJ. Ruled in ***R.K. Sabharwal v. State of Punjab***[22] that roster would be operative only till all the roster points in the cadre are filled and quota prescribed by the instruction is achieved and not thereafter. In this case one of the arguments of petitioners was that once the posts earmarked for the Scheduled Castes/ Tribes and Backward classes on the roster are filled the reservation is complete. Roster cannot operate any further and it should be stopped. Any post falling vacant, in a cadre thereafter, is to be filled from the category – reserve or general – due to retirement etc. of whose member the post fell vacant. The Constitution Bench found much force in the argument.

In this case 16 per cent reservation was given to SCs/STs/OBCs. In a lot of 100 posts those falling at serial nos. 1, 7, 15, 22, 30, 37, 44, 51, 58, 65, 72, 80, 87, and 91 had been earmarked and reserved in the roster for the Scheduled Castes. Roster points 26 and 76 were reserved for the members of Backward classes. Punjab Government's instruction dated 4.5.1964 further read that "the reservation prescribed shall be given effect to in accordance with a roster to be maintained in each Department. The roster will be implemented in the form of running account from year to year. "The Supreme Court gathered two-fold significance of 'running account', first its purpose is to make sure that the Scheduled Castes/

Scheduled Tribes and Backward classes get their percentage of reserved posts, and second, the concept of running account is to be so interpreted that it does not result in excessive reservation. The Supreme Court categorically ruled that-

"The running account" is to operate only till the quota provided under the impugned instructions is reached and not thereafter. Once the prescribed percentage of posts is filled the numerical test of adequacy is satisfied and thereafter roster does not survive."[23]

The Court further classified that-

> "The percentage of reservation is the desired representation of the Backward classes in the State services and is consistent with the demographic estimate based on the proportion worked out in relation to their population. The numerical quota of posts is not a shifting boundary but represents a figure with due application of mind."[24]

The Court placed main emphasis on equality of opportunity and explained.

> "the only way to assure equality of opportunity to the Backward classes and general category is to permit the roster to operate till the time the respective appointments/promotes occupy the post meant for them in the roaster. The operation of the roster and the 'running account' must come to an end thereafter – As and when there is a vacancy whether permanent or temporary in a particular post the same has to be filled from among the category to which the post belonged in the roster."[25]

The main object of the Court was to assure equality of opportunity and it arrived at conclusion that by adopting the above said procedure there shall neither be shortfall nor excess in the percentage of reservation. Clarifying the difference in the meaning of 'posts' – an appointment, job office or employment and 'vacancy' – an unoccupied post or office, the Court ruled that the cadre strength is always measured by the number of posts comprising the cadre. It made clear that right to be considered for appointment can only be claimed in respect of a post in a cadre and concluded that –

> "As a consequence the percentage of reservation has to be worked out in relation to the number of posts which form the cadre-strength. The concept of vacancy has no relevancy in operating the percentage of reservation."[26]

Much depends on emphasis. In ***Indra Sawhney v. Union of India***[27] in leading majority decision B.P., Jeevan Reddy, J. ruled that "for the purpose of applying the rule of 50 per cent a year should be taken as the unit and not the entire strength of the cadre of service or unit."[28] The decision in *Sabharwal case* by the constitution bench speaks of counting percentage of reservation in relation to the number of posts which form the cadre strength and vacancies in a year have no relevance. There appears to be contradiction between the two decisions. What is common in both is keeping of balance of 50 per cent in favour of general category under Article 16(1). The *Sabharwal case* reached the conclusion based on equality of opportunity in form of cadre-strength as has been discussed earlier. The Supreme Court's stand in *Mandal case*[29] is clear from the observations of Jeevan Reddy, J. which reads:

> "Take a Unit/service/cadre comprising 1000 posts. The reservation in favour of Scheduled Tribes, Scheduled Castes and Other Backward Classes is 50 per cent which means that out of the 1000 posts, 500 must be held by the members of these classes i.e. 270 by Other Backward Classes, 150 by Scheduled Castes and 80 by Scheduled Tribes. At a given point of time, let us say, the number of members of OBCs in the unit/service/ category is only 50, a shortfall of 220. Similarly, the number of members of Scheduled Castes and Scheduled Tribes is only 20 and 5 respectively, shortfall of 130 and 75. If the entire service/cadre is taken as a unit and the backlog is sought to be made up, then the open competition channel has to be chocked altogether for a number of years until the number of members of Backward Classes reaches 500, i.e., till the quota meant for each of them is filled up. This may take quite a number of years because the number of vacancies arising each year are not many. Meanwhile, the members of open competition category would become age-barred and ineligible. Equality of opportunity in their case would become a mere mirage. It must be remembered that the quality of opportunity guaranteed by clause (1) is to each individual citizen of the country while clause (4) contemplates special provision being made in favour of socially disadvantaged classes. Both must be balanced against each other. Neither should be allowed to eclipse the other. For the above reason, we hold that for the purpose of applying the rule of 50 per cent a year should be taken as the unit and not the entire strength of the cadre, service or the unit as the case may be."

In *Sabharwal case* the Court was mindful of the emphasis changed by it from year-wise assessment to cadre strength and therefore, it made an effort to distinguish *Indra Sawhney's case*: "These observation (at p. 737, para 814 of S.C.C.) in *Indra Sawhney case* are only in relation to posts which are filled initially in a cadre. The operation of a roster, for filling the cadre-strength by itself ensures that the reservation remains within the 50 per cent limit. *Indra Sawhney* is not authority for the point that the roster survives after the cadre-strength is full and the percentage of reservation is achieved."[30]

Instead, the Court relied with approval on the decision of Division Bench of the Allahabad High Court in ***J.C. Malik v. Union of India***.[31] In this case Allahabad High Court ruled that percentage of reservation is in respect of the appointment of the posts in a cadre and expressed the view that "if the reservation is permitted in the vacancies after all the posts in a cadre are filled then serious consequences would ensue and the general category is likely to suffer considerably." The Supreme Court in *Sabharwal case* examined the likely result if roster is PERMITTED IN RESPECT OF VACANCIES ARISING AFTER THE total posts in a cadre are filled. Explained, the Court:

> "In a 100-point roster, 14 posts at various roster points are filled from amongst the Scheduled Caste/Scheduled Tribe candidates. 2 posts are filled from amongst the Backward Classes and the remaining 84 posts are filled from amongst the general category. Suppose all the posts in a cadre consisting of 100 posts are filled in accordance with the roster by 31.12.1994. Thereafter in the year 1995, 25 general category persons (out of the 84) retire. Again in the year 1996, 25 more persons belonging to the general category retire. The position which would emerge would be that the Scheduled Castes and Backward Classes would claim 16 per cent share out of the 50 vacancies. If 8 vacancies are given to them in the cadre of 100 posts the reserve categories would be holding 24 posts thereby increasing the reservation from 16 per cent to 24 per cent. On the contrary, if the roster is permitted to operate till the total posts in a cadre are filled and thereafter the vacancies falling in the cadre are to be filled by the same category of persons whose retirement etc. caused the vacancies then the balance between the reserve category and the general category shall always be maintained."

The only concession made by the Court was that in the event of non-availability of a reserve candidate at the roster point it would be open to the State Government to carry forward the point in a just and fair manner. It is most humbly submitted that interpretation put forward by the Court is not very much favourable to OBCs. If due to dereservation the increase in quota of general category is to be tolerated at the cost of the low percentage of the reserved category, why not some, increase in their percentage be tolerated if it exceeds due to vacancies based implementation. The overall representation of reserved category in services is still poor and power sharing which itself is a cherished constitutional value, must be encouraged for national cohesion and solidarity.

The restrictive attitude of the judiciary may also be seen in ***Madan Lal and others v. State of J. and K. and others***[32]. In this case appropriate rule provided for preparation of the merit list of 20 member – 16 candidates from general category +2 from S.C. and 2 from ST. Government of Jammu and Kashmir, Civil Secretariat, Law Department issued notification for selection of candidates for appointment as Munsifs in the Judicial Department vide No. LD(A)92/78 dated 22.7.1992. The Public Service Commission was required to prepare list of 11 candidates for the existing vacancies. The notification read, "However, considering the fact that only 11 vacancies are presently available, only a select list of twenty candidates inclusive of Scheduled Castes/Scheduled Tribes candidates as per reservation quota may kindly be prepared and furnished to the Government. No waiting list of candidates is required". The issue related to the determination of seats for SCs/STs as 1/5 of the total available posts. Speaking through Majumdar, J., the division bench of the Supreme Court point out, "if this list has to operate, as we have held only till 11 vacancies are filled up, then on the ratio of 1/5 of the total vacancies to be filled up, the posts to be reserved for Scheduled Castes and Scheduled Tribes candidates as 1/5 of 11 would be 2.5 which would yield either 2 reserved candidates or maximum 3 candidates."[33] But the Court clarified its value preference: "But as maximum 3 candidates may tilt the interse balance between the Scheduled Castes and Scheduled Tribes, if either of these two category is given 2 posts out of 3, the interest of justice would be served if we direct the respondents to reserve 2 posts, in all out of 11 for being filled up by one Scheduled Caste and Scheduled Tribe candidate each, in order of interse merit of Scheduled Caste and Scheduled Tribe selected candidates."[34] It is submitted that there is problem or issue of maintaining interse balance between SC and ST are instead of making one post general it could have been conceded to SC as the ideal proportion prescribed is 15 per cent + 7 per cent for SC and ST respectively. Any way it reaffirms status quoist approach.

In *National Federation S.B.I. and others v. Union of India and others*[35] a three judge bench of the Supreme Court maintained a distinction between reservation and concession for SCs/STs in relation to promotion by selection to posts within clause I. The concession given was that those SC/ST officers who were senior enough in the zone of consideration for promotion so as to be within the number of vacancies for which the select list had to be drawn up would be included in the select list provided they were not considered unfit for promotion, i.e., there is nothing adverse against the candidate. The concession was that within required number if they fell they could be included in the select list without further ado, i.e. without subjecting them to the process of selection and without comparing their merit and grading with the merit or grading of the other officers within zone of consideration. The Court ruled that the status of such candidates would be same as was assigned to them by the Department Promotion Committee on the 'basis of record of service.' In a nutshell, they were not to be given one grading higher than the grading otherwise assignable to them on the basis of record of service, record, as was in the case of reservation. The Court explained and applied concession conceded by the Supreme Court in *Mandal case* under Article 16, i.e., concession designed and intended to help SC and ST officers to obtain promotion which they might not otherwise get. Thus, concession was conceded as something not equal to the status of reservation.

Anyway the Court has been watchful to the protection of the interests of the SC/ST. In ***P. Seshadri v. Union of India***[36] dealing with the issue whether promotion on the basis of seniority-cum-fitness would be denied to lone candidate in view of reserved vacancy available but his placement in combined select list being too low, the Division Bench of the Supreme Court speaking through Faizan Uddin, J. ruled that such candidates have to be picked up from the select lists of SC/ST candidates according to availability of reserved vacancies and their turn in those lists. In this case 22 vacancies were to be filled in by promotion. The placement of the concerned ST candidate was at 26 in the combined select list. The Court ruled, "it is beyond comprehension to say that not even a single post will go to the member of the Scheduled Tribe out of 22 posts which were available for promotion to the post of Deputy Director/ Executive Engineer on relevant date, i.e., on the date when 22 officers were promoted to that grade.[37] It further made clear that any other interpretation of the Memoranda would not only frustrate the scheme but it would render the reservation policy nugatory and no effect to reservation quota could be given. Similar spirit prevailed in ***Ritesh Sah v. Dr Y.L. Yamul and others***[38], wherein speaking for the Division Bench G.B. Patnaik, J. ruled that candidates belonging to reserved category candidates admitted on the basis of open merit, should be treated as open category candidates for the purpose of computing percentage of reservation. But they should be given option for admission to graduate and post-graduate course in colleges where seats kept reserved for reserved category and thereafter less meritorious reserved category candidates should be considered for admission in whichever colleges reserved seats are available. It was further held that such candidates would also be entitled to the concessions or scholarships and other benefits according to Government rules or instructions.

Roster method is used to ensure participation of all General and reserved category candidates in a balanced way. But roster upto 100 points has been found to be unwieldy. In ***Raj Kumar v. Gulbarga University***[39], the full bench of Karnataka High Court pointed out that in many cases due to paucity of vacancies the roster upto 100 point does not serve a meaningful purpose. Speaking for the Court Rama Jois, J. said:

"As number of posts available in each of the departments in each of the cadres is generally less than ten, and once a person is appointed against a vacancy, normally he continues in service for several years, it appears to us that 100 point rosters is unwieldy because, for the completion of the roster it might take a few centuries."[40] The Court suggested that it would be reasonable to fix the roster for points as minimum as possible for cadres in which the posts available are only a few and therefore the roster requires to be reviewed and modified."[41]

In ***Mohan Singh v. State of Punjab***[42] the question to be decided for the Supreme Court arose whether a particular post falling vacant was reserved for Scheduled Castes. In this case the question arose whether appellant was entitled for promotion from the post of Assistant to the post of Superintendent Grade I. The respondent's contention was that the post which fell vacant on the promotion of Gurdev Singh was not reserved. It was fifth post and therefore appellant was not entitled to the post. In this case first vacancy had occurred on 3.6.1970 and on 17.7.75 a second post was created which was occupied by PA to Advocate General. Since the incumbent was promoted along with creation of post, it was said that vacancy did not arise. The Supreme Court repelled this argument and ruled that it should be treated as a clear vacancy. Counting in that manner the post under challenge became 6th post and therefor, it was declared reserved for member of the Scheduled Castes as per the roster. The Supreme Court ruled that new post created and simultaneously filled up is to be counted as a post for the purpose of determining the roster point of the post in question.[43]

Promotion Sans Seniority

In a series of cases,[44] the Supreme Court has shown its value preference in cases of accelerated promotion through reservation. In ***Ajit Singh Januja v. State of Punjab***[45] it ruled that right to equality enshrined in the

Sl. No.	Name of Department	Professor				Reader				Lecturer			
		Total	Gen.	SC	OBC	Total	Gen.	SC	OBC	Total	Gen.	SC	OBC
	1	2	3	4	5	6	7	8	9	10	11	12	13
1.	English	2P	1	1	-	-	-	-	-	4P 1T 1Lv	2 1T 1Lv	1 - -	1 - -
2.	Urdu	1P	1	-	-	1P	1	-	-	-	--	-	-
3.	Sociology	1P	1	-	-	-	-	-	-	2P	1	1	-
4.	Economics	1P	1	-	-	3P	1	1	1	2P	1	1	-
5.	Botany	2P	1	1	-	2P	1	1	-	2Lv	1	1	-
6.	Computer Science	1P	1	-	-	-	-	-	-	1P	1	-	-
7.	Maths	1P	1	-	-	1P 2Lv	1 1Lv	- 1Lv	- -	2Lv	1	1	-
8.	Physics	1P	1	-	-	2P	1	1	-	1P	1	-	-
9.	Pol. Science	1P	1	-	-	2P	1	1	-	1Lv *3P	1Lv 1	- 1	- 1

(Contd...)

10.	Education	1P	1	-	-	2P	1	1	-	*2P 1P 1Lv	1 1 1	1 - -	- - -
11.	Hindi	2P	1	1	-	-	-	-	-	2P	1	1	-
12.	Commerce	1P	1	-	-	3P	1	1	1	1P	1	-	-
13.	Anc. History	--	-	-	-	4P	2	1	1	-	-	-	-
14.	Zoology	-	-	-	-	1P	1P	-	-	2P	1	1	-
15.	Chemistry	-	-	-	-	1P 5P	1P 2	- 2	- 1	2P 1P	1 1	1 -	- -
16.	Electronics	-	-	-	-	1P	1	1	-	2P	1	1	-
17.	Statistics	-	-	-	-	1P	1	-	-	2(part time)	1	-	-
18.	Philosophy (Specl. In Indian Philos.)	-	-	-	-	1T	1T	-	-	-	-	-	-
19.	Law	-	-	-	-	-	-	-	-	6	3	2	1
20.	Geography	-	-	-	-	1Lv	1Lv	-	-	1P	1	-	-

(Contd...)

26.	Home Science	-	-	-	-	-	-	-	-	1T	1	--	-
27.	Physical (Atheletic) Education	-	-	-	-	-	-	-	-	1P	1	-	-
28.	System Manager/ System Engineer (Temporary)	-	-	-	-	-	-	-	-	1	-	-	-
29.	Librarian (Central Library) Permanent	-	-	-	-	-	-	-	-	1	-	-	-
30.	Progammers (Temporary)	-	-	-	-	-	-	-	-	2	1	1	-
31.	Director (Adult & Continuing Education-Temporary)	-	-	-		-	-	-	-	1			
32.	Asstt. Director (Adult education) Temporary	-	-	-	-	-	-	-	-	1			
33.	Asstt. Director (Continuing Educn.) Temporary	-	-	-	-	-	-	-	-	1			
34.	Director, Allahabad Bank Chair in Centre of Integrated Rural Development (Temporary)	-	-	-	-	-	-	-	-	1			

* The appointment will be subject to the decision of the Chancellor.

Constitution is to be preserved by preventing reverse discrimination. The rule of reservation gives accelerated promotion but it does not give accelerated "Consequential seniority." The Court explained that if a reserved category candidate is promoted earlier because of the rule of reservation/ roster and his senior belonging to the general category is promoted later to that higher grade the general category candidate shall regain his seniority over such earlier promoted reserved category candidate.[46]

8.2 Dereservation of Reserved Posts

The mandate of Article 16(4) has to be read with Article 335. If reserved category is not filled by candidates of that group then the problem arises – how to tackle the issue. One of the method is to dereserve the post, i.e., to convert a reserved post into unreserved post. Reservation is rule, dereservation is exception. Chapter X of Constitutional and other Miscellaneous Provisions concerning Scheduled Castes and Scheduled Tribes 1978, deals with dereservation. It provides detail scheme and requirement for dereservation.

P- Permanent; T- Temporary, Lv- Leave Vacancy

Pay Scale:

Professor	4500-150-5700-200-7300
Reader	3700-125-4950-150-5700
Lecturer	2200-75-2800-100-4000
Librarian	3200-100-3500-125-4875
Director	4500-150-5700-200-7300
Asstt. Director	3700-125-4950-150-5700
System Manager System Engineer	3000-100-3500-125-4500
Programmers	2200-75-2800-EB-100-4000

Dereservation

10.1 A vacancy reserved for Scheduled Castes or Scheduled Tribes should not be filled by a general candidate without its being dereserved in accordance with the prescribed procedure. Prior approval of the Department of Personnel and Administrative Reforms should be contained for dereservation of a vacancy reserved for Scheduled Castes or Scheduled Tribes, which is included in the roster for permanent appointments and temporary appointments likely to become permanent or to continue indefinitely. Reserved vacancies included in the roster for purely temporary appointments which have no chance whatever of becoming permanent or continuing indefinitely can, however, be deserved by the Ministries themselves after ensuring that the steps prescribed in paras 8.1 to 8.4 have been duly taken to secure suitable Scheduled Caste and Scheduled Tribe candidates and that such candidates are still not available.

M.H.A. O.Ms. No. 31/10/63-SCT(1), dt. 27.3.61, 31/10/63- SCI(1), dt. 20.7.65, 1/6/1(1)65-E Est. (c), dt. 20.7.65, 1/6/67-Est. (C). Dt. 18.3.68, 8/1/69, Est. (SCT), dated 28.1.69 and Deptt. Of Personnel O.Ms. No. 16/1/72. Est. (SCT), dated 11.8.1972, No. 163/74 Est. (SCT), dated 26.4.74, No. 10/27/74 Est. (SCT), dated 12.11.1975 and No. 28/14/74 Est. (SCT), dated 12.11.1975 and No. 28/14/74 Est. (SCT), dated 12.7.1976.

10.2 Proposals for reservation of reserved vacancies included in the roster for permanent appointment and temporary appointments likely to become permit or to continue definitely should be made to the Department of Personnel and Administrative Reforms have been prescribed in this regard.

Proforma 1(a):	For posts filled by direct recruitment through Union Public Service Commission.
Proforma 1 (b):	For posts filled by direct recruitment through Employment Exchange etc.
Proforma II:	For posts filled by promotion on the basis of selection/seniority-cum-fitness/limited departmental competitive examination.
Proforma III:	For confirmation (in posts filled by direct recruitment only).

Ministries /Departments should observe the following procedure while sending proposals for dereservation to the Department of Personnel and Administrative Reforms:-

(i) The proposal should contain a certificate that is being made with the full knowledge and concurrence of the Liaslon Officer of the Ministry/Department.

(ii) Proposals for dereservation of reserved vacancies in respect of posts under attached/subordinate officers, etc. should not be sent to the Department of Personnel and Administrative Reforms direct. Such proposals should be sent to Administrative Ministry/ Department who will examine the proposals and send them to the Department of Personnel and Administrative Reform after satisfying itself that the prescribed procedure had been followed.

(iii) A copy of the proposal (in appropriate proforma) for reservation should be endorsed by the Ministry/Department concerned, simultaneously to the Commissioner for Scheduled Castes and

Scheduled Tribes, West Block No. 1, Wing No. 1, Wing No. 7, (Ist Floor, Ramakrishnapuram, New Delhi-22); and the fact thereof should be indicated in the proposal made to the Department of Personnel and Administrative Reforms.

10.3 In the case of reserved vacancies included in the roster for purely temporary appointments, which have no chance whatever of becoming permanent or continuing indefinitely, the Commissioner for Scheduled Castes and Scheduled Tribes should be informed about the dereservation made together with the details and reasons necessitating the dereservation in the appropriate proforma mentioned in para 102.

10.4 It should be ensured that before reference is made by a Ministry/ Department to the Department of Personnel and A.R. for dereservation of reserved vacancy/vanacies included in the roster for permanent appointments and temporary appointments likely to become permanent or to continue indefinitely, all the steps prescribed to secure Scheduled Caste/ Scheduled Tribe candidates for appointment against these reserved vacancies are invariably taken and fully followed by the appointing authority concerned and that the claims of eligible candidates of these communities have been duly considered. Dereservation should be proposed only when such a course becomes inevitable due to non-availability of Scheduled Caste/ Tribe candidates for appointment against reserved vacancies after having fully observed the procedures prescribed in this behalf and after applying the relaxed standards in the case of such candidates. These procedures are detailed in Chapters 7, 8 and 9 in respect of posts filled by direct recruitment and in Chapters 7 and 12 of this brochure, in respect of posts filled by promotion. Similarly, care should also taken by the Ministries/Departments before vacancies reserved for Scheduled Castes/Scheduled Tribes included in the roster for purely temporary appointments which have no chance of becoming permanent or continuing indefinitely, are dereserved by them in accordance with paras 10.1 and 10.3 of this Brochure.

Deptt. Of Personnel A.R.O.M. No. 16/2/74-Est. (SCT), dated 8.5.74 and No. 36022/18/76-Est. (SCT), dated 25.9.1976.

10.5 Annual statement of dereservation of purely temporary vacancies – Each Ministry/ Department should send to the Department of Personnnel and Administrative Reforms as soon after the Ist of January every year as possible, in any case cannot later than the Ist of April, a consolidated statement in respect of the Ministry/Department and all its attached and subordinate offices, in the form at Appendix 8, showing the reserved vacancies included in the roster for purely temporary appointments which were dereserved by the Ministry/Department under its own powers during the preceding year.

Notes: (1) After dereservation of a reserved vacancy and its being filled by a general candidate, the reservation is to be carried forward to subsequent three recruitment years. (The detailed procedure for carrying forward reservations is given in Chapter 11).

(2) For reserved vacancies in non-technical and quasi-technical posts, every effort should be made to recruit a candidate of the reserved category and dereservation in such vacancies may be proposed or made only when such a course becomes inevitable (In this connection para 7.6 may also be seen).

Deptt. of Personnel and A.R.O.M. No. 36034/16/76-Est. (SCT), dated 5.3.1977.

10.6. Unfilled reserved vacancies, though they are carried forward, should be formally got dereserved by the Department of Personnel and Administrative Reforms before they are filled by other candidates not belonging to Scheduled Castes and Scheduled Tribes, in accordance with the procedure laid down for this purpose.

Deptt. Of Personnel and A.R.O.M. No. 36011/3/76-Est. (SCT), dated 22.1.1977.

10.7. *Dereservation of reserved vacancies in posts/services under the Union Territory Administrations.* – Powers of dereservation of reserved vacancies in posts/services under the control of the Union Territory Administrations will be exercised by the authorities in the manner specified in this behalf of the Ministry of Home Affairs Letter No. U.15038/35/76-PLG, dated 20.12.1976.

Ministry of Home Affairs Letter No. U.15038/35/76-PLG, dated 10.12.1976.

The issue of dereservation has two-fold impact – first, it may create feeling among general category candidates that if for any reasons the post is dereserved, their chances would be fair, and second, leads reserved category members to charge the governmental inaction in implementing the reservation scheme effectively.

(1) The first has led the issue of fundamental right of general category candidates to get the unfilled posts of reserved category declared dereserved. In ***S.S. Sharma v. Union of India***[47] the Supreme Court of India held that if candidates belonging to reserved categories

are not available at a given recruitment, there was no rights in the candidates belonging to the general category to seek a direction to the state to dereserve the posts and make them available for open competition and that it was lawful for the State to make a fresh attempt to fill up those posts only from among persons belonging to reserved category. The relevant except from the judgment reads:

"Dereservation as a process should be resorted to only when it is not reasonably possible within the contemplation of law to fill the reserved vacancies. The process of dereservation would otherwise be antagonistic to the principle embodied in the Article 16(4) and Article 46 of the Constitution."[48]

Thus the Court explained:

"Paragraph 10.4 in the Brouchure on Reservation on Scheduled Castes and Scheduled Tribes in the series prepared by the Government of India provides that dereservation should be proposed only when such a course becomes inevitable due to non-availability of Scheduled Castes and Scheduled Tribes candidates for appointment against the reserved vacancies after having fully observed the procedure prescribed in this behalf and after applying relaxed standards in the case of such candidates. Once a decision has been taken to reserve vacancies for a backward class of citizens, the programming effected to that end should not be disturbed unless the avenues for fulfilling it have been explored and have failed.[49]

(2) The second leads to charge that government does not take any interest in filling up the vacancies in the reserved quotas and there have been persistent demands to provide for methods to ensure effective implementation of the Scheme. This led the Government of India to introduce a ban on dereservation in respect of reserved share of vacancies to be filled through direct recruitment vide letter dated 25.4.1989. Further in 1989 the U.G.C. and the Central Government issued directions to launch a drive for filling up the backlog of vacancies reserved for S.Cs and S.Ts. State Governments also issued the same instructions. All these were done in pursuance of the Letter of Secretary, Ministry of Personnel, Government of India dated 09.5.1989. It reads *inter alia*:

"Please refer to this Department's O.M. of even number dated 25.4.1989 which introduces a ban on de-reservation in respect of reserved share of vacancies fell through direct recruitment. As per this O.M. vacancies which are reserved for SC and ST for which suitable candidates are not available at the initial recruitment are to be treated as "back log" vacancies and repeated attempts are to be made to fill up those vacancies."

The above referred orders were intended to carry forward the unfilled vacancies/posts reserved for reserved category, so that those posts be made available to the persons belonging to reserved category as and when they become available. In *Raj Kumar* v. *Gulbarga University*,[50] the Karnataka High Court elaborated the philosophical purpose behind carry forward formulation instead of de-reservation:

> "if vacancies reserved for Scheduled Castes and Tribes are not carried forward and are dereserved the ideal with which the reservation of posts is provided for in Article 16(4) stands unfulfilled, which would not only be to the disadvantage of the backward classes but also detrimental to National interest as a whole."[51]

Speaking through Rama Jois, J., the full bench of Karnataka High Court made it clear that with a view to ensure that the reservation of posts in favour of backward classes is not frustrated the State is left with two options.

1. If the exigencies of public administration require, for instance, in the case of teaching posts filling up of the posts in any given subject cannot wait till the candidate of the reserved category becomes available, as otherwise students would suffer without a teacher, in such cases it would be open to the state to dereserve the vacancies and fill up the posts from among persons belonging to open category. In order to make equal number of vacancies available for the benefit of the persons belong to the reserved category at a subsequent recruitment in addition to the number of posts required to be reserved normally. In *Raj Kumar's case* the Karnataka High Court attached pragmatic interpretation to 50 per cent rule limit. To quote the Court: "If as a result of making the said number of vacancies as are equal to the number of vacancies dereserved at an earlier recruitment available in favour of persons belonging to the reserved category, the number of posts advertised on a given case exceeds 50 per cent it cannot be said that the reservation was excessive as the number of posts reserved in favour of reserved categories cannot be considered without reference to the action taken earlier by de-reserving vacancies and making them available in favour of persons belonging to open competition.[52]

2. Another course open for the state is not to de-reserve the posts when recruitment is made on a given occasion and to make a second attempt in respect of vacancies reserved for reserved categories against which no

selections were made earlier for want of candidates among the reserved categories. The High Court explained the situation: "in such cases also the mere fact that all the vacancies are made available for reserved categories is no ground to say that the reservation was excessive, for it cannot be considered without reference to the action taken earlier at which the vacancies reserved for reserved candidates were not fill up."[53]

The problem of reservation as a matter of right again arose in ***Harich Chandra Ram v. Mukh Ram Dubey and others***.[54] In this case a plea was taken of automatic de-reservation if reserved vacancies were not filled for three successive years. In this case post No. 2 was reserved for S.Cs. and appellant being S.C. with criteria for promotion was given promotion. In roster vacancy No. 2 was reserved for SCs and vacancy No. 4 was general. The contention of opposite party was that in the roster vacancy No. 3 was for general category and No. 4 was reserved for S.Cs. Since it was not filled up for three successive years, it must be deemed that the vacancy has been de-reserved and thrown open to the respondent and other general candidates who alone should be considered for promotion. This contention was ruled out. The Court's view was supported by Government Resolution dated 30.6.1983 which read: "Reservation is Government's policy and dereservation is not included in it. Dereservation is an exception for which the Chief Minister's approval through the Reservation Commissioner of Cabinet Secretary is essential. In anticipation of the order of the Chief Minister the reserved posts could be dereserved." Likewise the Government of Bihar resolved on 21.11.1990 that in any case the general category candidate would not be promoted against a reserved vacancy, even if in the first instance a reserved category candidate is not available. The Supreme Court ruled that even the non-availability of the candidate does not make any difference. Said, the Court "it is settled law that unless dereservation is done the vacancy will not be through open to general category. It was also pointed out that it is not incumbent upon the Government, as soon as the vacancy arises, that it must be filled by recruiting the candidates either by direct recruitment or from promotion from feeder cadre or by transfer.[55] The Supreme Court quashed the High Court decision that the rule of carry forward was for three years and since no one belonging to SC candidates was promoted for three years the vacancy becomes available to general candidate. Dereservation could not be automatic. The Supreme Court of India made clear that-

> "the recruitment years is the year in which recruitment takes place, but not each three successive years in which the vacancy exists. The same yardstick would apply to fill in the reserved vacancy.

De-reservation will be considered only at the end of third recruitment year provided reserved candidates are not available, or considered at the recruitment and found not fit for promotion or carried forward for three successive recruitment years. Then that matter should be placed before the competent authority for consideration for dereservation of the posts and a resolution or order should be made de-reserving the posts. Then those alone reserved posts or vacancies will be thrown open for recruitment by the general candidates."[56]

References

1. M.H.A.O.M. No. 31/10/63-SCT(1) dated 27.3.63 and 2.5.63.
2. M.H.A.O.M. No. 1/11/69.Ert.(SCT), dated 22.4.1970.
3. Department of Personnel and AROM No. 10/52/73-Est(SCT) dated 24.5.1974.
4. (1995) 1 S.C.C. 184 (D/-23.11.1994).
5. *Ibid.*
6. (1995) IS.C.C. 184 at pp. 186-187.
7. *Ibid.*, p. 187.
8. *Ibid.*
9. *Ibid.*, p. 187.
10. *Ibid.*
11. (1994) 4 S.C.C. 434.
12. (1988) Supp. S.C.C. 747.
13. A.I.R. 1996 S.C. 703.
14. (1995) 5 S.C.C. 367.
15. (1994) 6 S.C.C. 38.
16. *Ibid.*, p. 45.
17. *Ibid.*
18. *Ibid.*
19. *Ibid.*
20. *Ibid.*
21. (1) Union of India v. Vinay Kumar (1994) 6. S.C.C. 46; (2) Union of India v. Sanjay Kumar (1994) 6. S.C.C. 46; (3) Union of India in Savita Vikas Handa (1994) 6 S.C.C. 47; (4) Union of India v. Shankar Jinal (1994) 6 S.C.C. 47; (5) Union of India v. T. Vanudhar Reddy (1994) 6 S.C.C. 48; (6) Union of India v. Alka Bhargava (Smt.) I.P.S. (1984) 6 S.C.C. 48; (7) Union of India v. Anok Kumar (1994) 6 S.C.c. 49; (8) Union of India v. Anju Gupta (1994) 6 S.C.C. 50; and (9) Supriya Sahu v. Union of India (1994) 6 S.C.C. All cases including Rajiv Yadav's case were decided on July 21, 1994.
22. (1995) 2 S.C.C. 745.
23. *Ibid.*
24. *Ibid.*

25. *Ibid.*
26. *Ibid.*, p. 752.
27. (1992) Supp. 3 S.C.C. 217.
28. *Ibid.* p.737(para 814), 1992 S.C.C. (L. and S.) Supp. P. 1 at p. 441 (para 814).
29. *Ibid.*
30. (1995) 2 S.C.C. 745 at p. 752.
31. (1998) ISLR 844 (AU.).
32. (1995) 3 S.C.C. 486.
33. *Ibid.*, p. 506.
34. *Ibid.*
35. (1995) 3 S.C.C. 532.
36. *Ibid.* p. 557.
37. *Ibid.*
38. (1995) 3 S.C.C. 253.
39. A.I.R. 1990 Kant. 320.
40. *Ibid.*, p. 242 (para 32).
41. *Ibid.*, p. 343 (para 32).
42. (1995) 4 S.C.C. 151.
43. *Ibid.*, p. 152.
44. R.K. Sabharwal v. State of Punjab (1995) 2 S.C.C. 745; Union of India v. Virpal Singh Chauhan (1995) 6 S.C.C. 684; Ajit Singh Januja v. State of Punjab (1996) 2 S.C.C. 715.
45. (1996) 2 S.C.C. 715.
46. *Ibid.*, p. 734.
47. *Ibid.*
48. *Ibid.*
49. *Ibid.*
50. A.I.R. 1990 Kant. 320.
51. *Ibid.*, p. 340 (para 24).
52. *Ibid.*, p. 342.
53. *Ibid.*, p. 342 (para 29).
54. (1994) Supp. 2 S.C.C. 490. See also SBI SC/ST Employee's Welfare Assn. v. State Bank of India (1996) 4 S.C.C. 194. In this case court ruled out the possibility of giving retrospective effect to relaxed norms for SC/ ST after the vacancies had lapsed due to non-availability of reserved category candidates.

55 *Ibid.*, p. 492.

56 *Ibid.*, p. 493. In SBI SC/ST Employee's Welfare Association's case after three years dereservation was upheld.

Chapter - 9

Conclusions and Suggestions

Our study started with the crucial problem of the hierarchical Indian society. Coming through various governmental measures, judicial interpretation and overall impact of reservation policy on the status of the Scheduled Castes and the Scheduled Tribes the conclusions are required to be drawn and suggestions be given in view of the overall national interest in the amelioration of the conditions of the Scheduled Castes and the Schedule Tribes. Dr Ambedkar was correct when he observed "Annihilation of untouchability is our birth right. The untouchability has ruined the untouchables, the Hindus and ultimately the nation as a whole. To have the national objective achieved two great men of the twentieth country the Indian constitutional history had different outlook on attacking the social evil of untouchability. The magnetic personality like Mahatma Gandhi believed in the emergence of socially conscious will through change in attitude of Hindus towards untouchable and removal of the rigidity of the caste system. Bapu said, "To remove untouchability is a penance that Caste Hindus owe to Hinduism and to themselves. The purification is required not of 'untouchables' but of the so-called superior castes. There is novice that is special to our untouchables, not even dirt or insanitation. It is our arrogance which binds us, superior Hindus, to our blemishes and which magnifies those of our downtrodden brethren whom we have suppressed and whom we keep under suppression."[1] Dr Ambedkar was more practical on the issue of untouchables. He made clear "some men say that they should be satisfied with the abolition of untouchability only, leaving the caste system alone. The aim of abolition of untouchability alone without trying to abolish the inequalities inherent in the caste system is a rather low aim [and] it is a crime. Let us probe the evil to its very roots and not to be satisfied with mere palliatives to assuage our pain. If disease is not rightly diagnosed, the remedy will be useless and the cure may be delayed.[2] Both Mahatma Gandhi and Dr Ambedkar aimed equality which is the message of Rigveda – "All human beings are equal. The king should have the same regard for his subjects that a mother has for her sons." On 29th November 1948 while resolving to abolish untouchability, the Constitution Assembly echoed the Mahatma Gandhi wish, "I do not want to be reborn, but if I am reborn, I wish that I should be born as a Harijan, as an untouchable, so that I may lead a continuous struggle, life long struggle against the oppressions and indignities that have been heaped upon these classes of people."[3]

There are many slips between reservational cups and its beneficiaries' lips

The constitutional scheme of reservational justice to the SCs/ STs and OBCs is well intentioned ideology of the founding fathers. Parliament enacts laws with comparatively less intentioned and commitment to implement such schemes and make the reservation policy effective by leaving certain loopholes. The power that be, of the elite class exploit those loopholes to ineffectuate the reservation schemes. The implementation of such schemes is entrusted to administrators that are lashed with elitist mind set, corruption and social prejudices and frustrate the honest implementation. In most of the cases government announces reservation to pacify and satisfy sentiments of the beneficiaries of the social reservation without doing field work and identifying the real beneficiaries in tune with judicially evolved norms and like Jat reservation, the announcement withers away. The role of judiciary is intermittent. But, it is also problematic in three ways. *Firstly,* what Marc Galanter viewed, "the individualised weighing of multiple factors that is attractive in the judicial setting is worrisome in the administrative setting. It may lead to misunderstanding and lack of information; it many confer discretion, where that is wanted, and it may make administration slow and costly. Further judicial resolution is possible in theory but in practice informed and continuing monitoring by the judiciary is possible only if the beneficiaries are capable of bringing to the court cases and the data required for such control."[4] The reality is that the beneficiaries are not capable of that and the government becomes lukewarm. *Secondly,* judiciary itself becomes instrument in frustration of reservation schemes. Beneficiaries of reservation become unequal in court, as they are not in a position to contest the cases and government itself contest the cases half hearted by conceding some point before the court like role of attorney general in famous **Mandala** case - easily conceding the opponent's views and assuring court to get SEBCs identify a fresh within three months and clearing plea of stay against the government memorandum implementing 27 per cent reservation for OBCs in services which had been rejected by Chief Justice Sabya Sachi Mukerjee court earlier observing that the responsibility to maintain peace/

law and order in society was on the police, not on the court. *Thirdly,* the judicial interpretation is put in such a way that the whole scheme of reservation because infructuous and meaningless. The government started applying roster treating the whole institution as unit. The Supreme Court rules that department should be treated as unit. More particular, in U.P. since the enforcement the U.P. Public Services (Reservation for SCs, STs and other Backward classes) Act, 1994 (enforced from 11.12.1993), the power that be is apprehension that fifty per cent posts will go to the social reservation group, have taken the help of judicial wing to get posts not filled. In some universities no selection has been held for the last fifteen years. The sufferer are the students who are starved of teacher – in department of law with 23 sanctioned posts of 1 Professor + 2 Reader + 16 Lecturers + 4 part-time Teacher, there are only 5 Assistant Professor's substantive post holders and one associate professor's post holder, that in quite astonishing situation, that is to say after appointment being quashed by its Excellency the chancellor vide order no. E- 7098/ G.S, dated 09.08.19999, confirmed by the High Court order in *Raj Kishore Pathak* v. *Chancellor,* Deen Dayal Gorakhpur University and other, Dated Nov. 21 2007 (C.M.W.P . of 34774 of 1999) and reaffirmed by the Hon'ble Supreme Court in appeal vide S.L.P No. 23361/2007 on 16.08.2013 and remaining out of job for many years was suddenly allowed by the V.C. to join on 3.3.2016. Anyway department is run 6 out of 23 teachers i.e. about 26 per cent staff. Sometimes the Hon'ble Hight Court decisions have added fuel to the fire of social reservations injuries. The obvious interpretation has been that at least 4 posts will be need for application of reservation i.e. 2 GC + 1 OBC + 1 SC. But on 9.07.2010, a special bench of the High Court of Allahabad took the view that such arrangement would increasing the percentage of quota SCs, that is to say 21 per cent reservation for S.C would become 35 per cent in U.P. Out of 3 Posts one post was claimed by S.C. the full bench took the view that reservation could not apply if posts were less than 5.[5]

The repercussion of this holding was such that a division bench strongly differed requesting the Chief Justice of the High Court to constitute a bigger bench. Chief Justice constituted a five judge bench to decide over the issue, but the Petitioner Archana Mishra[6] went to the Supreme Court in appeal and the operation of division bench decision was stayed by the Supreme Court and uncertainty is looming large to the detriment of the social reservation group. It is to be noted that out of 67 posts of Associate Professors advertised by the Lucknow University only 2 posts go to the OBCs and none to the SCs. The possibility of ST even against the Assistant Professors posts is only after filling up of 181 posts so is the position in the case of the advertisements by Dr Ram Manohar Lohia University, Faizabad and another University, newly created, Siddhartha Vishwavidyalaya, Kapilvastu, Siddhartha Nagar U.P. A further damaging trend against the social reservation is developing that in some institutions instead of the single integrated Professors' carder artificial division between different schools are being made so as to avoid the implementation of reservation policy.

The further dilution of social reservation and every effort to disrepute the social reservation is the plea of substitution of economic criterion are grant of 10 per cent reservation in favour of economically backward classes of the Upper Caste people. It is becoming a political stunt adopted by almost all parties including BSP that the upper castes poor people will be given 10 per cent reservation in educational institutions and services. It is so inspite of the repeated frustration of any effort in this direction and finally decided by the nine-judge bench in the famous **Mandal case**. The argument is very deceptive, problematic and full of misuse of this concession if provided. Though it appears to be very attractive and being adopted by many corners including the judicial one, but, our experiences, rational thinking and study in this book has drawn the conclusion that it may prove more disastrous than the caste criterion.[7] A very alive research on point was done by Marc Galanter during 1980's exposing in grievances of income certificate. To quote him, "In a 1964 sample investigation of 15,438 beneficiaries in one state, it was found that 4,491 (29.1 per cent) had given false statement of income. False income ran as high 58.9 per cent in one of the four district samples; none had less than 5.6 per cent false statement". Only income of only salaried people income can be easily known. Income of businessmen, agriculturists, professional and self employed is impossible to be known. In one of the cases – **Nataraja v. Selection Committee**[8], the Mysore High Court found that certificates had been issued by Tehsildars indiscriminately without proper investigation into the bonafides of the claims"[9]. In D.D.U. Gorakhpur the student leaders enjoying use of bullet motor-cycle and four-wheeler were able to capture benefits meant for poor students from amongst upper caste/classes. Not only this different cheques were issued in the usual name of the student i.e. Ram Krishan Mishra and in the name R.K. Mishra.[10]

In view of the two heart burning issues – how long reservation will continue and why to reserve posts SCs and STs at the promotional level, the books concludes keeping the framers' objective alive.

1. According to, by far the best available evidence, preferential treatment is not counterproductive. On the contrary, it seems

impressively successful. Nor is preferential treatment unfair, it violates no individual fundamental rights and compromises no moral principle. All allegations against reservation that it has bypassed poor, it has reduced efficiency or economic criteria are better than caste and reservation should be self liquidating and not perpetuating have been ingenuine and motivated and are based on deep rooted elite prejudice against social reservation.

2. In spite of hue and cry of danger to upper caste interest, the position is that the systematic caste discrimination of the past and its invisible continuance at the present, has created a nation in which position of power and prestige have been largely reserved for the upper caste (and most probably for a single dominant caste) people.
3. The objective of full and effective participation of the SCs and STs on equal footing with other brethren has not yet been achieved. The gap between the haves and haves not has not been reduced to the withering stage, the human values of human brotherhood have not been established that is the reason why the judiciary has wisely deferred the issues of abolition of reservation through quota and creamy layerisation among the SCs/STs to opportune time and that too for the popular branches to take decision as to the policy measures.
4. The Continuation of Article 334 raising 10 years limit for SCs/STs reservation in Lok Sabha and Vidhan Sabhas upto 70 years with every likelihood of further increase establishes the failure of our democratic paties to ensure their representation is Lok Sabha and Vidan Sabhas as a general category candidate.
5. The decision of the Gajendragadkar J. in **Rangachari**[11] permitting reservation at promotional stage, five year extension conceded by nine judge bench decision in **Mandal Case**[12] and constitution Amendments[13] safeguarding the interest of SCs/STs employees in tune with the constitutional aspiration to make these people equal partner in the governance of the country to quote Justice V.R. Krishna Iyer:

   "The real power could be shared by the weakest sections only if the doors of the higher decks are opened to them. The higher echelons are real controllerates not the menial levels. Obviously Article 16(4) was not designed to get more Harijans in to the government services as scavengers and sweepers but as officers and "bosses" so that administrative power may become the common property of the high and the low. This is no doubt true that the Scheduled Castes, in the administrative services at the promotional level remained a paper hope, teasing illusion and a promise of unreality."[14]

6. The preferential treatment to SCs/STs, many a times, has fallen victim of see-saw game between the legislature and the executive. The Parliament enacts law to provide benefits to SCs/STs, the executive does not appropriately implement them. Sometimes, it does not provide for benefits to SCs/STs. They go to the courts for compelling executive to implement the policy. The court refuses to do so as that action falls within the discretion of the executive and, that is also a policy matter which court does not like to interfere with. On the other occasions, the executive issue the half -heartedly notifications regarding the benefits to the SCs/STs without complying with the judicially evolved preconditions for the exercise of such powers. As a consequence such efforts fail. In a nutshell, Parliament proposes, executive disposes. Not only this, on certain occasions, the judiciary contributed towards confusion. The case of backlog clearance of the reserved seats is the obvious example. Prior to Aug. 29, 1997, the vacancies for the SCs/STs posts, which could not be filled on account of unavailability of suitable candidates were to be treated as backlog vacancies. Such vacancies were treated as a distinct group and were excluded from the ceiling of fifty per cent reservation…. Some confusion was created by the Mandal case decision which ruled that fifty per cent ceiling would also include carried forward posts. Consequently on August 29, 1997 the executive issued official memorandum implementing fifty per cent ceiling for special recruitment drive. Considering the seriousness of the matter due to many representation made by members of parliament, it amended the constitution. The Constitution Eighty- First Amendment Act made clear that the unfilled vacancies would be filled in any year or years as a separate class being immune from fifty per cent ceiling. Similar has been the impact of catch up–rule in determination of the seniority of the promotee SCs/STs.

7. The SCs/STs candidates are victim of not only apathy but antipathy of the upper class employer. To quote A.K. Vakil, "Commissioner for Scheduled Castes and Scheduled Tribes smelled something wrong to reject the S.C. candidates on account of inadequate qualifications."[15] In one case in Commerce Department of

Gorakhpur University one Scheduled Caste bright candidate with first class career was not appointed for being only one candidate against the post.[16] Some incidents of knowingly avoiding SCs appointments are done with a view to appoint some caste Hindus. To quote Mumtaj Ali Khan, "quite often the qualifications are fixed in such a manner that no Scheduled Caste candidate is available; though relaxation can be done in their case, it is generally observed in the case of the caste Hindu candidates. Even when qualified candidates are available, relaxation is made in the case of the caste Hindus on some ground on the other."[17]

8. There is no doubt that preferential treatment policy have produced substantial redistributive effect. The presence of the representative SCs and STs in Parliament and legislatures of the different States has influenced the legislature to pass many favourable laws to SCs and STs. Job reservation has given job security and also some standard of decent life. Education is also spreading among them. But desired goal is yet to be achieved in view lack of proper implementation. In spite of the availability of the posts SCs/STs posts are left vacant on one pretext or the other. Scholarships are not released in time. Their fee is not reimbursed to the educational institution and sometimes SCs students are threatened to not to be allowed in the examinations due non-recovery of fee from the education department of the government. The Ambedkar Colonies, hostels and other places given to the Scheduled Castes are not in up to mark hygenic conditions.

9. In spite of acceptance of the problems of the SCs/STs groups on the policy level, at implementation level they do not attract respectful attention. The overall hostility to the SCs and STs has become taboo in legislative and other forums. There is no change in the position, as pointed out by the great scholar on preferential Treatment, Marc Galanter in late 1970s and the 2014 general election exercising NOTA (None of the Above) by electors in reserved constituency in sizable number. Galantar pointed out, "...... there is evidence that SC and ST are not accepted politically. Very few members of these groups are nominated for non-reserved seats, and only a tiny number are elected. There is massive withdrawal by voters from participation in election for reserved seats in the legislative assemblies. Apparently, large numbers of people do not feel represented by these legislators and do not care to participate in choosing them."[18]

10. In spite of our constitutional commitment under Article 39(b) towards securing that 'the ownership and control of material resources of the community are so distributed as best to subserve the common good, the last nearly seven decade experience shows that there has been development at upper end and stagnation at the bottom. Something has been done, more is needed.
11. In spite of their differences on social problems in India between Bapu and Ambedkar Saheb – former to achieve social harmony through change of heart, the latter wishing annihilation of caste system, there was agreement between them on the point of attacking social evils through inter-marriages. But in reality, there is also agreement that their hopes have been belied with elimination of couples or at least the male partner of intercaste marriage. Often news flares about the killing of SC husband or even prior to marriage, the S.C. lover of higher caste girl. The terror of Khap Panchayats in Haryana and Andhra and Tamil Nadu are well known in this respect. Recently a news of killing of a S.C. boy marrying with a Thevar dominant community in Southern Tamil Nadu appeared in the Indian Express dated 14.3.2016. A 28 year old engineering graduate from Dalit family, Sankar had married Kauslya, a second year Engineering student, eight months earlier. Sankar family was happy and they were living with that family. But father of the girl was pressing for his girl's return to the parental family. She had filed F.I.R. and ultimately they were severely attacked – Sankar died, Kaushlya survived.[19]
12. In spite of well-intentioned Protection of Civil Rights Act, 1955 and SCs/STs (Prevention of Atrocities) Act, 1989, the main objective is not achieved. The Acts are laudable but implementation/application is deplorable due to two obvious reasons. *First*, legal system functions with restitutive sanctions, rather than the repressives ones.[20] As Nandu Ram views, 'it operates with the spirit of correcting the offender and not eliminating him or her from the social scene.'[21] Marc Galanter has very well pointed out that the failure of law is not due to unawareness of its existence that inhibits its use but awareness of the hazards and weaknesses. *Second*, there is all round antipathy. Inspite of many laws relating to the protection of human rights of dalits, as National Public Hearing on Dalit Human Rights pointedout after hearing of over 50 cases of violation of dalit human rights pointed out situation is not encouraging at all. The

conclusion showed that: (i) the state is continuing to perpetuate violence against dalits; (ii) The state is colluding with dominant castes. State agencies, especially police even oppresses the dalits; (iii) State inaction encourages dominant castes to perpetuate atrocities on dalits; and (iv) even the judiciary has not responded to the violation of the rights of the Dalits with adequate sensitivity and urgency.[22] Victims do not dare to pursue case due to financial vulnerability and witnesses are threatened. Police is bribed. And, accused is let free.[23]

13. The root cause of the scheduled caste agony, due to violent reactions, is the rising consciousness among SCs towards their rights. They have developed some identity, learnt Dr Ambedkar's message to educate, organise and agitate in letter and spirit. They have left the path of suffering meekly without a whisper. They protest, assert their right and rise for their claims through active involvement which Dr Ambedkar taught. Since they have come to know the genuine requirement of the time what a Shayar has said, "VAKT KA TAKAZA HAI TOOFAN SE JUJHO, KAB TAK CHALOGE KINARE KINARE," The society is not mentally prepared for such realism, i.e., translating assurances into reality of life. It still believes in sloganism, not realism. Dr Ambedkar and his principles are celebratively propagated for political gains without any intendment to observe or allow to be observed by others in the actual life. Dalit consciousness is met with violent reactions from rural villages to the high echelon of the Central Universities.

Suggestions

1. Social mind set need to be changed through proper education about constitutional commitments so as to avoid thrashing of Dalit woman for touch the image of some god, as it happened in Allahabad in November, 2015; fines as well as social boycott for entering into the premises of some of the temples in Andhra Pradesh and attack as well as beating of the MP leading Dalit entry in temple by villagers in May, 2016 in Uttrakhand.
2. Economic vulnerability of SCs/STs is the root cause of their helplessness and non-assertion of their rights. If they assert, they have to face with boycott and exclusion by co-villagers. Therefore, it is suggested that Social boycott, Economic boycott and economic blackmail should be made punishable as atrocities against SCs/STs.

3. With a view to tackle caste prejudices among PCR and Protection Against Atrocities Police, at least 50 per cent of police personnel employed in PCR police station should be from the SCs/STs.
4. In order to achieve the object of fair trial and tackle caste prejudices in judiciary, in all cases registered under POA Act/ PCRA, out of two judge bench at least one member must be from SCs/STs category. In cases of rape the presence of one woman SCs/STs judge be ensured.
5. The Judicial pronouncements have been favourable to the SCs/ STs by attaching finality to the Presidential orders under Articles 341 and 342 of the Constitution. They obviously intend to safeguard the interests of SCs and STs and do not allow dilution of preferential treatment by usurpation of facilities by other groups using similar caste name. But, sometimes, the courts have become too literal and legalist to confine the benefits strictly to those which are mentioned in the Presidential order in spite of the ground reality that some groups of the same caste are more vulnerable than those mentioned in the Order. The example of 'mochi' is obvious. In rural and distant areas mochi's status is more vulnerable than 'Chamars'. Secondly, by allowing benefit of fraudulent caste certificate by the non-SCs, if sufficient time has elapsed, in educational courses, has emerged into bad tendency of taking chances by other caste groups. In most of the cases, in absence of challenge, the incumbents continue to enjoy such benefits and kill the chance of genuine SCs/STs.
6. With a view to make a reality, the constitutionally envisioned policy to abolish untouchability, there is need to eradicate it in all its manifestation to establish Dalits' lost humanity, dignity and security; to liberate Dalits from the continuing bondage to poverty, deprivation, suffering, gender and other discrimination.
7. To make the constitutional schemes for SCs/STs effective some shift is needed in emphasis on too much individual liberty based on western human rights aspirations to the security of the community liberty for whose life is an eternal struggle for survival.
8. The denial of the material needs of the Dalits should be treated as denial of Dalit Human Rights. On legislative side on policy matter there is express desire to provide preferential treatment to SCs/STs. The failure lies on the side of governance. In order to

make preferential treatment honest, effective and sympathetic, proper implementation needs be ensured.

9. Much water has flown under the bridges when dining with SCs/ STs was aimed to social assimilation. Such efforts have lost significance in view of politicisation i.e. organising such meets with a hidden view to attract votes of Dalits. Now they demand of participation in decision-making and governance. The pressing need of social interest is that Dalits should be ensured of an equal access to all state institutions - in legislative they have, in executive they have no decisive number at important decision making centres and in judiciary they are drop in the ocean. O. Chinnappa Reddy's question, posed in K.C. Vasantha Kumar,[24] still speaks allowed on demand of participation of SCs/STs in different agencies of governance. The learned judge posed very realistically serious question. "Why not ask ourselves why 35 (now 69) years after Independence, the position of the Scheduled Castes etc. has not greatly improved? Is it not a legitimate question to ask whether things might have been different, had the District Administrators and the State and Central Bureaucrats been drawn in larger numbers from these classes?"[25]
10. Government Jobs and seats in government run or aided educational institutions are most meager (the colleges are in most vulnerable conditions). Preferential treatment through reservation to SCs/ STs should be ensured in Private Sector services and in unaided private educational institutions too. In this respect American Affirmative Action Policy should be followed in the letter and the spirit.
11. The rights of the Dalits to identify themselves as culturally different from other groups need guarantee. The commercialisation of their cultural form must be stopped. Enough financial allocation should be made for the promotion and preservation of the cultural forms of the SCs and STs.[26]
12. The Dalit women are the most vulnerable creature on the earth They are discriminated, misused, abused and tortured in three different ways. They are discriminated because, they are women (gender); they are discriminated because they are Dalits (Caste) and they are discriminated by their own Dalit folk (gender and caste). Therefore, special measures need to be taken for protection of the rights, dignity and individuality of the Dalit women in all the mentioned areas.

13. The prompt actions need be taken to ensure the SCs/STs from all indignities. Political advantage of icon like Dr Ambedkar through birthday celebration on large scale in grand manner will serve no purpose, unless the heart of the people changes. The meaningful way to do all these would be, what Dr Upendra Buxi suggests, "by declaring war on these unconstitutional evils and developing where it is posted at present."[27]
14. The government scheme to finance and make arrangement for separate CREMATION GROUND for Dalits is sophisticated form of discrimination which Gujarat and some other states have adopted. For God sake such discriminatory sympathy must be stopped without any further delay and leave the soul of Dalits live in peace without any discrimination.
15. The recent move of the P.M. Modi to change the Dalits lives with new jobs through distribution of e-rickshaws is a very laudable and welcome gesture.[28] But, much more and more schemes are needed in this regard.
16. Very disheartening and disturbing trend is developing that the SC/ST employees are not getting respectable accommodations and more disturbing incidents are like the committing of suicide by a Dalit junior clerk in a Magistrate's office in Rajasthan due to the very humiliating conduct of his fellow employees who had always been humiliating by calling him names and discriminating by asking him to go out of the room while they were taking the lunch in office. Every effort should be made that such miserable and discriminatory incident do not take place in future otherwise the Constitution and the relevant laws enacted under Article 35 (a) to give effect to Article 17 declaring the practice of untouchbaility as an offence shall remain a rope of sand and teasing illusion. It is welcome development that Parliament recently amended 1989 Act making it more effective and beneficial to SCs. and STs. But, its real fruits will depend on the effective and unbiased implementation.
17. The present practice of holding separate Selection Committees for S.Cs./S.Ts., O.B.Cs.and General Categories, must be abandoned, as it mars/ends the chances of even the most brilliant social reservation group scholars to be appointed on the open/merit posts. It encourages the practice of impermissible and unconstitutional three types of reservations viz., (i.) for S.Cs./S.Ts., (ii) for O.B.Cs., and, (iii) for upper classes candidates.[29]

18. In view of the threat to the extinction of the reserved category species in some states, the alarming situation must be avoided by ensuing the truthful irriplementation of the constitutional commitment towards the weak, meek and bewildered downtrodden people. After the decision of the Honourale High Court of Allahabad in *Heera Lal* v. *State of U.P.* dated 9.7.2010, the advertisement of Lucknow University showed that out of 68 Associate Professors only one O.B.C. would find chance and S.C./S.T. WOULD HAVE NO CHANCE at all. S.T. CANDIDATE WILL HAVE CHANCE AFTER 181 candidates in the appointments of Assistant Professors. Siddhartha Nagar, University and R.M.L. University, Faizabad, will sale on the same boat .The formula of SC/ST RESERVATION IF ATLEAST 5 posts in a cadre In a particular department are available and OBC RESERVATION ONLY IF at least 4 posts are available will result into total extinction of social reservation in near future which the framers of the Constitution would have never *thought j* dreamt of. It is sincerely suggested that serious thought should be given so as to avoid total ouster of social reservation group from some services like higher seats of learning (Universities).[30]

May all our endeavours be towards the above and may we be able to say with the Australian Aboriginal poet;

To our father's father
The pain, the sorrow,
To our children's children
The Glad tomorrow.

References

1. M.K.Gandhi, Untouchability (Edited by Baratan Kamarappa) 3 (1964)
2. M.L Sharare, Dr Bhim Rao Ambedkar His Life and Works, 31 (1988).
3. C.A.D Vol VII p. 666.
4. Marc Galanter, Competing Equalities, Oxford University Press, 1984, p. 359.
5. Heera Lal v. State of U.P., (FB) Decided on 9.7.2010, 2010 Law Suit (All) 3053.
6. Archana Mishra v. State of U.P., decided on December 23, 2010; 2010 Law Suit (All) 1745.
7. In addition to our study, the study of Marc Galanter, Competing Equalities, 1984, p, 343-348 and Sukhdev Thurat, Nitin Tagade, Ajay Naik, "Prejudice against reservation policy- how and why", Economic and Political Weekly, February 20, 2016 p. 61-68 are worth noting.
8. 1972 (1) Mys. L.J. 226, 227 (NIC)

9. Marc Galanter, competing Equalities (1984) pp. 343.
10. This had got much coverage in newspapers during the Vice-Chancellor ship of Professor Arun Kumar.
11. G. M. Southern Railway v. Rangachary, AIR 1962 SC 36.
12. Indra Sawheny v. Union of India, 1192 Supplementary (3) SCC 217: AIR 1993 SC 477.
13. Constitution (77th Amendment) Act 1995, Section 2 inserted Clause 4-A after Clause 4 of Article 16 providing for reservation in favour of SCs and STs in the matters of promotion and the Constitution (85th) Amendment Act, 2001 Section 2 further amended Article 4-A with a view to further insure promotion with consequential seniority. Constitution 81st Amendment Act added Clause 4-B with a view to fill effectively the vacancies unfilled without being effected by 50 per cent limit.
14. A.B.S. K. (Rly) v. Union of India AIR 1981 SC 298 (Krishna Iyer J.)
15. V.K. Vakil, "Reservation Policy and Scheduled Castes in India (1985) p. 42.
16. Anirudh Prasad, Reservation Policy and Practice in India, Deep and Deep Publications (1991) p. 68.
17. Mumtaj Ali Khan, Protective Discrimination: Implementation of Reservation Policy (in) Shah and Agrawal (ed.) Rservation Policy, Programme and Issues, 1986, p. 157.
18. Marc Galanter, "Compensatory Discrimination in Political Representation: A Preliminary Assessment of India's Thirty year Experience with Reserved Seats in Legislatures." Economic and Political Weekly 14:437-454; Competing Equalities (1984) p. 549.
19. "Eights months after he married Thevar Woman, Dalit hatked to Death in Tamil Nadu."

    The Indian Express, March 14, 2014 p. 8. It is good point that Suo Molu congnisance was taken by the National Human Rights Commission, New Delhi who issued notices to the Chief Secretary, Tamil Nadu and Director General of Police as the matter was very serious involving security of low castes people. The Hindu, 15.3.2016, p. 9.
20. Emile Durkheim, cited from Nandu Ram, Beyond Ambedkar : Essays on Dalits in India, Har-Anand Publications, New Delhi, 1995, p. 309.
21. *Ibid.*
22. See, A. Ramaiah, Laws for Dalit Rights and Dignity, Rawat Publications, 2007, pp. 7-8.
23. For detail see, Ramaiah, ibid. Chapter 4 – Law and Justice pp. 64-129 and Chapter 5 – Implementation of Special laws pp. 130-226.
24. K.C. Vasantha Kumar v. State of Gujrat A.I.R. 1985 S.C. 1985.
25. *Ibid*, p. 1509 (para 36).
26. Dr Ambedkar asserted, "We are different people and all attacks on the cultural heritage must be stopped forth with. India is a multi-cultural society, and there must be room for the cultural expression of all people living in it. While attacking the homogenisation of cultures at the global level, the Indian State as well as the

dominant caste civil society seeks to impose its cultural forms on the Dalits in the name of the nation culture. At the same time the cultural forms of the Dalits and other indigeneous people are commercialised through the media for greater economic benefits of the dominant caste society."

27. Constitutional Day After.
28. Hindustan Times 6.4.2016 p. I, PM promises to change Dalit lives with new jobs.
29. In Uttar Pradesh, UP Higher Education Commission advertised posts vide Advertisement No. 46, dt/4/3/20 14.50 per cent seats were left for social reservation. The figure of reservation was as under Total posts 1652, G.C. 828; OBC 449; SC 348; ST 29 = Total 1654 (2 exceeding due to adjustments). In view of the High COUl1 decision and direction in Pratima Mishra v State of UP I Writ Petition No. 28255 /20 14 dated 22.5.2014, the Commission made amendments and necessary changes. The corrected/modified advertisements of 1652 posts appeared as G.C. = 1101; OBC= 319; SC = 232; ST = 0, Total 1652. The result being there was increase of 373 in General Category. and decrease of 130 number in OBC category,116 in SC category, and 29 in ST category. The result being the percentage of G.C. is raised to 66.64 per cent and percentage of OBC fell to 19.3 per cent and SC to 14.04 per cent and ST to 0 per cent.

    The modified advertisement gave option to social reservation group to change their category, that is to say, social reservation groups candidates were given option to opt for General Category. It clearly establishes that the governmental policy of reservation speaks of three categories of reservations i.e., reservation for I. SCs/STs 2. OBC and 3.G.Cs. As a result reducing the over and above social reservation to a guaranteed minimum in spite of the clear verdicts of the apex court of the country.
30. A study conducted by Rakesh Gupta, Advocate Allahabad High Court in relation to the Govt, aided U.G, and P.G. college teachers position is that representation of G.C. is 86 per cent; a.s.c 9 per cent: S.C. 5 per cent, S.T.O per cent. (This data has been submitted by Mr Gupta in Ram Prakash v. State of U.P. Petition No. 41899 Of 2014 to the Honourable High Courtj. Detailed data on the already precarious representation of the social reservation groups have been given in Volume-2 of the book.

Glossary

1. **Backward Class:** The expression "backward class" is used in Article 16(4) and it has three components -the scheduled castes, the scheduled tribes and other backward class. Thus, SCs and STs are definitely backward, yet there are classes which have a little better position than them but are not forward.
2. **Other Backward Class:** Other backward class connotes backward class other than SCs and STs, who need state boost for their upliftment. In Constitution they are known as socially and educationally backward class [Article 340 and Article 15(4)] (SCBC). But in common use and in media it is termed as backward class.
3. **Benign Discrimination:** The governmental efforts to eliminate the continued effects of past segregation and discrimination arousing compassionate treatment.
4. **Brandeis -Brief:** It is termed after the innovative brief submitted by Louis D. Brandeis in *Muller v. Oregon,* 208 U.S. 415 (1912) to support the constitutionality of a legislation limiting the working hours for women in factories. The brief contained reference to the legislation of many states and countries, extracts from over ninety reports of Committees, bureaus of statistics, commissioners of hygiene, inspectors of factories both in United States and in Europe, to the effect that long hours of labours are dangerous for women primarily because of their special physical organisation. In a nutshell, the brief contained statistical account in more than hundred seven pages and legal brief within two and half pages.
5. **Carry- Forward-Rule:** If sufficient number of eligible candidates from reserved category are not found in a particular year, the posts are de-reserved and filled in from the general category candidates and unfilled posts of reserved category are added in

next year reserved number. They are carried forward up to two years.

6. **Compensatory Discrimination:** Preferential treatment to safeguard the interests of historically disadvantaged sections of the population so as to compensate harm done to them. Through historical prosecution and discrimination and present day accumulated effect making them vulnerable.
7. **Hierarchical Social Structure:** A social structure based on Varnashram system with caste hierarchy –Brahmins at the top and Shudras at the bottom. The social structure is based on the sequential upside order, that is to say, Shudras at the bottom, Vaishyas superior/higher to shudras, Kshatrias superior to both shudras and vaishyas, and Brahmins superior to all the three-shudras, vaishyas and kshatrias.
8. **Invisible Reservation:** In addition to the social reservation for SCs/STs and OBCs (Vertical Reservation)) and permissible reservation cutting across social reservation (horizontal reservation) there is a peculiar category of invisible reservation which has neither any constitutional basis nor any statutory nor executive order's basis. In practice it is most prevalent whereby dominant class experts appoint their own class candidates with quite inferior qualifications in preference to far superior careerists of the other classes/categories. Sometimes, even eligibility is not insisted upon. Once appointed by or crook the dominant class consolidation defends such legally indefensible appointments up-to the lost.
9. **Positive Discrimination:** Eradication of present institutionalised effects of past discrimination, through positive governmental steps awarding preferential treatment in favour of certain weaker sections of the society.
10. **Protective Discrimination :** It denotes the idea that the object of special or preferential treatment is not so much to give any special privileges as to extend protection to those who have been exploited due to centuries of oppression and ill-treatment and but for the special treatment are vulnerable to exploitation.
11. **Reservation:** It is one of the mechanisms of protective discrimination, as a social policy of the State enshrined in the Constitution to ensure the participation of the traditionally neglected section of the society. It involves fixation of quotas in

the Legislative Bodies, in Educational Institutions and in the public employments.

12. **Social Reservation:** Reservation made by the government in favour of the Scheduled Castes/Scheduled Tribes and Socially and Educationally Backward Classes (OBCs).
13. **Vertical and Horizontal Reservation:** Vertical reservation refers to reservations given by the government under constitutional commitment to SCs/STs and OBCs. Horizontal reservations cuts across the vertical one like that women, disabled (differently abled/specially-abled) persons, sport-persons, wards of freedom fighters, institutional students, inhabitants of hilly and under developed areas, ex-servicemen, etc.
14. **Reverse Discrimination:** It connotes the idea of discrimination in favour of those who until recently had been the victim of discrimination and involves discrimination against those who had not suffered discrimination so far. In other words, it is a situation created by preferential treatment which results into denial of employment opportunity of a qualified applicant of a non-preferred group.
15. **Scheduled Castes:** The castes, races or tribes or parts of or groups within castes, races or tribes which have been publically notified to be deemed so by an order of the President after consultation with the Governor of a State. The separate order is issued for the Union Territory e.g. (i) The Constitution Scheduled Castes) Order, 1950 (C.O.19) and (ii) the Constitution (Scheduled Castes) (Union Territories) Order 1951 (C.O. 32) Article 366(24) read with Article 341.
16. **Scheduled Tribes:** The tribes or tribal communities or parts of or groups within tribes or tribal communities which have been publically notified to be deemed so by an order of the President after consultation with the governor of a State. A separate order is issued with respect to Union Territories e.g., the Constitution (Scheduled Tribes) Order 1950 (C.O.22): The Constitution (Scheduled Tribes) Union Territories) Order 1931 (CO33) Article 366(25) read with Article 342(1).
17. **Social Engineering:** A balancing or adjustment process between the different competing interests in the society.
18. **Special Drive to Fill-up the Unfilled Reserved Posts:** Unfilled vacancies of a year which are reserved for being filled up in that year as per permissible reservation policy are treated as a separate

class of vacancies to be filled in any succeeding year or years. Such classes of vacancies are not considered together with the year in which they are being filled up for determining the ceiling of 50 per cent reservation on total number of vacancies of that year. They are deemed to be filled under special drive scheme.

Index